Tables

Foreword

Leaders at all levels now understand the vital importance of having talented employees who are motivated and aligned with the organization's strategy, but relatively few have a deep understanding of how to be systematic in planning for and achieving this important condition for sustained success.

When leaders lack a well-developed perspective on the specific relationship between talent strategy and organizational strategy, their talent strategies may merely be to tweak existing processes (staffing, development, goal setting, compensation, etc.) to their perception of "fit," or they may imitate what they hope are best practices from other organizations. Even more problematic is when they apply simplistic reward systems or focus on the immediate financial impact of the decisions, without an understanding of the impact on the culture and employees within the firm. Without a well-grounded and clear perspective on the critical success factors, they may make incorrect adjustments or fail to understand the keys to success in the practices they emulate or the organizational consequences of financially motivated decisions.

This book will help future leaders develop a more rigorous perspective of their organizational and talent decisions, improving the success of their organizations and their own individual careers as well. In one short and easy-to-read volume, the authors provide both frameworks and vivid examples that will help leaders within and outside the HR profession better understand and create better human capital strategies.

John Boudreau and Wayne Cascio are both seminal contributors to a more comprehensive understanding of strategic human resources. Over the last three decades they have established envied reputations with academics and HR executives alike for their disciplined, systematic, and logical analysis of issues of real significance. Their distinctive and insightful perspectives are well displayed in this book.

Short Introduction to Strategic Human Resource Management

The *Short Introduction to Strategic Human Resource Management* provides a concise treatment of the key elements of strategic HRM using an innovative risk-management approach. It emphasizes the importance of the decisions, processes, and choices organizations make about managing people, and shows how workforce management directly affects strategic organizational outcomes. It provides guidance for managers on how to make better human capital decisions in order to achieve strategic success more effectively. Reflecting an increasing uncertainty in global business, Cascio and Boudreau consider ways of dealing with risk in managing human capital. Numerous examples in every chapter illustrate key points with real business cases from around the world.

WAYNE F. CASCIO is the Robert H. Reynolds Distinguished Chair in Global Leadership at the University of Colorado, Denver. His work is featured regularly in business media, including *The Wall Street Journal*, *Newsweek*, *Time*, *The New York Times*, *Harvard Business Review*, and National Public Radio, among others.

JOHN W. BOUDREAU is Professor of Management and Organization at the Marshall School of Business of the University of Southern California (USC), based in Los Angeles, and Research Director at the USC's Center for Effective Organizations. His work is featured in *Fast Company* and *Harvard Business Review*, and in his regular columns for *UFO* magazine and *Talent Management* magazine online.

CAMBRIDGE SHORT INTRODUCTIONS

Series editors: Cary L. Cooper CBE, Lancaster University
                  Thomas G. Cummings, University of Southern California

The purpose of this innovative series is to provide short, authoritative, reasonably priced books for students taking a first course in management, particularly at MBA and masters levels. The books include concise coverage of the key concepts taught in the core subjects, as well as suggestions for further study. Written by a team of experts from the world's leading business schools, these books are highly recommended for anyone preparing to study for an advanced management qualification.

For supplementary materials, visit the series website: www.cambridge.org/csi

About the series editors:
Cary L. Cooper is Distinguished Professor of Organizational Psychology and Health, and Pro Vice Chancellor at Lancaster University. He is the author/editor of over 120 books and is a frequent contributor to national newspapers, TV and radio. Professor Cooper is past President of the British Academy of Management, is a Companion of the Chartered Management Institute and one of the first UK-based Fellows of the (American) Academy of Management. In 2001 Cary was awarded a CBE in the Queen's Birthday Honours List for his contribution to occupational safety and health.

Thomas G. Cummings is a leading international scholar and consultant on strategic change and designing high-performance organizations. He is Professor and Chair of the Department of Management and Organization at the Marshall School of Business, University of Southern California. He has authored over seventy articles and twenty-two books. Dr. Cummings was the 61st President of the Academy of Management, the largest professional association of management scholars in the world, with a total membership of over 19,000.

Short Introduction to Strategic Human Resource Management

Wayne F. Cascio and
John W. Boudreau

CAMBRIDGE
UNIVERSITY PRESS

CAMBRIDGE
UNIVERSITY PRESS

University Printing House, Cambridge CB2 8BS, United Kingdom

Cambridge University Press is part of the University of Cambridge.

It furthers the University's mission by disseminating knowledge in the pursuit of education, learning and research at the highest international levels of excellence.

www.cambridge.org
Information on this title: www.cambridge.org/9781107608832

First published 2012

A catalogue record for this publication is available from the British Library

Library of Congress Cataloguing in Publication data
Cascio, Wayne F., author.
  Short introduction to strategic human resource management /
Wayne F. Cascio, John W. Boudreau.
    pages   cm. – (Cambridge short introductions)
  Includes index.
  ISBN 978-1-107-02781-7 (hardback) – ISBN 978-1-107-60883-2 (paperback)
  1. Personnel management.   2. Strategic planning.
  I. Boudreau, John W., author.   II. Title.
  HF5549.C2977   2012
  658.3′01–dc23   2012016908

ISBN 978-1-107-60883-2 Paperback

Contents

Figures

I am quite fortunate to have worked with both of the authors, beginning in the late 1990s, when I was chief financial officer at Personnel Decisions International (PDI). I was introduced to them by the late Marvin Dunnette (a respected professor at the University of Minnesota and chairman of PDRI, a PDI subsidiary at the time). Wayne was a member of the PDRI board, and, as I began my journey to understand the economic value of HR tools such as assessment, development, etc., Marv directed me to the works of John and Wayne to learn about the state of the art, and I worked with each of them in the years that followed.

Five years ago I became a Vice President at the Toro Company, an organization in which a deep understanding of the importance of people to strategy was established long before my arrival. In my role I have both HR and business-development responsibilities, and as a result I frequently have the opportunity to be involved in issues at the intersection between business and HR strategy. In dealing with such situations, I have been able to deploy many insights that I gained from my interactions with John and Wayne. This book will provide important perspectives on these issues for future leaders of dynamic organizations, whether inside or outside the HR function.

Much of executive education is focused on the analytical tools of strategy, finance, and marketing. This book provides an important additional analytical perspective on talent issues, which play an increasingly important role in organizational success.

Peter M. Ramstad
Vice President – Human Resources and Business Development
The Toro Company
Bloomington, Minnesota, United States

1 What is strategy?

This book is about human resource (HR) strategy – *the decisions, processes, and choices that organizations make about managing people.* It is designed as a primer for students in master of business administration (MBA) or HR programs, as well as for HR and organization leaders and general managers. It aims to provide an overview of the elements of human resource plans at the strategic, operational, unit, and functional levels.

It is more than that, however. A unique aspect of this book is that we have incorporated a consistent perspective that human resource or human capital strategy is also about risk optimization and management. It is difficult to consider any arena of management without attention to risk, and this is especially true in the arena of human capital. Integrating risk into human resource strategy is a less traditional way to approach the topic, but an increasingly uncertain world demands such a perspective.

Not only is it important to incorporate risk more explicitly into the framework of human capital strategy, but also, we believe, doing so will enhance and extend the paradigms of human capital planning in new and useful directions, producing a unique perspective for leaders inside and outside the HR function. We will have much more to say about risk optimization and management in later chapters. The purpose of this opening chapter is to explore some of the fundamental ideas that underpin organizational strategy in general, because organizational strategy is the foundation of human resource strategy.

Strategy consists of the decisions, processes, and choices that organizations make to position themselves for sustainable success.[1] These decisions, processes, and choices define a firm's competitive position in the marketplace. This is the most common perspective, and one that we adopt frequently in our examples. This definition also includes organizations that are not companies, that operate in non-market environments, and that may define strategic success differently from financial or competitive outcomes. Nonetheless, the fundamental elements of strategy, including relative positioning, decisions, stakeholders, and dynamism, apply to all organizations.

Think of the automobile industry, for example. Think about the differences between the cheapest cars available (Chevy Aveo, Tata Nano), mid-priced offerings (Honda Accord, Toyota Camry), luxury cars (BMW, Mercedes, Lexus), and ultra-luxury cars (Rolls-Royce, Bentley, Aston Martin). Think about the differences between sedans, sports cars, and sport-utility vehicles, and between convertibles, hard tops, and hard-top convertibles. It is all about positioning a product or service in the marketplace (competitive positioning) so that it appeals to different customer segments.

Strategy answers the following questions. Why should customers buy from your company, as opposed to one of your competitors? What do you do better than anyone else? What do you offer that is valuable, rare, and difficult to imitate? Do you offer products or services that no other competitor can match, such as a patent-protected miracle drug? Do you offer the cheapest products or services? Are your products or services the highest-quality ones available? Do they fill a specialized niche? Do you deliver your products or services more rapidly than any competitor can? Does your company distinguish itself by providing the very best customer service? Competitive strategy is about the choices and trade-offs that firms make. It is about being different. It means deliberately choosing a different set of activities in order to deliver a unique mix of value to the customer.[2]

To appreciate how differences define competitive strategy, consider that a full-service airline is configured to get passengers from almost any point A to any point B. To reach a large number of destinations and serve passengers with connecting flights, full-service airlines employ a hub-and-spoke system centered on major airports. To attract passengers who desire more comfort, they offer first-class or business-class service. To accommodate passengers who must change planes, they coordinate schedules and check and transfer baggage. Because some passengers will be traveling for many hours, full-service airlines serve meals.[3]

In contrast, Southwest Airlines Company offers short-haul, low-cost, point-to-point service between midsize cities and secondary airports in large cities. It does not fly great distances, and, at least in its early years, it avoided large airports. Its customers include business travelers, families, and students. Southwest's frequent departures and low fares attract price-sensitive customers who otherwise would travel by bus or car, and convenience-oriented travelers who would choose a full-service airline on other routes.[4] As you can see from this brief introduction, strategy is the foundation for all organizational decisions.

Strategy provides an overall direction and focus for the organization as a whole, including for each functional area. In this book our primary focus is on one functional area: HR strategy. Overall business strategy, through its hierarchy of goals – vision, mission, and strategic objectives – provides helpful guidance about the type of talent that will be necessary to fulfill the organization's strategic objectives, and to move toward its mission and vision. HR strategy is much more specific with respect to the selection, deployment, and management of that talent.

Corporate identity: fundamental enabler of strategy

A distinctive, coherent corporate identity is the fundamental enabler of strategy and the source of competitive advantage.[5] It is the quality that attracts customers, allies, stakeholders, investors, employees, and suppliers. It is grounded in the things that an organization can do with distinction (its internal capabilities) and in market realities (based on its assessment of the external environment and the industry or industries in which it chooses to compete). To develop its own capabilities-driven strategy, each organization must be able to answer questions such as the following. How do you capture value, now and in the future, for your chosen customers? What are your most important capabilities, and how do they fit together? How do you align them with your portfolio of products and services? The more clearly and strongly a company makes these choices, the better its chances of creating a corporate identity that allows it to win in the long run.[6]

Strategy formulation

Strategy formulation answers the basic question "How will we compete?"[7] Answering this question is a vital role of senior leaders within an organization, and to do so they typically consider trends and forces in the competitive environment, customer wants and needs, competitive positioning, and their firms' internal strengths and weaknesses. In this section we consider frameworks for analyzing the external environment, and in the following section we do the same with respect to internal strengths and weaknesses.

A popular framework for analyzing environmental opportunities and threats in an industry is the "five-forces model" that Michael Porter and his associates have developed. It considers the threat of new entrants, the power of suppliers, the power of buyers, the threat of substitutes, and rivalry among competitors.[8]

Typical steps in the analysis include: (1) definition of the industry (products, geographic scope); (2) identification of participants (buyers, suppliers, competitors, substitutes, potential entrants); (3) identification of the overall industry structure (forces that control profitability, understanding why the level of profitability is what it is); (4) analysis of recent and likely future changes in each force; and (5) identification of aspects of industry structure that might be influenced by competitors, new entrants, or your company. The overall objective is to understand the underpinnings of competition and the root causes of profitability. This is the job of the strategist: to understand and cope with competition.[9]

Strategy can also usefully be viewed as building defenses against competitive forces or finding a position in the industry at which the forces are weakest. Here is an example presented by Porter.[10] Paccar Inc. manufactures premium commercial vehicles sold around the world under the Kenworth, Peterbilt, and DAF nameplates. The heavy-truck industry is structurally challenging. Many buyers operate large fleets or are large leasing companies, with both the leverage and the motivation to drive down the price of one of their biggest purchases. Most trucks are built to regulated standards and offer similar features, so price competition is rampant. Capital intensity causes rivalry to be fierce, especially during recurring cyclical downturns. Unions exercise considerable supplier power. Although there are few direct substitutes for an eighteen-wheeler, truck buyers face important substitutes for their services, such as cargo delivery by rail.

In this setting, Paccar, a company based in Bellevue, Washington, with about 20 percent of the North American heavy-truck market, has chosen to focus on one group of customers: owner-operators – drivers who own their trucks and contract directly with shippers or serve as subcontractors to larger trucking companies. Such small operators have limited clout as truck buyers. They are also less price-sensitive, because of their strong emotional ties to and economic dependence on the product. They take great pride in their trucks, in which they spend most of their time.

Paccar has invested heavily in order to develop an array of features with owner-operators in mind: luxurious sleeper cabins, plush leather seats, noise-insulated cabins, sleek exterior styling, and so on. At the company's extensive network of dealers, prospective buyers use software to select among thousands of options to put their personal signature on their trucks. These customized trucks are built to order, not to stock, and delivered in six to eight weeks. Paccar's trucks also have aerodynamic designs that reduce fuel consumption, and they maintain their resale value better than other trucks. Paccar's roadside-assistance program and its system for distributing spare parts, which is supported by information technology (IT), reduce the time a truck is out of service. All these are crucial considerations for an owner-operator. Customers pay Paccar a 10 percent premium, and its Kenworth and Peterbilt brands are considered status symbols at truck stops.

Paccar illustrates the principles of positioning a company within a given industry structure. The firm has found a portion of its industry in which the competitive forces are weaker – in which it can avoid buyer power and price-based rivalry – and it has tailored every single part of the value chain to cope well with the forces in its segment. As a result, Paccar has been profitable for sixty-eight years consecutively and has earned a long-run return on equity of more than 20 percent.

Strategy formulation may be quite formal and last for long periods, or it may be highly dynamic and adaptive, as was the case during the Great Recession of 2007–9. In response to sharp swings in consumer demand during the recession, many firms discovered that increased flexibility and accelerated decision making were preferable to static five-year strategic plans. What was new was a heavy dose of opportunism based on rough "adaptive strategies" that considered multiple scenarios. For example, before the recession and the housing crisis, appliance maker Whirlpool Corporation considered scenarios based on a 5 percent increase or decrease in consumer demand. During the recession, however, the firm discovered that the rate of change and the width of volatility were considerably greater than it had assumed previously. The company now considers alternative scenarios in response to swings as wide as 15 percent.[11] In the process of strategy formulation, analysis of the competitive environment is necessary, but not sufficient. A complete understanding of the sources of competitive advantage also requires analyses of a firm's strengths and weaknesses.

Analyzing internal strengths and weaknesses

Internal strengths and weaknesses arise from "resources" and "capabilities." In their quest to develop bases for competitive advantage, firms try to offer something that is valuable, rare, and difficult to imitate. This section considers each of these.

A firm's resources and capabilities add value by allowing it to exploit opportunities or to neutralize threats.[12] 3M, for example, used its skills and experience in substrates, coatings, and adhesives – along with an organizational culture that rewards risk taking and creativity – to exploit numerous market opportunities in six broad areas: consumer and office; display and graphics; electro and communications; healthcare; industrial and transportation; and safety, security, and protective services. Some of its notable products include Scotch-Brite™ cleaning products, Scotch® tapes, Nexcare™ skincare products, Scotchguard™ fabric protection, Microtouch™ touch screens, Fastbond™ adhesives, Filtrete™ air filters, O-Cel-O™ sponges, and Post-it® notes.[13]

Strategically, 3M's managers linked their analysis of the firm's internal resources and capabilities with their analysis of environmental opportunities and threats. Those resources are not valuable on their own, but they become valuable when they exploit opportunities or neutralize threats. For example, Post-it® notes exploited an untapped opportunity in the marketplace for adhesive-backed notepads that do not lift the print off of the paper on which they are stuck. The "five-forces model" that we discussed earlier can be used to isolate potential opportunities and threats that can be exploited or neutralized by the resources a firm controls.

As Jay Barney has noted, valuable but common resources and capabilities are sources of competitive parity.[14] To be a genuine source of competitive advantage, a firm's resources and capabilities must be rare among competing firms. Consider, for example, Apple Inc.'s meticulous attention to product design and functionality. These features have made products such as the iPod, iPhone, iPad, and Macintosh computers favorites among consumers. In fact, in 2012 Apple topped *Fortune* magazine's listing of "World's most admired companies" for the fifth year in a row. What makes Apple so admired? Well, for starters, this is the company that changed the way we do everything from buying music to engaging with the world around us (think about instant access to the internet from mobile devices, such as the iPhone and iPad). Its track record for innovation and fierce consumer loyalty translates into tremendous respect across the highest ranks of business; or, as BMW chief executive officer (CEO) Norbert Reithofer put it, "The whole world held its breath before the iPad was announced. That's brand management at its very best."[15]

Firms that possess valuable, rare resources and capabilities can gain at least a temporary competitive advantage – unless or until competitors are able to imitate them. If competing firms face a cost disadvantage in imitating these resources and capabilities, however, then firms with these special abilities can obtain a sustained competitive advantage over time.[16] Such is the case with operating systems for personal computers (PCs), which are exceedingly complex and difficult to imitate. This helps to explain why Microsoft's Windows™ and Apple's MAC OS X™ operating systems have a near-monopoly on the PC market worldwide.

Finally, to exploit its potential fully for competitive advantage, a firm needs "complementary resources," in the form of organizational structure and management systems. These include reporting relationships, management control systems, and compensation policies.[17] To appreciate the importance of these organizational resources, consider an example presented by Barney. Through the 1960s and early 1970s Xerox invested in a series of innovative technology-development research efforts through its stand-alone research laboratory, Xerox PARC, in Palo Alto, California. The innovative scientists and engineers who worked there developed an amazing array of technological innovations, including the personal computer, the mouse, windows-type software, the laser printer, and Ethernet, among others. These technologies were rare, and their market potential was enormous.

Unfortunately, Xerox did not have an organization in place to take advantage of these resources. No structure existed by which Xerox

PARC's innovations could become known to managers at Xerox. When managers finally did become aware of these innovations, in the mid-1970s, very few of them survived Xerox's highly bureaucratic product-development process. Moreover, Xerox managers failed to exploit fully those that did, because their own compensation depended on maximizing current revenue, not developing markets for future sales and profitability. Xerox's formal reporting structure, its explicit management-control systems, and its compensation policies were all inconsistent with exploiting the valuable, rare, and costly-to-imitate resources developed at Xerox PARC.[18] Not surprisingly, then, Xerox failed to exploit any of these potential sources of sustained competitive advantage.[19]

Broad strategies for achieving competitive advantage

At a broad level, firms may achieve competitive advantage through strategies such as cost leadership, differentiation, or speed, or by focusing narrowly on a market segment. For instance, differentiation as a strategy seeks to exploit differences in a firm's products or services by creating something that is perceived industry-wide as unique and valued by customers; examples include:

- prestige (Ritz-Carlton hotels or BMW automobiles);
- technology (Bose sound systems, Apple's iPad);
- innovation (Apple, 3M, Medtronic medical equipment, Intel); and
- customer service (Lexus, Amazon.com).

FedEx CEO and founder Fred Smith claims that the key to his firm's success is innovation. He contends that his management team did not understand its real goal when the firm started operating in 1971: "We thought that we were selling the transportation of goods; in fact, we were selling peace of mind."[20] To that end, by 2000 FedEx was providing each driver with a hand-held computer and a transmitting device, so as to make it possible for customers to track their packages right from their PCs (and, today, from their mobile devices).

While it is possible to provide examples of each of the broad strategies that enable firms to differentiate themselves from competitors, pure forms of them are rare. Consider Amazon, for example, the king of e-commerce, and one of *Fortune* magazine's top five "World's most admired companies" in 2011.[21] Amazon excels in innovation, in cost leadership, and in customer service. Founded in 1994 as an online bookstore, Amazon is now the internet's largest retailer, with some 33,700 employees and 2011 sales of $48.1 billion. In the area of innovation, consider Amazon's e-reader, the Kindle. In 2011 the company sold more than 12 million Kindles, making it Amazon's best-selling product. More importantly, the Kindle allowed Amazon to stake out an early lead in e-books. Since 2010 it has sold three times as many e-books as hardcovers, and it dominates the fast-growing new market. Indeed, creating the hardware helped create the market.

In terms of cost, in a Morgan Stanley survey of fifty products, Amazon sold items for 6 percent less, on average, than Wal-Mart and 9 percent less than Best Buy. Finally, Amazon's customer service (along with that of its subsidiary, Zappos) ranked higher than any other retailer's, according to a recent National Retail Federation survey. Amazon recognizes the need to continue to innovate, for that is the only way to outrun the competition. Recently it introduced Amazon Prime, which offers free shipping for a $79 annual fee. The program is a hit with customers and a way for Amazon to boost repeat sales across its categories – a difficult feat for online retailers to achieve.[22]

Strategy analysis

Strategy analysis is the process that defines the crucial (or pivotal) elements for the strategy's success. It answers the question "Where does superior execution most enhance our strategic success?" Analyzing the overall strategy to reveal the implications of these pivotal elements focuses attention on the execution of the broader business strategy.

As an example, consider Sysco Corporation of Houston, Texas. Sysco is the number one food service marketer and distributor in North America. In fiscal year 2010 its revenues exceeded $37 billion, it employed almost 50,000 people, and it served 500,000 customers with approximately 300,000 different products. What makes Sysco special is that it excels in innovation as well as in the execution of a well-developed strategy. That strategy is based on differentiation. To do that, the company serves not just as a vendor to its customers, but also as a partner, for its objective is to help its customers succeed. One way it does this is by providing third-party financing for its customers – restaurant owners who seek financing for a new kitchen, for example.

In terms of strategy execution, consider just one business process: order fulfillment. Of the more than 4 million cases of food and related products that Sysco ships every day, it receives about 85 percent of its orders after 5:30 p.m. the day before they are supposed to be delivered. The company relies on an enterprise resource planning (ERP) system, an integrated computer-based application, to process orders and to set up routing. Warehouse employees wear wrist computers to ensure correspondence between customers' orders and the items that actually are loaded onto trucks for delivery. This process results in more than 99 percent accuracy.[23]

ERP systems facilitate the flow of information among all business functions inside the boundaries of the organization, and they manage the connections to outside stakeholders.[24] At Sysco, delivery trucks are loaded in the middle of the night from warehouses, and they are dispatched up to 150 miles away, beginning at 5:00 a.m. Such dedication to process has resulted in high levels of control as well as transparency. Beyond that, Sysco's compensation system for drivers – activity-based compensation – rewards them for delivering customers' orders on time and in good condition. This is strategy analysis that leads to strategy execution.

The process of accurate, timely order fulfillment is aligned with incentive compensation to ensure end-to-end excellence in the overall process of order realization. Such alignment leads to solid execution of a critically important aspect of Sysco's well-developed strategy. Execution represents the implementation of strategy and makes it real, so that an organization can sustain its competitive advantages. At a broader level, how firms compete with each other, and how they attain and sustain competitive advantage, constitute the essence of what is known as strategic management.[25]

Before we leave the subject of execution, which focuses on operational effectiveness (OE), it is important to emphasize that OE is not strategy.[26] OE means performing similar activities better than rivals. Execution-oriented ideas, such as reengineering, benchmarking, outsourcing, and change management, all have the same strategic limit; that is, they all lead to better operations, but ignore the question of which businesses to operate in the first place. This is why strategy formulation must precede strategy analysis. First choose industries or markets in which overall conditions are favorable – most companies are relatively weak, suppliers have relatively little clout, and aspiring entrants are few – or in which a company can differentiate itself.[27] Then focus on the pivotal elements of the overall strategy and their implications for operational effectiveness. Outside the corporate world, it is important to note that other organizations, such as the Red Cross or UNAIDS, also consider the vital factors that matter to stakeholders, and then position themselves for strategic success along those factors. We return to the notion of strategy formulation and analysis later, in Chapter 5, when we provide an explicit framework for connecting talent implications to each level of strategy.

A brief history of strategic thought[27]

At a broad level, there are four basic schools of thought regarding strategy: position, execution, adaptation, and concentration (see Figure 1.1). Each has something significant to offer, so long as it is adopted in an appropriately balanced way. Here is a brief description of each approach.

Position – winners select favorable markets as defined by external forces.
Execution – winners gain advantage through operational excellence.
Adaptation – winners develop an overall direction through experimentation and rapid change.
Concentration – winners make the most of current core strengths and businesses.

From the 1960s to today, many companies have bounced from one quadrant to another.

Cesare Mainardi and Art Kleiner built Figure 1.1 from three earlier books on the history of strategy: Walter Kiechel's *The Lords of Strategy*;[28] Kleiner's *The Age of Heretics*;[29] and Henry Mintzberg, Bruce Ahlstrand, and Joseph Lampel's *Strategy Safari*.[30] The grid itself reflects views as to the best approach for developing business strategy. The X-axis represents the point of view on authorship: who is responsible for major strategy decisions? The left side depicts those who favor collective choice (strategic thinking is instilled among as many people throughout the company as possible). The right side depicts those who favor top-down formulation (strategy is developed by the few, the designated expert planners and senior executives, while the rest of the enterprise is dedicated to execution).

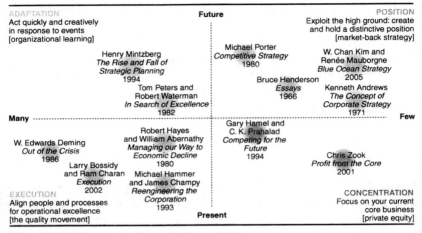

Figure 1.1 A landscape of strategy concepts
Source: Mainardi, C., and Kleiner, A. (2010). The right to win. *Strategy and Business*, 61: 1–12, 4.

The Y-axis depicts time orientation: the degree to which strategy is seen as present- or future-oriented. At the top are those who favor moving toward a long-term destination that may be different from the company's current position. At the bottom are those who favor letting the company's strategic direction emerge from its current state.

Conflicting business realities

Despite their differences, all four schools of strategy represent attempts to resolve the same basic underlying problem: the tension between two conflicting business realities.[31] The first reality is that advantage is transient. Even the most formidable market position can be vulnerable to technological disruptions, upstart competition, shifting capital flows, new regulatory regimes, political changes, and other features of a chaotic and unpredictable business environment.

It might therefore appear that the answer is to become completely resilient, changing to match the shifting demands of the market. Companies cannot do that, however, because of the second reality: corporate identity is slow to change. The innate qualities of an organization that distinguish it from all others – its operational processes, culture, relationships, and distinctive capabilities – are built up gradually, decision by decision, and continually reinforced through organizational practices and conversations. Very few companies have reinvented themselves thoroughly, and those that have managed it typically have had to force many people out, including top executives, and to replace them with new recruits chosen for a different set of attitudes and skills. Even when leaders recognize the need for change or know that the company's survival is at stake, this identity is difficult to shift.[31] In short, it is tough for an incumbent leadership team to refloat the boat. Now let us consider briefly each of the four major schools of thought that have influenced the development of business strategy.

Four major schools of thought

School no. 1: position is the key to winning   Starting in the mid-1960s, and based on the early thinking of Napoleon Bonaparte, Carl von Clausewitz, and Sun Tzu, strategy was seen as an overarching plan for growth, usually written up in a formal document and endorsed by the CEO, aimed at creating an unassailable position for the company in the marketplace.[32] These early efforts by the position (or positioning) school assumed that winning companies comprehensively analyzed all critical factors: external markets, internal capabilities, and the needs of society. Inevitably, such analyses evolved into a complex checklist of strengths, weaknesses, opportunities, and threats (the origin of the SWOT analysis still prevalent today).

In the days before the advent of spreadsheets, big companies hired armies of planning staffers to compile all this information into elaborate documents, which were debated in annual strategy sessions that became exercises in bureaucratic complexity. Only gradually did it become clear that the plans did not correlate with real-world performance or issues. For example, Ford and General Motors (GM) both experienced losses of more than $500 million in 1979 and 1980 – their first such losses in decades. In the aftermath of these and other sharp reversals, mainstream business leaders began to question the wisdom of the position school.

School no. 2: execution is the key to winning   The first serious contrary reaction came from those in operations management, specifically from Robert Hayes and William Abernathy, both of the Harvard Business School. They introduced a competing school of strategic thought, based on the idea that execution and operational excellence were the real keys to winning in the marketplace. The message to companies was clear: develop and deploy better practices, processes, technologies, and products. The execution message was bolstered by companies such as General Electric (GE) and Motorola, both of which provided examples of operations-oriented strategies, with their reliance on executive training and such practices as six sigma.[33]

Operational excellence was also a basic tenet of the quality movement – the continuous improvement practices that were developed at the Toyota Motor Corporation and a few other Japanese companies in the 1950s and 1960s and are now generally known as "lean management." The most influential strategic thinker associated with the quality movement was W. Edwards Deming, an American statistician who began consulting with Japanese companies after World War II had ended. Deming's most prominent book was entitled *Out of the Crisis*.[34] In his view, winning companies honed and refined their day-to-day processes and practices, eliminating waste, training people throughout the company to use statistical methods, and cultivating the intrinsic "joy in work" that people feel when they are truly engaged in their jobs.

In the early 1990s the execution school received a big boost from Michael Hammer and James Champy, in an approach called "reengineering."[35] This approach encouraged companies to look afresh at all their processes, as if redesigning them from scratch. Unfortunately, many companies used reengineering as a launching pad for across-the-board layoffs that left them weaker. By the end of the 1990s execution-based strategy was largely relegated to the production side of the business.

The idea of building value through managerial methods returned to strategic relevance after the dot.com bubble burst. Its return was symbolized by Larry Bossidy and Ram Charan's business bestseller *Execution: The Discipline of Getting Things Done*.[36] By this time, however, many leaders understood, through experience, the value of improving execution, as well as its challenges. It generally required major changes in managerial and employee behavior.

Porter: new vitality for the position school Harvard Business School professor Michael Porter – probably the most influential thinker on corporate strategy in the institution's history – identified the other major limit of the execution school. In his early publications, from the late 1970s to the early 1990s, Porter brought positioning to a level of unprecedented sophistication. He recast the turbulence of a company's business environment into a "value chain" and "five forces" (as we noted earlier) – two frameworks that could be used to analyze the value potential and competitive intensity of any business.

To Porter, execution-oriented ideas such as reengineering, benchmarking, outsourcing, and change management all had the same strategic limit. They all led to better operations, but, as noted earlier, they ignored the question of which businesses to operate in the first place. After all, the core strategic decision is the pursuit of simplicity through a clear market strategy.

The position school became a major driver of the resurgence of corporate competitiveness in the West during the 1980s and through the mid-1990s, but its limits became evident in the late 1990s and 2000s. Although Porter took pains to explain that industry structures can change and can be shaped by the actions of leading companies, to many his message was that some industries are innately good and others are irredeemably bad. Some companies tried to escape by entering new businesses in which they had no distinctive capabilities, so-called "blue oceans," where they did not know how to swim.[37] These efforts generally failed. As the 2000s unfolded, companies with solid market positions, such as Microsoft, also saw their advantage fade when new competitors, such as Google, emerged. This did not disprove Porter's hypothesis, but it gave others an opening to criticize his thinking.[38]

School no. 3: adaptation and experimentation   Perhaps Porter's best-known critic was Henry Mintzberg of McGill University, in his history of strategic planning,[39] who presented strategy as the art of perpetual adaptation and experimentation. In this line of thinking, executives win in the marketplace not by analysis and planning but by experimenting with new ideas and directions, discarding those that do not work, and adjusting their efforts to meet new challenges.

The adaptation school is also limited, though, because its freewheeling nature may lead to incoherent, uncoordinated efforts. As Mainardi and Kleiner note:[40]

> A multitude of products and services that all have different capability needs and different market positions cannot possibly be brought into sync. The more diverse a company's efforts become,

the more it costs to develop and apply the advantaged capabilities they need. Letting a thousand flowers bloom can lead to a field full of weeds – and to businesses that can't match the expertise and resources of more focused, coherent competitors.

School no. 4: concentration The shortcomings of the adaptation school led to the appeal of the fourth group of strategy thinkers – the concentration school – whose early proponents were Gary Hamel and C. K. Prahalad, authors of *Competing for the Future.*[41] They argued that the most effective companies owed their success to a select set of "core competencies": a foundation of skills and technological capabilities (such as new forms of hardware, software, systems, or biotechnology) that allowed companies to compete in distinctive ways. Companies that focused on these would win in the marketplace.

More recently, Chris Zook of Bain & Company, drawing on his firm's experience with private equity, has been the most prominent proponent of this school. In his view, companies that win stick to their core businesses and find new ways to exploit them for growth and value. This means differentiating a company by starting with its central capabilities. For example, Enterprise, Dollar/Thrifty, and Avis all prospered by focusing on, respectively, rentals for people with car repairs, vacationers, and business travelers.[42]

In practice, the concentration strategy often becomes a way of holding on to old approaches, even when they become outdated. To hold on, many companies (and private-equity firms) resort to slash-and-burn retrenchment. They cut costs and minimize investments in research and development (R&D) and marketing. Such a pared-down company produces more profits at first, but cannot sustain the growth required for long-term profitability. Truly successful game-changing leaps, such as Apple's into consumer media or Tata's into the inexpensive Nano automobile, cannot be managed from a concentration strategy alone.[43]

Strategy today

It is important to note that most of the thinkers who introduced the four schools of thought that we have just discussed recognized the challenges and limits of their approaches, and even warned against misapplying them. Businesspeople still misapplied them, however. When actual results failed to match those that each theory predicted, opportunities were created for the next theory to emerge.

Where is the field today? Stepping back, it is important to consider a concept that we identified earlier as the fundamental enabler of business strategy: company identity. This approach encompasses the way a company expects to compete, the capabilities with which it will compete, and the portfolio decisions that fit. Such a capabilities-driven strategy process takes into account the position the leaders want to hold as well as the company's ability to deliver. Today, more than fifty years after the field of business strategy emerged, we recognize that each of the four schools of thought that we have discussed provides important insights that can help a company find and hold competitive advantage relative to its competitors. At the same time, however, each company, with its unique identity and circumstances, has got to find its own answers.

Ensuring coherence in strategic direction: vision, mission, and objectives

Organizations are more likely to be successful if everyone from the mailroom to the boardroom is striving for common goals and objectives. From general to specific, stated goals form a hierarchy that includes each organization's vision, mission, and strategic objectives.

An organization's vision should be massively inspiring, overarching, and long term.[44] Emotionally driven, it is a fundamental statement of an organization's values, aspirations, and goals. Here are some examples.[45]

- "To be the happiest place on earth" (Disneyland).
- "Restoring patients to full life" (Medtronic).
- "To be the world's best quick-service restaurant" (McDonald's).
- "To be our customers' most valued and trusted business partner" (Sysco).
- "Zero new HIV Infections. Zero discrimination. Zero AIDS-related deaths" (UNAIDS).

A vision may or may not succeed. It depends on whether everything else happens according to a firm's strategy.

A mission statement differs from a vision statement, in that it includes the purpose of the company as well as the basis of competition and competitive advantage. Here is FedEx's: "To produce superior financial returns for our shareholders as we serve our customers with the highest-quality transportation, logistics, and e-commerce."[46]

The most important audience for a mission statement is employees, as it helps build a common understanding of an organization's purpose and the basis of its intended competitive advantage in the marketplace. Strategic objectives operationalize the mission statement. They may be either financial or nonfinancial, but in both cases they need to provide guidance on how the organization can fulfill or move toward the higher-level goals: vision and mission. For example, Walgreen's set itself a strategic objective of operating 6,000 stores by 2010, up from 3,000 in 2000. Fortune Brands set the strategic objective of reducing corporate overhead costs by $30 million a year. These objectives are SMART – that is, they are specific, measurable, appropriate (consistent with the vision and mission), realistic (challenging but doable), and timely.

SMART objectives have several advantages. They help to channel the efforts of all employees toward common goals. They can motivate and inspire employees to higher levels of commitment and effort. Finally, they can provide a yardstick to measure performance, and thus the distribution of rewards and incentives.

Although planning business strategy clearly offers a number of benefits, there is also a potential downside, in that it may lock companies into a particular vision of the future – one that may not come to pass. This poses a dilemma: how to plan for the future when the future changes so quickly. The answer is to make the planning process more democratic.

Instead of relegating strategic planning to a separate staff – as in the past – it needs to include a wide range of people, from line managers to customers to suppliers. Top managers must listen and be prepared to shift plans in midstream, if conditions demand it. This is exactly the approach that Cisco Systems takes. It is not wedded to any particular technology, because it recognizes that customers are the arbiters of choice. It listens carefully to its customers and then offers solutions that customers want.

Our final section addresses the relationship between HR and business strategy in more detail.

Relationship of HR strategy to business strategy

Human resource strategy parallels and facilitates the implementation of the strategic business plan. HR strategy refers to the processes, decisions, and choices the organization makes regarding its human resources and how they are organized. HR strategies are often formulated to align with the organization's strategy, by creating the capacity in the workforce and how it is organized that is necessary to achieve the organization's strategic objectives. It requires a focus on planned major changes in the organization and on critical issues, such as the following:

- What are the HR implications of the proposed organizational strategies?
- What are the possible external constraints and requirements?
- What are the implications for management practices, management development, and management succession?
- What can be done in the short term to prepare for longer-term needs? In this approach to the strategic management of human resources, a firm's business strategy and its HR strategy are interdependent.[47]

Figure 1.2 is a simple model, which we elaborate more completely in later chapters, that shows the relationship of HR strategy to the broader business strategy.[48] Briefly, the model shows that planning proceeds top down, while execution proceeds bottom up. There are four links in the model, beginning with the fundamental question "How do we compete?" As we noted earlier, firms may compete on a number of non-independent dimensions, such as innovation, quality, cost leadership, or speed. From this, it becomes possible to identify business or organizational processes that the firm must execute well in order to compete (e.g., speedy order fulfillment). When processes are executed well, the organization delights its internal and external customers through high performance. This may occur, for example, when an employee presents a timely, cost-effective solution to a customer's problem.

At a general level, high-performance work practices include the following five features:[49]

(1) pushing responsibility down to employees operating in flatter organizations;
(2) increased emphasis on line managers as HR managers;
(3) instilling learning as a priority in all organizational systems;
(4) decentralizing decision making to autonomous units and employees; and

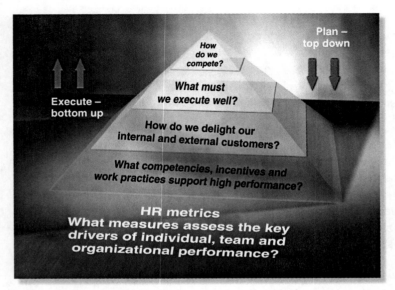

Figure 1.2 The relationship of HR strategy to the broader strategy of a business
Source: SHRM Foundation (2004). *HR in Alignment*, DVD. Alexandria, VA: SHRM Foundation (available at www.shrm.org/Foundation).

(5) linking performance measures for employees to financial performance indicators.

To manage and motivate employees to strive for high performance, the right competencies, incentives, and work practices must be in place. Execution proceeds from the bottom up, as appropriate competencies, challenging incentives, and work practices inspire high performance, which delights internal and external customers. This, in turn, means that business processes are being executed efficiently, enabling the organization to compete successfully for business in the marketplace.

HR metrics serve as a kind of overlay to the model itself. HR metrics should effect the key drivers of individual, team, and organizational performance. When they do, the organization is measuring what really matters. Like any other aspect of business, HR issues, sometimes called talent-related issues, carry risk. Prudently managing those risks is a never-ending challenge. It is also a critical component of value creation, as the next section makes clear.

Strategy and risk

When we use the term "risk," we are referring to an undesirable outcome and its consequences, usually when that outcome or its consequences are uncertain. While risk cannot be eliminated, given the many uncertainties in the environment and the sudden, violent changes that sometimes occur in the business world, it is possible to optimize the kinds of risks that organizations face. Chapter 4 provides a framework for integrating risk optimization into human capital strategy. Here we note simply that the concept of risk management is rapidly becoming an integral feature of business strategy and operational management. As we move deeper into the twenty-first century, a variety of outside agencies and observers are beginning to recognize talent-related risks as important features of organizations.

Thus the global accounting firm Ernst & Young identified this category of risk as "one of the key business risks of our time."[50] Its survey of Fortune 1000 executives from finance, HR, and risk management reported that the top five HR risks are: talent management and succession planning; ethics and tone at the top; regulatory compliance; pay and performance alignment; and employee training and development.

At a general level, the recent global financial crisis exposed the weakness of risk-management systems in many organizations: boards that did not consider macroeconomic factors when assessing risks, and risk committees that did not receive accurate information regarding mission-critical risks and the effectiveness of their organizations' responses to mitigate them. It is not surprising, then, that the global spotlight on risk management has intensified. The US Securities and Exchange Commission now requires that proxy statements filed by public companies include the role of the board of directors in risk oversight, the nature of communications between executives and the board on risk issues, and the disclosure of risk-based compensation policies. The US National Association of Corporate Directors' report on risk governance urges boards to assess strategic risks, closely monitor risks in culture and incentives, and consider emerging global risks to the firm's business. In a related development, the International Organization for Standardization's recent ISO 31000 guidance defines a common global approach to risk management.[51]

Finally, a 2010 Korn/Ferry survey of several hundred executives in more than sixty-five countries found that boards and CEOs are reporting that the overriding lesson of effective risk management is that it must become an integrated element of strategy. Corporate leaders increasingly see the levels of risk and the metrics of risk as inherent components of developing and executing strategies, and in evaluating the appropriate tolerance for risk.[52] As we noted earlier, risks tend to fall into one of two classes: (1) those associated with the protection of existing assets (e.g., intellectual property [IP], physical assets); and (2) those associated with the creation of value (e.g., new products or services). Both inherently incorporate the potential for failure if they are not managed well.

The 2004 risk-management report of the Committee of Sponsoring Organizations of the Treadway Commission (COSO) provided a more specific framework of risk categories. The commission notes that risk mitigation is only one element of a complete approach to risk:[53]

> Events can have negative impact, positive impact, or both. Events with a negative impact represent risks, which can prevent value creation or erode existing value. Events with positive impact may offset negative impacts or represent opportunities. Opportunities are the possibility that an event will occur and positively affect the achievement of objectives, supporting value creation or preservation. Management channels opportunities back to its strategy or objective-setting processes, formulating plans to seize the opportunities.

Figure 1.3 shows enterprise risk management (ERM) in three dimensions, with the top face of the cube reflecting the risk-management objectives:

* *strategic* – high-level goals, aligned with and supporting the company's mission;
* *operations* – the effective and efficient use of its resources;
* *reporting* – the reliability of reporting; and
* *compliance* – compliance with the applicable laws and regulations.

The front face of the cube reflects the risk-management activities (objective setting, event identification, etc.), and the side face of the cube reflects the organizational entity or level of analysis at which

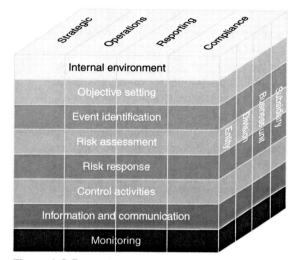

Figure 1.3 Enterprise risk-management framework
Source: COSO (2004). *Enterprise Risk Management – Integrated Framework: Executive Summary.* Chicago: COSO, 5.

the risk management occurs (subsidiary, division, etc.). The risk-management "cells" represent the intersection of each of the three dimensions, and COSO suggests this as a way to describe the domain across which opportunity, risk, and uncertainty can be managed.

With regard to human resource strategy, we return to apply the COSO "cube" in later chapters. For now, simply understand two general points: (1) human resource or human capital "risk" management should distinguish among uncertainty, risk, and opportunity; and (2) human resource strategy can address risk management either by managing the HR issues that affect the elements of the risk "cube" (e.g., by preparing the workforce to be better at event identification) or by applying the elements of the cube directly to HR issues (e.g., by evaluating the operational risk associated with HR processes such as staffing and payroll).

Conclusion

Strategy comprises the decisions, processes and choices that organizations make to position themselves for sustainable success. These decisions, processes, and choices define a firm's competitive position in the marketplace. Strategy provides an overall direction and focus for the organization as a whole, including for each functional area. At a broad level, there are four basic schools of thought regarding strategy: position (winners select favorable markets as defined by external forces); execution (winners gain advantage through operational excellence); adaptation (winners develop an overall direction through experimentation and rapid change); and concentration (winners make the most of current core strengths and businesses). Each has something significant to offer, so long as it is adopted in an appropriately balanced way.

With respect to HR, overall business strategy, through its hierarchy of goals – vision, mission, and strategic objectives – provides helpful guidance about the type of talent that will be necessary to fulfill the organization's strategic objectives, and to move toward its mission and vision. Nonetheless, there are significant risks associated with managing talent. These risks can be managed, but, to do so, HR professionals need to act now to raise awareness in their organizations about current and impending talent risks, to identify workable strategies to address emerging needs, and to implement action plans to operationalize those strategies. To do otherwise is to ignore human capital risks that can threaten the success of the business strategy that the enterprise has worked so diligently to develop. In order to develop a framework for addressing these risks, our next two chapters address the external environment that underpins decisions about business and HR strategies (Chapter 2), and the context and levels at which HR strategies develop (Chapter 3). Following that, we consider more explicitly how risk optimization and management can be incorporated into HR strategy (Chapter 4).

Notes

1 Lawler, E. E., and Worley, C. G., with Creelman, D. (2011). *Management Reset: Organizing for Sustainable Effectiveness*. San Francisco: Jossey-Bass.
2 Porter, M. E. (1996). What is strategy? *Harvard Business Review*, 74(6): 61–78.
3 Porter (1996).
4 For more on Southwest Airlines, see O'Reilly, C. A., and Pfeffer, J. (2000). *Hidden Value: How Great Companies Achieve Extraordinary Results with Ordinary People*. Boston: Harvard Business School Press, 21–48.
5 Mainardi, C., and Kleiner, A. (2010). The right to win. *Strategy and Business*, 61: 1–12.

6 Mainardi and Kleiner (2010).
7 Boudreau, J. W., and Ramstad, P. M. (2007). *Beyond HR: The New Science of Human Capital.* Boston: Harvard Business School Press.
8 Porter, M. E. (2008). The five competitive forces that shape strategy. *Harvard Business Review*, 86(1): 79–93.
9 Porter (2008).
10 Porter (2008); see also www.Paccar.com.
11 Lublin, J. S., and Mattioli, D. (2010). Strategic plans lose favor. *Wall Street Journal*, January 25: B7.
12 Barney, J. B. (1995). Looking inside for competitive advantage. *Academy of Management Executives*, 9(4): 49–61.
13 Society for Human Resource Management [SHRM] Foundation (2008). *Seeing Forward: Succession Planning at 3M*, DVD. Alexandria, VA: SHRM Foundation.
14 Barney (1995).
15 World's most admired companies: the 50 all-stars. *Fortune*, March 19, 2012: 140. Tkaczyk, C. (2010). World's most admired companies. CNNMoney, http://money.cnn.com/magazines/fortune/mostadmired/2010/snapshots/670.html (accessed January 26, 2011).
16 Barney (1995).
17 Amit, R., and Schoemaker, P. (1993). Strategic assets and organizational rent. *Strategic Management Journal*, 14(1): 33–46.
18 Barney (1995).
19 Kearns, D. T., and Nadler, D. A. (1992). *Prophets in the Dark: How Xerox Reinvented Itself and Beat Back the Japanese.* New York: HarperCollins; Smith, D. K., and Alexander, R. C. (1988). *Fumbling the Future: How Xerox Invented, then Ignored, the First Personal Computer.* New York: William Morrow.
20 Rosenfeld, J. (2000). Unit of one. *Fast Company*, April: 98.
21 Cendrowski, S. (2011). How Amazon keeps cranking. *Fortune*, February 28: 18.
22 Cendrowski (2011).
23 SHRM Foundation (2004). *Sysco: HR in Alignment*, DVD. Alexandria, VA: SHRM Foundation.
24 Bidgoli, H. (2004). *The Internet Encyclopedia*, vol. I. New York: Wiley, 707.
25 Dess, G. D., Lumpkin, G. T., and Eisner, A. B. (2007). *Strategic Management: Text and Cases*, 3rd edn. Burr Ridge, IL: McGraw-Hill/Irwin.
26 Porter (1996).
27 Material in this section is adapted from Mainardi and Kleiner (2010).
28 Kiechel, W. (2010). *The Lords of Strategy: The Secret Intellectual History of the New Corporate World.* Boston: Harvard Business School Press.
29 Kleiner, A. (2008). *The Age of Heretics: A History of the Radical Thinkers Who Reinvented Corporate Management*, 2nd edn. San Francisco: Jossey-Bass.

30 Mintzberg, H., Ahlstrand, B., and Lampel, J. (2009). *Strategy Safari: The Complete Guide through the Wilds of Strategic Management*, 2nd edn. Upper Saddle River, NJ: FT Prentice Hall.

31 Mainardi and Kleiner (2010).

32 Mainardi and Kleiner (2010).

33 Six sigma is a fact-based, data-driven philosophy of quality improvement that values defect prevention over defect detection. In simple terms, six sigma quality performance means no more than 3.4 defects per million opportunities. Source: http://asq.org/learn-about-quality/six-sigma/overview/overview.html.

34 Deming, W. E. (1986). *Out of the Crisis*. Boston: MIT Press.

35 Hammer, M., and Champy, J. (2003). *Reengineering the Corporation: A Manifesto for Business Revolution*, rev. edn. New York: Harper Business.

36 Bossidy, L., and Charan, R. (2002). *Execution: The Discipline of Getting Things Done*. New York: Crown Business.

37 See, for example, Kim, W. C., and Mauborgne, R. (2005). *Blue Ocean Strategy: How to Create Uncontested Market Space and Make the Competition Irrelevant*. Boston: Harvard Business School Press.

38 Mainardi and Kleiner (2010).

39 Mintzberg, H. (1994). *The Rise and Fall of Strategic Planning: Reconceiving Roles for Planning, Plans, Planners*. New York: Free Press.

40 Mainardi and Kleiner (2010: 10).

41 Hamel, G., and Prahalad, C. K. (1994). *Competing for the Future*. Boston: Harvard Business School Press.

42 Zook, C. (2010). *Profit from the Core: A Return to Growth in Turbulent Times*. Boston: Harvard Business School Press.

43 Mainardi and Kleiner (2010).

44 Lipton, M. (1996). Demystifying the development of an organizational vision. *Sloan Management Review*, 37(4): 83–92.

45 Dess, Lumpkin, and Eisner (2007).

46 Dess, Lumpkin, and Eisner (2007).

47 Becker, B. E., Huselid, M. A., and Ulrich, D. (2001). *The HR Scorecard: Linking People, Strategy, and Performance*. Boston: Harvard Business School Press. See also Huselid, M. A., Becker, B. E., and Beatty, R. W. (2005). *The Workforce Scorecard: Managing Human Capital to Execute Strategy*. Boston: Harvard Business School Press.

48 SHRM Foundation (2004).

49 Cascio, W. F., and Boudreau, J. W. (2011). *Investing in People: Financial Impact of Human Resource Initiatives*, 2nd edn. Upper Saddle River, NJ: Pearson Education/FT Press.

50 Ernst & Young (2008). *Global HR Risk: From the Danger Zone to the Value Zone*, webcast. London: Ernst & Young.

51 Bhatt, N. (2010). Despite global crisis, companies unprepared for risk management. *Economic Times* [India], October 8 (available at http://economictimes.indiatimes.com; accessed October 12, 2010).

52 Sorkin, A. R. (2010, Aug. 10). Crisis-shaken executives sharpen focus on risk. *New York Times*, August 10 (available at http://dealbook.blogs.nytimes.com; accessed August 12, 2010).

53 COSO (2004). *Enterprise Risk Management – Integrated Framework: Executive Summary.* Chicago: COSO.

2 The external environment

HR should be every company's "killer app." What could possibly be more important than who gets hired, developed, promoted, or moved out the door? Business is a game, and as with all games, the team that puts the best people on the field and gets them playing together wins. It's that simple.[1]

Jack Welch, former CEO of General Electric

Among the choices and results of HR strategy are which people to "put on the field," "when and where they play," and "getting them to play together." Today, the people who work for an organization may come from down the street or from across the sea. Moreover, they may be physically co-located or only "meet" virtually. "Getting them to play together" has never been more challenging, especially when the game is being played on a field and in a context that includes changing fan preferences, changing rules and regulations, global franchises, and the technology that enables, records, and broadcasts the game. In this chapter we identify some of the challenges that businesses face in today's world. Our objective to is identify key forces and trends that are helping to shape how business is transacted, and how it will be transacted in the future, with particular emphasis on forces and trends that have implications for how strategy and human capital connect. Let us begin by considering two mega-trends: the effects of globalization and technology on organizations. Figure 2.1 illustrates other aspects of the external environments of organizations that we discuss in this chapter.

Globalization

Perhaps the single most dominant trend that will continue to play a major role is globalization – the free movement of goods, services, and people across international borders. Globalization is a fact

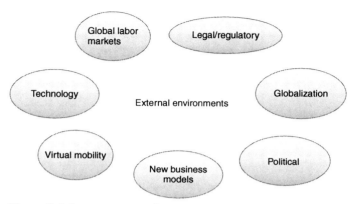

Figure 2.1 Some aspects of the external environments of organizations

of organizational life, as countries, companies, and workers are interconnected as never before. Global trade connects the fate of every industry and laborer, no matter how small or seemingly self-sufficient, to the decisions of bureaucrats in China, shipbuilders in South Korea, and bankers everywhere.[2] To illustrate, consider how the ripple effects of the Japanese earthquake of 2011 affected automobile manufacturers. When the quake shut down parts suppliers in Japan, the assembly of General Motors vehicles in Shreveport, Louisiana, and Buffalo, New York State, also shut down, and workers were laid off. Production slowdowns in Spain, France, and Germany affected GM, Toyota, and PSA Peugeot-Citroën.[3] As another example, consider how the financial crisis in Greece, a member of the European Union, depressed stock markets everywhere in 2011, and threatened to cause a second global financial crisis. Indeed, a global marketplace has been created by factors such as the following.[4]

- Global telecommunications, enhanced by fiber optics, satellites, and computer technology.
- E-commerce that makes firms global from the moment their websites are up and running, as customers from around the world log on.
- Giant multinational corporations such as AstraZeneca, Unilever, and Nestlé, which have begun to lose their national identities as they integrate and coordinate product design, manufacturing, sales, and services on a worldwide basis. For example, IBM generates 65 percent of its sales outside the United States.[5]

- Growing free trade among nations (e.g., the European Union; the North American Free Trade Agreement linking Mexico, the United States, and Canada; and the Association of Southeast Asian Nations).
- Financial markets are now open twenty-four hours a day around the world.
- Cost pressures (which prod firms to move where labor and other resources are cheapest), coupled with a search for new markets (as firms and consumers around the world seek foreign goods and services).
- The integration of cultures and values through international travel, as well as the spread of goods such as music, food, and clothing. In combination, these have led to common consumer demands around the world.
- The emergence of global standards and regulations for trade, commerce, finance, products, and services.

Global labor markets

Another feature of globalization is that cheap labor and plentiful resources, combined with ease of travel and communication, have created global labor markets. This is fueling mobility as more companies expand abroad and people consider foreign postings a natural part of their professional development. In the aggregate, more than 500 million people, double the number today, will legally work outside their home countries in the next twenty years. Why? Experts point to factors such as conflict, natural disasters, climate change, and economic opportunism.[6] The implication, of course, is that there will be a great need for employees and leaders with well-developed cross-cultural skills and the ability to adapt to changing circumstances, to embrace change, and to listen to promising ideas from anyone, anywhere. Characteristics such as these have direct implications for strategy development and implementation, as more and more companies develop global staffing strategies. As examples, consider the following.[7]

- At heavy-equipment maker Caterpillar Inc. more than a half of the 15,000 people hired in 2010 were outside the United States. UPS is also hiring more aggressively overseas. For both companies, sales in international markets are growing twice as rapidly as sales in domestic ones.

- At fiber and chemicals giant DuPont, the number of US employees shrank by 9 percent from 2005 to 2009; during the same time period the number of employees in the Asia-Pacific region grew by 54 percent.
- Among Coca-Cola's 93,000 global employees, fewer than 13 percent of them were located in the United States in 2009, down from 19 percent five years earlier. This trend is unlikely to reverse course anytime soon, as the company is completing a three-year, $2 billion investment in China and a five-year, $1 billion investment in the Philippines.

Why is this happening? The short answer is the rise of the middle class in developing countries such as India, China, and Brazil. Companies are striving to meet the growing demands of global consumers, and this often means that they need to locate factories and operations close to those consumers. In light of that demand, many of the products manufactured overseas (and the jobs created to fulfill that demand) are not coming back to the United States. Fully one-half of the revenue of the S&P 500 companies has come from outside the United States in recent years. Indeed, by 2015 the number of consumers in Asia's middle class will equal the number in Europe and North America combined. Is it any surprise, then, that the number one worry of Mike Duke, CEO of Wal-Mart, is "continuing to grow the talent for a company that's growing around the world"?[8]

To be sure, global labor markets enable employment opportunities well beyond the borders of one's home country. This means that competition for talent will come not only from the company down the street but also from the employer on the other side of the world. It will be a seller's market, with talented individuals having many choices. Countries as well as companies will need to brand themselves as employers of choice in order to attract this talent.[9]

Along with these trends, expect to see three more. The first is increasing workforce flux, as more roles are automated or outsourced, and more workers are contract-based or mobile or work flexible hours. This may allow companies to leverage global resources more efficiently, but it also will increase the complexity of management's role. Second, expect more diversity as workers come from a greater range of backgrounds. Those with local knowledge of an emerging market, a global outlook, and an intuitive sense of the corporate culture will be particularly valued. Not surprisingly, talented young people will more frequently choose their employers on the basis, at least in part, of opportunities to gain international experience. Finally, technical skills, while mandatory, will be less defining of the successful manager than the ability to work across cultures and to build relationships with many different constituents.[10]

Technology

Perhaps it is Thomas Friedman, author of *The World Is Flat*, who has expressed the effects of technology best when he writes: "You know the 'IT revolution' that the business press has been touting for the last 20 years? Sorry, but that was only the prologue. The last 20 years were just about forging, sharpening, and distributing all the new tools with which to collaborate and connect. Now the real IT revolution is about to begin, as all the complementarities between these tools start to really work together to level the playing field."[11]

In fact, there are two aspects to the technological revolution that is taking place.[12] The first is the rapid and continuous fall in the cost of computing. This has impacted the ease with which work has been outsourced to low-cost economies, and has also seen some work replaced by complex data analytics and robotics. The fact is, workers are getting more expensive while technology is getting cheaper, and this combination is encouraging companies to spend money on machines rather than on people. Equipment and software prices have dipped 2.4 percent since the end of the 2007–9 recession, but labor costs have risen 6.7 percent.[13] Nor does that trend seem to be lessening, as money spent on software, data, storage, and other functions delivered via the internet is projected to climb from $30 billion in 2011 to more than $160 billion by 2020.[14]

The second technological trend that executives believe is currently shaping work is increased connectivity across the world. This connectivity, combined with the trend of rapid digitalization of the world's knowledge, has created the opportunities for billions of people in both megacities and rural areas to share ideas and to begin to create the possibility of a "global consciousness." Mass collaboration through file sharing, blogs, and social networking services is making leaps in creativity possible, and changing the way companies in a variety of industries do business. Here are some examples.[15]

- *Research and development*. Procter & Gamble makes use of outside scientific networks to generate 35 percent of new products from outside the company, up from 20 percent three years ago. This has helped boost sales per R&D person by 40 percent.
- *Software development*. By coordinating their efforts online, programmers worldwide volunteer on more than 100,000 open-source projects, such as Linux, thereby challenging traditional software.
- *Telecommuncations*. More than 41 million people use Skype software to share computer-processing power and bandwidth, allowing them to call each other for free over the internet. This has cut revenues sharply at traditional telecom providers.
- *Retail*. With 61 million active members, eBay has created a self-sustaining alternative to retail stores.

The internet gives everyone in the organization, at any level and in every functional area, the ability to access a mind-boggling array of information – instantaneously from anywhere. Instead of seeping out over months or years, ideas can be zapped around the globe in the blink of an eye.

Connectivity and the continuous fall in the cost of computing have also created a novel connection between technology and work, namely the increasing prevalence of data storage in "the cloud" – that is, in web-connected servers rather than on desktop or laptop computers. Cloud technology will create a global infrastructure for storing services, applications, and resources. It will allow anyone with a computer or handheld device to "rent" services on a minute-by-minute basis.

Lynda Gratton notes that as these applications become more advanced we can expect more of the talent of a company to be held in the "ecosystem" of the myriad of small businesses, some of which will be involved in complex intellectual property development. In essence, this is a "cloud" approach to human capital and talent. Cloud technology has enormous potential to bring sophisticated technology to every corner of the world, and this will impact where work takes place as well as how it takes place. Low-cost, ubiquitous connectivity will certainly reduce the barriers to the emergence of micro-entrepreneurs, while also creating ever more opportunities for open innovation.[16]

What will companies look like in 2020?

According to recent research from the Economist Intelligence Unit, companies will become larger and more global, handling operations in more countries than they do today. At the same time, they will be more globally integrated, with better information flow and collaboration across borders. They will be less centralized, but not fully decentralized either. Local operations will be free to move on opportunities that will advance the interests of the global organization, while headquarters will continue to play an important role in setting the tone and values of the company.

Companies will also be flatter, with employees being given more opportunities for decision making, often at an earlier stage in their careers. The size of the workforce may fluctuate in response to shifting talent needs across global operations. Such flexibility will have a cost, however, as the average worker feels less loyalty to the organization, which may lead to greater employee churn over time.[17]

Effects of globalization and technology on labor markets

A labor market is a geographical area within which the forces of supply (people looking for work) interact with the forces of demand (employers looking for people), and thereby determine the price of labor.[18] Labor markets, in turn, may be internal (within an organization, where employees peddle their skills to available buyers) or external. External labor markets may be local, regional, national, or global. Globalization and technology have created labor markets that are truly global in scope. Consider how times have changed:

> During the agrarian revolution, the most important resource was land. During the industrial revolution it was capital and machinery. In post-industrial society, it is increasingly knowledge. Consequently, the growth of the "knowledge class" will constitute a larger part of the labor force, if not the largest.[19]

Competition – among companies and countries – for highly skilled workers will intensify in the coming decade. There will be abundant opportunities for well-educated people with critical expertise. Indeed, the World Economic Forum predicts significant global talent risks – deep and widespread talent shortages by 2020 in both the Northern and Southern Hemispheres – over the next decade. In the Northern

Hemisphere, the expected talent gaps will be caused mainly by demographic shifts, notably the retirement of the baby boomers. For example, in the United States, Germany, Canada, and the United Kingdom, immigration and expected birth rates will not balance the workforce losses caused by aging populations. In the Southern Hemisphere, talent gaps are anticipated due to lower skill levels. In short, human capital is replacing financial capital as the engine of economic prosperity.[20]

To appreciate just one dimension of this issue, consider that the United States, often perceived as the best location for top scientists and engineers, is strongly reliant on immigrant contributions. Foreign nationals are authors on the majority of patent applications filed by many US companies: 65 percent at Merck, 64 percent at GE, and 60 percent at Cisco.[21] Geographical and virtual mobility will define many highly skilled workers in the coming decade. They will be technologically savvy, mentally flexible, and committed to learning new skills and reinventing themselves to achieve meaningful careers. Many, especially younger workers, will be willing to move either temporarily or permanently to new locations to pursue opportunities. Any organization that continues to rely on conventional learning and routine work done in silos, without fostering a culture of continuous learning, will face ever-deepening talent gaps.

Talent risks are real, for instance, as young people's expectations for their work lives contrast dramatically with those of their parents. Instead of adjusting their lives to the job, these new workers expect to adjust their jobs to their lives. Instead of long-term relationships with employers, they will be satisfied with a planning horizon of two to five years.[22] Strategic choices about where to compete and to locate operations are heavily influenced by legal, regulatory, and political considerations. The next sections explore these issues at a general level.

Legal and regulatory environments

It goes without saying that legal and regulatory environments affect the strategic choices that firms make. Many of these choices involve people-related business issues. Although a detailed, country-based treatment of legal and environmental concerns is beyond the scope of this chapter, consider just one dimension of this issue: the prerogative of managers to hire and fire at will and the ability of firms to lay off employees. Employees in many countries other than the United States have employment contracts with rules regarding severance and notice of termination. Here, in brief, are the requirements in eight of them.[23]

- *Mexico*. Employees receive three months' pay plus an additional twenty days of pay per year of service.
- *France*. Employees get at least thirty days' severance pay for each year of service, though companies usually pay more to avoid labor tribunals.
- *Russia*. Employers must give at least two months' notice, and employees are entitled to at least one month's severance pay.
- *United Kingdom*. Employers must give one week's notice per year of service, up to twelve weeks. Employees receive a minimum of £299 per year of service.
- *Japan*. Employers must give employees thirty days' notice.
- *India*. Employers must give laid-off workers once month's salary, plus fifteen days' wages for every year of service.
- *Germany*. Employers must give notice of up to seven months, along with two weeks' pay for each year of employment.
- *China*. Employers must give thirty days' notice or at least one month's wages.

In many cases, the determination of who goes and in what order is determined by statute. In the Netherlands, the rule is "Last in, first out." In other countries, social criteria determine layoffs. In Germany, for example, it is a legal obligation to select employees for downsizing using objective criteria. These criteria may include personal factors, such as family size and employability. Thus employees with disabilities or those nearing retirement often enjoy a higher level of de facto job protection than do other employees.[24] Considerations such as these may have significant effects on the decisions of companies to operate in particular countries. So also do political considerations.

The political environment

At a general level, political risk is a key consideration for managers in deciding whether, and to what extent, to operate in a given country. As a senior manager, do you really want to commit assets and people to a country where the rule of law is in question or where property rights, including intellectual property rights, are not well developed? In general, unstable political regimes or countries characterized by high levels of corruption are red flags to companies about doing business there.

A somewhat different aspect of this issue, however, is the effect of political pressures to locate work in countries that consume an organization's products or use its services. As an example, consider some of the problems Boeing faced in building its "Dreamliner" 787 aircraft, the first examples of which were delivered in 2011 after many delays. Flag carriers (national airlines) in many countries around the world would like to be able to claim that their country's people helped to build the planes the carrier is flying. To lower the $10 billion or so that it would cost to develop the plane by itself, Boeing authorized a team of parts suppliers to design and build major sections of the craft, which it planned to assemble at a Seattle-area factory. This posed a major operational risk, in that control of the assembly of various sections of the airplane was now outsourced, and, unfortunately, outsourcing so much responsibility turned out to be far more difficult than anticipated.[25]

The supplier problems ranged from language barriers to problems that developed when some contractors themselves outsourced chunks of the work. For their part, some suppliers complained that the company was three to eight months late in giving them final specifications for structures and systems. The lesson? Program managers thought they had adequate oversight of suppliers, but learned later that there were many details that they knew nothing about. They needed insight into what was actually going on in suppliers' factories so they could help suppliers deal with the challenges they faced.

This underscores a key finding from a global outsourcing study, namely that managing such an extended network of relationships requires more transparency, better communication, greater trust, and genuine reciprocity, as client–service-provider relationships shift from adversarial to collaborative, from procurement to partnership.[26] We will have more to say about the human resource risk elements in this example in Chapter 5.

Whether it is outsourcing business processes or managing knowledge, one thing is clear: intellectual capital will be critical to business success. The advantage of bringing breakthrough products to market first will be shorter than ever, because technology will let competitors match or exceed them almost instantly. To keep ahead of the steep new-product curve, it will be crucial for businesses to attract and retain the best thinkers. Companies will need to build a deep reservoir of talent – including both employees and free agents – to succeed in this new era. One way to do this is by harnessing the power of virtual mobility.

Virtual mobility

Mobility need not imply that one changes geographical locations, as the following quote from David Arkless, president of Manpower Inc., suggests: "According to our research, roughly 30% of tasks in multinational corporations could be done virtually. Virtual mobility can also take the lead in the inclusion and enablement of women, who have previously been excluded from the labor force."[27]

Women's work opportunities matter, as shown by several studies that found significant correlations between gender diversity and corporate financial performance.[28] Women are one of the fastest-growing dynamic economic forces in the world today, with assets worth $20 trillion worldwide. In the United States alone, women-owned businesses generate $4 trillion, while women comprise nearly 14 percent of the entrepreneurs in Thailand, 12 percent in Argentina, 11 percent in Brazil, and 10 percent in Chile and Mexico. As women begin to make up more than a half of all university graduates in much of the developed world, there is an increased consciousness that this talent must be given the opportunity to lead.

Several countries have introduced legislation that mandates minimum requirements for women's participation, in both business and politics. Numerous multinational companies have aligned core elements of their businesses and products to support and provide opportunities for women in the communities in which they are active. Despite these encouraging statistics, in many countries and within many companies, women are an under-used and under-appreciated resource. Chapter 5 provides more detailed examples of how decisions about human capital practices are directly affected by the environmental context.

Another important trend that may affect organizations everywhere instantly, and sometimes with violent shocks, is disruptive technology, as reflected in new business models that no one anticipated, least of all the established players in a market. The following sections present several examples that rocked their industries.

New business models

As Gary Hamel notes in *Leading the Revolution*, we have entered a new age – the age of revolutions in business concepts. The age of incremental progress, little by little, in tiny steps – a little cheaper, a little better, a little faster – is over. Today, the nature of change has changed. No longer is it additive. No longer does it move in a straight line. In the twenty-first century change is discontinuous, abrupt, and distinctly non-linear.[29] A key reason for this is that the internet has rendered geography meaningless. At the same time, global capital flows have become a raging torrent. The cost of storing a megabyte of data has dropped from hundreds of dollars to essentially nothing. In this new age, a company that is evolving slowly is already on its way to extinction.

In the age of incremental progress, industrial giants such as DuPont, Mitsubishi, DaimlerChrysler, and General Motors harnessed the disciplines of progress: rigorous planning, continuous improvement, statistical process control, six sigma, reengineering, and ERP. Decade after decade they focused single-mindedly on getting better. If they happened to miss something that was changing in the environment, there was plenty of time to catch up. The advantages of being the incumbent – global distribution, respected brands, a deep pool of talent, cash flow – granted them the luxury of time. Thus, although Apple Computer got an early start in the microcomputer business in the late 1970s and early 1980s, IBM quickly reversed Apple's lead when it threw its worldwide distribution might behind the PC. In a world of discontinuous change, however, a company that misses a critical development may never catch up. Consider just one example.

Between 1994 and 2001 the number of mobile phones sold each year exploded, from 26 million to more than 400 million. By 2011 there were 5.3 billion mobile phone subscribers worldwide, led by China and India. That is 77 percent of the world's population! During the 1994–2001 timeframe, the technology changed from analog to digital. Motorola, the world leader in the cellular telephone business until 1997, missed the shift to digital wireless technology by just a year or two. In that sliver of time, Nokia, a hitherto unknown company perched on the edge of the Arctic Circle, became the world's new number one. In the late 1980s Nokia was making snow tires and rubber boots. Suddenly, it was one of Europe's fastest-growing high-tech companies. Motorola is no longer a top player. As of 2011, in mobile phones, Nokia was the world's leader, with a 32.6 percent market share, followed by Samsung at 20.2 percent and LG at 8.4 percent. In mobile smartphones, Nokia also dominated world market share, at 34.2 percent, while RIM had 16.7 percent and Apple 16.2 percent. Expect that situation to change, though, as Apple's iPhone sales are growing at a rate of better than 89 percent per year.[30]

Today, 100-year-old companies with venerated brands are as vulnerable as yesterday's internet darlings of the dot.com revolution. A common error is to mistake historical rivals for the enemy. Go to any large company in the music industry. Find its strategic plan from 2002. Look for any reference to the iTunes Music Store. You will not find any. This is because it was not until April 28, 2003, that Apple introduced the iTunes Music Store – and rocked the entire music industry with 99 cent pricing for downloadable songs.[31] The lesson: do not mistake historical rivals for future ones.

In a recent Gallup poll, 500 CEOs were asked: "Who took better advantage of change in your industry over the past ten years – newcomers, traditional competitors, or your own company?" The number one answer was "newcomers." Then they were asked whether the newcomers had won by changing the rules of the game or by executing better. Fully 62 percent of the CEOs said the newcomers had won by changing the rules of the game.

Despite this, how many times have you heard senior executives say "Our real problem is execution"? Or, worse, they will tell people: "Strategy is the easy part; implementation is the hard part." As Hamel notes in *Leading the Revolution*, that is nonsense. Strategy is easy if you are content to have an approach that is based on someone else's. Strategy is anything but easy if your goal is to be the author of an industry revolution. It is immensely rewarding, however, as you put your fingerprints all over the future, and in some cases, such as Steve Jobs and Apple Inc., radically reinvent entire industries, such as music (iPod, iTunes), movies (Pixar, animated films), and telecommunications (iPhone). Meanwhile, Apple's impact on its original industry, computers, has only grown (think iPad2, MacBook Air, MacBook Pro). As *Fortune* magazine noted in naming Jobs as its "Entrepreneur of the decade":

> Remaking any one business is a career-defining achievement; four
> is unheard of. Think about that for a moment. Henry Ford altered

the course of the nascent auto industry. Pan Am's Juan Trippe invented the global airline. Conrad Hilton internationalized American hospitality. In all instances, and many more like them, these entrepreneurs turned captains of industry defined a single market that had previously not been dominated by anyone. The industries that Jobs has turned topsy-turvy already existed when he focused on them.[32]

Our next section presents another example of a revolutionary business concept: a new car that commands a price tag of just $2,900. Does that sound impossible? Read on.

Nano, a people's car for the developing world[33]

As head of the Mumbai-based Tata Group, which employs 395,000 people in eighty countries, Ratan Tata has engineered a remarkable transformation at the enterprise that his great-grandfather founded in 1868. It encompasses ninety-eight operating companies that, among other things, make steel and chemicals, provide information technology, own hotels, produce tea, and build cars. Tata Group's 2010 revenues of $67.4 billion represented a twelvefold increase since 1991.

Tata Motors has been making passenger cars for only thirteen years and lacks the depth of experience of older companies, as well as an established supplier network. Although it also owns the Land Rover and Jaguar brands, most of its revenue comes from trucks, buses, and other commercial vehicles. The Tata Nano, with a beginning price of $2,900, is the world's cheapest automobile. It is designed to lure India's growing middle class away from their bicycles and motor scooters, and into safe, family-size, and weatherproof vehicles. It is a great example of market segmentation. India provides a solid base from which to grow, because just two new vehicles are sold annually for every 1,000 inhabitants, versus up to fifty-eight per 1,000 in the United States in some years. In short, India's population of 1.2 billion people represents an enormous untapped market. If it takes off in India, the Nano could eventually represent an export opportunity to the United States and Europe.

Consider some cost-saving tricks that the Nano's engineers used to build the car within price specifications. They used three lug nuts instead of four to hold each wheel to its axle. Components multitask, so the horizontal brace holding the front seats to the floor also serves as side-impact protection. There is no radio, there are no airbags, and there is only one windshield wiper. Air-conditioning is an option. When packaging and convenience conflict, packaging wins. The tiny engine is stowed beneath the back seat, and is accessible only after unscrewing six wing nuts. The car weighs just 1,320 pounds, about half as much as a compact car in the United States. Its engine generates 35 horsepower, and gets 50 miles per gallon of gas. Rajan Tata is considering "a more potent" vehicle for the US market that could sell for $7,000 to $8,000, with a bigger engine, a wider stance, and better crash protection. "If you have a vision, you can come pretty close to doing it, even if everybody tells you it can't be done," he says. The Nano is proof positive that he can deliver on his promises.

Business concept innovation

Yes, business concept revolutionaries such as the late Steve Jobs and Rajan Tata represent chief executive officers with vision. Many people believe that change *must* start at the top – but that is not always so. How often does a revolution start with the monarchy? Did Nelson Mandela, Václav Havel, Thomas Paine, Mahatma Gandhi, or Martin Luther King possess political power? No. Each disrupted history, however, and it was passion, not power, that allowed them to do so. This is where the link to company culture and values is forged. Never has there been a more propitious time for visionary leadership and business concept innovation – that can develop anytime, anywhere.

Consider some examples: in a flattening world, e-mail, corporate intranets, and corporate social media are creating an "information democracy." Beyond the boundaries of any single organization, perhaps the best examples of information democracy are Wikipedia and open-source programming. As another example, think of the brilliant business model that Apple (and, more recently, Google) has forged with applications developers. Hundreds of thousands of applications now exist for the iPhone and iPad, not to mention the Android operating system for mobile smartphones. The developers of those "apps" do not work for Apple or Google. They benefit from the revenues that their applications generate, but neither Apple nor Google is supporting them as employees. They work for Apple or Google, but are on the payroll of neither one.

Outdated management practices based on the "3Cs" – command, control, and compartmentalization of information – render companies immobile in their response to the demands of the marketplace. Conversely, as Hamel has noted, "In the age of business concept revolution, it doesn't matter whether you are the CEO or a newly hired administrative assistant, whether you work in the hallowed halls of HQ or in some distant backwater, whether you are entitled to a senior citizen discount or whether you're still struggling to pay off school loans. Never before has opportunity been so democratic."[34]

Management fads cannot last. As examples, consider theory Z, total quality management, reengineering, customer intimacy, and economic value added. Consultants make sure all firms know and try to implement these techniques. If all the firms in an industry do the same thing, however, how can there be any long-term competitive advantage? As we noted in Chapter 2, the tests of sustained competitive advantage lie in doing something valuable, rare, and difficult to imitate. In contrast, building corporate cultures (shared norms about what is important) that change the basis of competition is what visionary leadership is all about. It requires the courage to think and act outside the box, seizing opportunities to unlock the hidden value in all your people. HR strategy is central to the process of building a company culture that will last, and in subsequent chapters we show the links between elements of HR strategy and valuable business outcomes. For the present, however, let us consider two alternative approaches to creating and sustaining organizational values and identity.

Conventional versus values-based views of strategy

Figure 2.2 shows the conventional view of strategy. In this view, it is reasonable to ask "What business are we in?" – choosing the products, markets, and geographies in which the firm will operate. A second question is "How will we compete?" – positioning the company against the competition, and developing a value proposition for the customer – first mover, low cost, service, innovation, and so forth. Third, answers to these questions are used to identify the kinds of competencies or capabilities a company will need, such as service or quality.

Next, these decisions are translated into specific, functional plans and objectives that are delegated to functional managers (e.g., marketing,

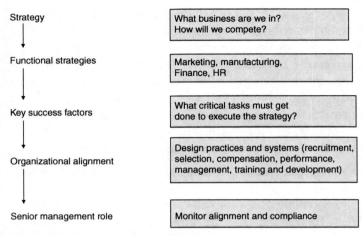

Strategy

What business are we in?
How will we compete?

Functional strategies

Marketing, manufacturing,
Finance, HR

Key success factors

What critical tasks must get
done to execute the strategy?

Organizational alignment

Design practices and systems (recruitment,
selection, compensation, performance,
management, training and development)

Senior management role

Monitor alignment and compliance

Figure 2.2 Conventional view of strategy
Source: O'Reilly, C. A., and Pfeffer, J. (2000). *Hidden Value: How Great Companies Achieve Extraordinary Results with Ordinary People*. Boston: Harvard Business School Press, 13.

HR, finance), who are held accountable for achieving them. Finally, senior management monitors and oversees the operation of these plans, intervening when necessary. Unfortunately, these questions will not engage people at an emotional level, especially those charged with implementing the strategy.

The conventional approach, though widely accepted, is not the only way to develop strategy. Consider an alternative view, a values-based approach to the development of business strategy. This approach, almost the reverse of what we have just described, is shown in Figure 2.3. The idea here is to build strategy around things that are long-lasting, in this case values.

The values-based approach begins with a set of fundamental values that are energizing and capable of unlocking people's human potential – values such as fun, fairness, challenge, trust, respect, community, and family. These values serve as the basis for evaluating management policies and practices that express the values on a day-to-day basis. For any value, the key question is: "To what extent is this practice consistent with our core beliefs about people and organizations?"

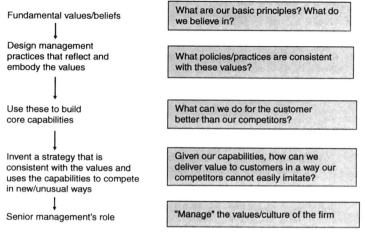

Figure 2.3 A values-based view of strategy
Source: O'Reilly and Pfeffer (2000: 15).

Examples of the values-based approach: Apple and UPS

Consider a firm that competes through innovation. Is it less likely to downsize employees when times get tough than one that competes through cost leadership? While the innovator focuses on product leadership and cycle time, the cost cutter emphasizes operational excellence and doing more with less of everything – including fewer people. For the innovator, people are a source of competitive advantage; for the cost cutter, people are an expense to be minimized.[35] To illustrate the difference in philosophy and in the values that underlie management practices, consider how Jobs, former CEO of Apple Inc., thought about managing in difficult economic times:

> We've had one of these before, when the dot.com bubble burst. What I told our company was that we were just going to invest our way through the downturn, that we weren't going to lay off people, that we'd taken a tremendous amount of effort to get them into Apple in the first place – the last thing we were going to do is lay them off. And we were going to keep funding. In fact we were going to up our R&D budget so that we would be ahead of our competitors when the downturn was over. And that's exactly what we did. And it worked. And that's exactly what we'll do this time.[36]

The management practices that are implemented have effects on people. Consequently, these practices come to produce core competencies and capabilities at companies that adopt a values-based approach to strategy. In turn, these capabilities and competencies can change the competitive dynamics of an industry and outflank the competition. As an example, consider that in November 2001, just before the dot.com crash ended, Apple began selling its first iPod as it reaped the fruits of its investment and innovation strategy during the dot.com bubble. Today it holds a 73 percent global market share in hand-held digital music players.[37] That is changing the competitive dynamics of an industry.

As another example, consider a key value of UPS, a company with 100,000 trucks and 550 airplanes, namely sustainability.[38] The company strives constantly to become more environmentally friendly and more efficient, both of which qualities benefit the company and its consumers. Consider UPS trucks. Bob Stoffel, UPS's senior vice president of supply chain, strategy, engineering, and sustainability, refers to the vehicle fleet as UPS's "rolling laboratory." He is experimenting with virtually every green technology and reducing the company's carbon emissions by millions of tons annually. UPS has all-electric vehicles, hybrid-electric, compressed natural gas, and liquid natural gas, as well as higher-efficiency diesel engines. All have merits in different situations. The result? UPS has improved the fuel efficiency of its domestic delivery fleet by 10 percent in the past ten years, and it wants another 10 percent improvement in the next ten years.

To improve overall efficiencies further, UPS uses telematics – sensors that monitor 200 different vehicle parameters, such as braking speeds, idling, doors open, seat belts, and engine components. One example of a payoff is that UPS relies on the sensors to indicate when it needs to change the oil in a truck. It now uses a lot less oil than when it stuck to a rigid schedule for changing, such as every 6,000 miles. UPS illustrates nicely how a key value, sustainability, leads to policies and practices that embody that value, and contributes directly to the company's long-term strategy to be the world's leader in integrated global supply-chain logistics.

In the values-based view of strategy, strategy comes last, after the values and practices have been aligned, and after the company has produced capabilities that set it apart from its competition. This is not to imply that strategy is unimportant. Both Apple and UPS, like all successful companies, have well-defined competitive strategies that help them make decisions about how and where to compete. These decisions are secondary, however, to living a set of values and creating the alignment between values and people. Strategy is critical, but so are values and management practices that produce implementation.

Konosuke Matsushita, founder of the giant electronics firm that bears his name and markets its products under the brand names National Panasonic, Technics, and Quasar, was a lifelong believer in values-based management. Here is a brief excerpt from his written philosophy of management:

> When my company was still small, I often told my employees that when customers asked, "What does your company make?" they should answer, "Matsushita Electric is making men. We also make electrical appliances, but first and foremost our company makes men."[39]

If the CEO's philosophy is to build men (and women), then how do we take that and connect it specifically to the choices necessary to support strategy? This is the topic that the next chapter addresses.

Conclusion

Clearly, there are many external influences that affect the strategic choices that firms make. In this chapter we have discussed seven such influences: globalization, technology, global labor markets, legal and regulatory environments, political environments, virtual mobility, and new business models and concepts. The list is by no means exhaustive, but it does reflect the myriad of factors that affect strategy formulation, outcomes, and human capital risk. Our next chapter addresses these issues in more detail.

Notes

1 Welch, J., and Welch, S. (2006). So many CEOs get this wrong. *Bloomberg Businessweek*, July 10: 92.
2 *Bloomberg Businessweek* (2011). 2011: year in review. *Bloomberg Businessweek*, December 26: 9.
3 Ramsey, M., and Moffett, S. (2011). Japan parts shortage hits auto makers. *Wall Street Journal*, March 24: B1–B2.

4 Cascio, W. F. (2010). *Managing Human Resources: Productivity, Quality of Work Life, Profits*, 8th edn. Burr Ridge, IL: McGraw-Hill.

5 Bloomberg (2009). IBM chief expects company to strengthen during slump. www.bloomberg.com, March 9 (accessed July 5, 2011).

6 Fox, A. (2010). At work in 2020. *HR Magazine*, 55(1): 18–23 (available at www.shrm.org/Publications/hrmagazine/EditorialContent/2010/0110/Pages/0110fox.aspx; accessed June 17, 2011).

7 Gogoi, P. (2010). Where are the jobs? For many companies, overseas. *USA Today*, December 28 (available at http//finance.yahoo.com; accessed January 4, 2011).

8 *Bloomberg Businessweek* (2010). Year in review. *Bloomberg Businessweek*, December 20 (accessed January 20, 2011).

9 World Economic Forum (2011). *Global Talent Risk: Seven Responses*. Geneva: World Economic Forum.

10 Lublin, J. S. (2011). Hunt is on for fresh executive talent: cultural flexibility in demand. *Wall Street Journal*, April 11: B1, B9. See also Economist Intelligence Unit [EIU] (2010). *Global Firms in 2020: The Next Decade of Change for Organisations and Workers*. London: EIU.

11 Friedman, T. L. (2005). *The World Is Flat: A Brief History of the Twenty-First Century*. New York: Farrar, Straus, & Giroux.

12 Gratton, L. (2011b). Workplace 2025: what will it look like? *Organizational Dynamics*, 40(4): 246–54. See also Gratton, L. (2011a). *The Shift: The Future of Work Is Already Here*. London: Collins.

13 Rampell, C. (2011). Bosses are hiring lots – of equipment. *Denver Post*, June 19: 3K.

14 *Fortune* (2011). Computing, untethered. *Fortune*, June 13: 112.

15 Hof, R. D. (2005). The power of us. *Bloomberg Businessweek*, June 20: 74–82.

16 Gratton (2011b).

17 EIU (2010).

18 Cahuc, P., and Zilberberg, A. (2004). *Labor Economics*. Cambridge, MA: MIT Press.

19 Khurana, R., quoted in World Economic Forum (2011: 15).

20 Khurana, R., quoted in World Economic Forum (2011: 15).

21 Wadhwa, V. (2008). America's other immigration crisis. *The American*, July/August (available at http://ssrn.com/abstract=1259154).

22 World Economic Forum (2011).

23 Thornton, E. (2009). The hidden perils of layoffs. *Bloomberg Businessweek*, March 2: 52–3.

24 Federation of European Employers (2010). Managing HR in an economic downturn (available at www.fedee.com/downturn.shtml; accessed October 7, 2010).

25 Boudreau, J. W. (2010). *Retooling HR: Using Proven Business Tools to Make Better Decisions about Talent*. Boston: Harvard Business School Press. See also Lunsford, J. L. (2007). Boeing scrambles to repair problems with new plane. *Wall Street Journal*, December 7: A1, A13.

26 Miller, S. (2007). Collaboration is key to effective outsourcing, in *2008 HR Trend Book*: 58–61. Alexandria, VA: SHRM.

27 Arkless, D., quoted in World Economic Forum (2011: 27).

28 World Economic Forum (2010). *The Global Gender Gap Report 2010*. Geneva: World Economic Forum (available at www.weforum.org; accessed July 5, 2011).

29 Hamel, G. (2000). *Leading the Revolution*. Boston: Harvard Business School Press. We draw heavily from this source in this section of the chapter.

30 MobiThinking (2001). Global mobile phone statistics, 2001. MobiThinking, http://mobithinking.com/mobile-marketing-tools/latest-mobile-stats (accessed July 2, 2011).

31 Lashinsky, A. (2009). The decade of Steve: how Apple's imperious, brilliant CEO transformed American business. *Fortune*, November 23: 93–100.

32 Lashinsky (2009: 94).

33 Information in this section comes from Taylor, A. (2011). Tata takes on the world: building an auto empire in India. *Fortune*, May 2: 87–92.

34 Hamel (2000: 28).

35 Cascio, W. F. (2006). Decency means more than "Always low prices": a comparison of Costco to Wal-Mart's Sam's Club. *Academy of Management Perspectives*, 20(3): 26–37.

36 Morris, B. (2008, March 6). America's most admired companies: Steve Jobs speaks out. CNNMoney, http://money.cnn.com/galleries/2008/fortune/0803/gallery.jobsqna.fortune/index.html.

37 Lashinsky (2009).

38 Colvin, G. (2010). The UPS green dream. *Fortune*, December 27: 44–51.

39 Matsushita, K. (1978). *My Management Philosophy*. Tokyo: PHP Institute, 45.

3

HR strategy in context: environmental, organizational, and functional elements

Human resource strategy occurs in a context that exists at different levels. HR departments and human capital decisions exist within organizations, which exist within competitive and social environments. Chapter 5 shows how human resource strategy must address questions such as how the HR department's activities produce the necessary results at the levels of individuals, groups, and organizational units, how those results affect the organization's execution of processes, and how that execution, in turn, produces sustainable strategic success in the competitive and social environment.

This chapter describes the key considerations, issues, and components of human resource strategy that characterize the environmental, organizational, and functional levels of context. Human capital permeates and affects every aspect of organizations, so leaders must understand the contextual levels of HR strategy to achieve a better formulation and evaluation of their HR strategy. Understanding the context of HR strategy is also important because it helps to define the appropriate contribution of the leaders and managers who serve different organizational roles in the HR strategy process. For example, the executive heading the HR department plays a significant leadership role in HR strategy, and usually defines and is accountable for executing the HR strategy processes. Other functional executives on the leadership team, such as the chief financial officer or chief operating officer, play a collaboration role in human capital strategy, but do not drive the HR strategy process.

As we shall see, the nature of human capital strategy also varies depending on the type of organizational unit. Strategy for a business unit, such as Disney theme parks, involves decisions about how Disney theme parks will compete against such other theme parks as Cedar Point, Great America, etc. We discussed this type of strategy in earlier chapters. Strategy for a value-chain functional unit, such as the entertainment division that supports Disney theme parks, involves decisions about how entertainment contributes to the theme park results, because the entertainment division does not generally provide services other than to Disney nor does it compete with entertainment divisions at Great America, Cedar Point, etc. Strategy for the Walt Disney Company itself involves decisions about how to create a portfolio of business units, ranging from theme parks to television to retail stores, that together create synergy beyond their individual value. Clearly, the human capital strategies will also involve different questions depending on the type of organization unit involved.

In this chapter, we first describe how HR strategy has to consider not just the HR department but its connection to the organization and even the surrounding environment. This multi-level approach provides both HR and non-HR leaders with guidance to consider arenas in which broader strategies must consider human capital issues, but also in which the perspective of human resources should inform the strategic issues themselves (such as when sustainability is heavily dependent on employment relationships to create a license to operate in developing economies, or when socioeconomic changes are detected and analyzed through labor markets and recruitment processes). Then we describe how HR strategy varies depending on the type of organization unit. This framework helps HR and non-HR leaders understand that the connection of human capital to strategic outcomes differs depending on how the organization unit itself contributes to the organization's strategic goals. Using the example of Disney's diversification into interactive gaming, we show how the risk-management framework introduced earlier can help clarify and organize the varied human capital and organization strategy issues that permeate different organization levels. Finally, we turn to the context of the HR department itself, and provide an "HR functional excellence" framework that describes the essential elements of an HR organizational strategy. Again, we show how a common risk-management framework can help clarify and organize the nature of risk, opportunity and uncertainty as HR organizations create their internal strategy, so that it fits and supports their role in supporting the larger organizational strategy.

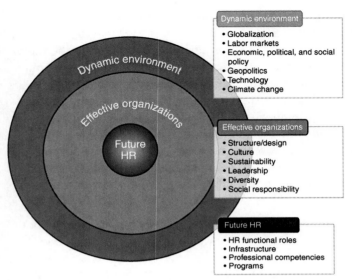

Figure 3.1 The multi-level context for HR strategy
Source: Boudreau, J. W., and Ziskin, I. (2011). The future of HR. *Organization Dynamics*, 40(4): 255–66; reprinted with permission.

A multi-level framework for the context of HR strategy[1]

Figure 3.1 shows a framework proposed by John Boudreau and Ian Ziskin to describe the multiple levels and multiple issues that an HR strategy must consider.[2] As the figure shows, they suggest that the HR function exists within an organization and an environmental context. Chapter 2 described the environmental trends that affect organizational strategy; here we focus on how HR strategy connects to the environment outside the organization. Each of these levels defines its own set of considerations. Some of them are a direct function of decisions made about the HR function and profession within the organization (such as the structure, competencies, and role of the HR function), while others are the joint concern of leaders in many areas of the organization (such as defining and achieving sustainability, or dealing with geopolitical changes).

The centermost circle, "Future HR," is meant to capture those issues that are primarily focused at the level of the HR function itself. This level of context includes important questions about the design of HR functions, HR's professional roles and competencies, how HR uses infrastructure such as IT and process delivery systems, and the specific programs and practices that HR enacts. Much attention of HR strategies is typically focused here, on the HR department or profession, and we return to it at the end of this chapter. Leaders focus exclusively on the HR functional strategy at their peril, however, because issues at this level need to be embedded within a broader strategic perspective for a full understanding of the implications of decisions in the inner circle to be reached.

The middle circle, "Effective organizations," is meant to capture the reality that HR must exist and optimize its role within a surrounding organizational context. HR will influence and be influenced by organizational elements such as structure and design, culture, and leadership, as well as such organization-level issues as sustainability, diversity, and social responsibility. The HR profession is often centrally involved, and can even be a primary driver of organizational success in areas such as diversity and leadership. These are prominent topics in HR strategy. Nonetheless, HR's involvement and leadership in these organization-level issues varies considerably. The evolution of HR's role in these areas will significantly define the evolution of the professional elements in the centermost circle.

For example, Boudreau and Ziskin note that it is still common – though our experience suggests less so than in the past – for the functions of organization effectiveness, design, and development (OD) to be separate from the HR function.[3] Indeed, it is not unusual to find professionals in the OD area who insist that they are not a part of HR, noting that they address more "strategic" issues of organization design and effectiveness, while HR addresses more tactical and administrative issues that support the strategy. Such a stark separation can create serious and important limitations for organizations and for the OD and HR professions.[4] The fact is, OD competencies are vital for HR, and vice versa.

Boudreau and Ziskin note a similar pattern in the area of leadership development, again with the trend appearing to be toward incorporating leadership into the HR profession, with a strong integration into the portfolio of HR practices for leaders, but also for the broader workforce.[5] In areas such as social responsibility and sustainability, the role of HR strategy varies. We see many organizations in which there are significant initiatives, such as including corporate social responsibility in recruitment or performance-management practices, but little presence of HR in formulating the agendas or implementing the key initiatives. Rather, the role of the HR profession seems to be more reactive, awaiting resolution of the thorny questions and then being ready to implement the requested HR programs and practices.[6] That said, there is an upwelling of books and articles suggesting a more central role for HR in defining such issues and their strategic role in the organization.[7]

Finally, the outer circle of Figure 3.1 reflects the "Dynamic environment" as a defining factor of consideration in effective organizations, and thus a significant determinant of HR's future. These are the trends and influences that will span organizations and affect entire industries, regions, and economies. Like the issue in the "Effective organizations" circle, these broader environmental trends are sometimes a central concern of the HR profession, but more often they appear only in the broadest strategy statements. The role of the HR profession in defining and responding to these issues remains to be determined, yet the HR profession's capability to play a significant role, when appropriate, will be key. Perhaps more important will be the profession's ability to pick its targets to engage on such issues. It is not yet clear that the HR profession must play a leadership role in such issues as climate change and geopolitics, but what is increasingly clear is that HR leaders have to understand such trends well enough to help their organizations craft strategic responses. HR's role may well emerge as one of a supporting player, with disciplines such as politics and economics being fundamental and organizational functions such as strategy and government relations taking the lead.

Boudreau and Ziskin also describe emerging examples, however, in which the effects of these trends manifest themselves primarily through the employment relationship, and thus thrust HR into a central role.[8] Global labor markets and collective action are often the organization's first tangible globalization challenge. Employment unrest or HR's role in crisis management and evacuating employees and their families can often be the first organizational challenges that require significant attention to geopolitics. Thorny issues of employee behavior in technologically enabled social networks and forums may often be the organization's first tangible challenges that require a considered position on emerging technology.

Not many leaders would jump to the conclusion that issues such as geopolitics, climate change, and emerging technology-driven social democracy are the focus of HR strategy! When you think about it, though, the employment relationship is often the most important, or even the first, place that such issues become tangible to the organization. Accordingly, it is important that decision makers and strategists not lose sight of the need to consider such issues in human resource strategy.

Several broad observations emerge as we use the boundary-spanning perspective of Figure 3.1 to engage HR leaders and constituents to think more broadly about the profession and its future role. The three observations are:

(1) HR success will incorporate other disciplines;
(2) HR success will rely on boundary spanning; and
(3) HR success will require accepting diverse definitions of the HR role.

HR strategy will incorporate other disciplines   Challenges such as diversity, sustainability, and socio-economic disparities require approaches that draw on disciplines well beyond the traditions of the HR profession. Traditional HR disciplines such as industrial and organizational psychology and labor economics are valuable, but increasingly we see HR organizations reaching beyond these traditional areas in an effort to address thorny but important challenges. Google employs analysts in its people analytics (HR) organization with disciplinary backgrounds including operations, politics, and marketing.[9] Human capital planning and strategy are increasingly carried out with the assistance of those with deep training in competitive strategy and scenario planning, whether they exist within the HR function or in a separate strategy group. The risk-based perspective on strategy offered in this book will make partnerships between experts on risk management and HR even more vital.

HR process excellence is often achieved with the involvement of operations management experts, or even by placing responsibility for HR processes within the operations management group itself. When IBM's HR organization wished to design its talent management system using the logical principles of a supply chain, it engaged its top experts in operations management to assist and help lead the project.[10] We are increasingly seeing the employee value proposition and employer brand being defined using tools from the disciplines of consumer behavior and marketing, and in some cases these efforts are contained within marketing organizations with deep expertise in branding and consumer research. At Starbucks, Melissa Graves, an industrial/organizational (I/O) psychologist, is the director of partner insights, which brings the best tools possible to questions about partners, stores, customers, and financials.[11] Prasad Setty of Google and Juha Äkräs of Nokia are two additional examples of non-HR professionals who came into the function to become effective HR leaders.[12]

Boudreau and Ziskin note that the answer is unlikely to be the same for all organizations.[13] Sometimes this trend will mean expanding the role of HR, such as when HR's effective handling of employment issues relating to communications and corporate social responsibility leads to expanded roles that incorporate responsibility for all these areas. In other organizations it may mean that things such as strategy, process excellence, and employment branding are primarily driven out of functions such as corporate strategy, operations, or marketing. The question in the future may be less about "What competencies must we in HR develop in order to address these multidisciplinary challenges within our own function?" and more about "What competencies exist, among the best and brightest in any discipline, that HR can skillfully draw upon to address these challenges best?"

HR success will rely on boundary spanning   Closely related to the first observation is the idea that HR strategies and the associated decisions will increasingly need to span boundaries of all types to be effective. Certainly, boundaries between disciplines and functions will need to be more permeable, as we noted above. Nevertheless, HR will also likely need to span the boundary of the organization itself. Work by Sue Mohrman and Chris Worley suggests that solving issues of sustainability requires considering organization designs that demand inter-organizational cooperation, resource sharing, and decisions.[14]

Boudreau and Ziskin foresee that such solutions will be necessary for virtually all the issues in Figure 3.1.[15] The "collective" is increasingly defined without the necessity of an organization boundary. Disciplines such as marketing and research and development routinely draw ideas from the "crowd" around the organization, and consider engaging that "crowd" to be as vital to their mission as engaging the employees within their organizations. Focus groups are widely employed to elicit opinions and feedback from customers (and potential customers) about a whole host of issues, including products, services, new product development, and advertising.[16] The Mattel Toy Testers program brings in children to play with, test, and comment on new toys not yet on the market.[17] Emerging markets increasingly require engaging constituents such as non-governmental organizations, governments, local collectives, and others that may exist both within and outside the organization.

Moreover, the boundaries will be more permeable between the HR function, the organization, and the environment depicted in Figure 3.1. At Gap Inc., HR professionals have the opportunity to take assignments that have them helping business owners in emerging economies learn the basics of such things as motivation, performance assessment, training, and communication. These assignments span the boundary between the HR function, the organization, and the economic environment, putting HR leaders in a direct position to carry out the boundary-spanning activity. The result: better-run businesses in emerging countries that happen to be direct suppliers of the essential components of Gap products. Lower costs, higher quality, and better employment relationships are all outcomes of this kind of boundary spanning. It is notable that it was the skills that HR leaders could teach that were most needed by these suppliers, and strategically significant for Gap.

HR success will require diverse definitions of the HR role   Any HR strategy must define the HR organization and the roles within that HR organization. This includes roles such as strategic partner, change catalyst, trusted advisor, employee advocate, and process architect.[18] Nonetheless, most strategies about such roles are focused within the center circle of Figure 3.1. In the context of an increasingly agile organization and dynamic environment, this will not be sufficient. HR leaders and non-HR leaders must consider questions such as these: When is it the role of HR to support the initiatives of others with strong traditional human capital programs and processes? When is it the role of HR to be the "face" of the organization on significant issues such as sustainability and environmental responsibility? When is it the role of HR to be the disciplinary expert on issues such as emerging social networks and harnessing the power of the crowd?

For example, when Bill Conaty wanted an executive to head up his new function of corporate responsibility in 2004, he reached out to the head of GE's Crotonville learning center, Bob Corcoran.[19] Bob soon found himself traveling the globe on projects such as bringing advanced healthcare to Ghana as part of GE's "Developing health globally" initiative – at a time when GE had no business interests, offices, or facilities in Ghana.[20] In his new role, would we say that Bob Corcoran is still in HR? Is corporate social responsibility still a separate function from HR? In the future, these questions will probably be less important than the questions of how HR leaders can best leverage their capabilities to make the biggest impact, regardless of the boundaries they must cross.

In sum, seeing the future of HR through a multi-level lens redefines some of the most basic premises about the meaning of HR, the role of HR professionals, and the meaning of the contribution of HR leaders, and vividly illustrates the need to think "beyond the center circle" when considering how to define, implement, and evaluate HR strategy.

Conclusion The Ernst and Young report on global human resource risk reflects the necessity of this multi-level understanding of the context for HR strategy.[21] The executives surveyed in the report identified issues such as the following as significant for their "human resources" risk:

- globalization;
- an aging workforce;
- a scarcity of skilled labor;
- the regulatory environment;
- the changing demographics of the workforce; and
- vendor management and sourcing.

It is difficult to see how any organization could address these issues without defining its human resources strategy to include the environment, organization, and HR function levels. Executives outside the HR profession appear to recognize that these vital issues have to be addressed in HR strategy. Figure 3.1 may provide a more specific framework for understanding how such issues span levels. Moreover, because issues such as these are already recognized by executives as legitimate arenas for HR risk management, it is a natural starting point to use these issues as a litmus test for the quality of HR strategies, and also as a vehicle to develop more comprehensive and boundaryless approaches to the HR-strategy development process.

Strategy level	Core concept		
Enterprise strategy	Portfolio optimization Creating a portfolio that is more competitive together than they would be independently, through strategic resource coordination	Building support resources and processes that optimally span the organization	Enterprise resource unit strategy Support optimization
Business unit strategy	Competitive optimization Building and executing compelling value propositions and business models to generate returns in targeted markets		
Value chain process strategy	Operational optimization Building specific operations that uniquely support the competitive positions within the targeted markets		

Figure 3.2 Core strategy concepts for different organization units
Source: Boudreau, J. W., and Ramstad, P. M. (2005). Strategic partnership with impact, executive education seminar. Center for Effective Organizations, Los Angeles; adapted with permission.

Human resource strategy depends on the type of organization unit

Not only does human resource strategy encompass the context of the organization and the environment, it must also consider the internal organizational environment. Different types of organization units often approach strategy very differently, and the human resource strategy implications are thus also very different. Figure 3.2 describes several types of organization units, and the core concept of their strategies. Figure 3.3 shows how these concepts apply to the Walt Disney Company, with examples of the different Disney units in each box.

Most of the classic strategy models discussed in Chapter 2 focus on the *business unit*, in the second row of Figures 3.2 and 3.3. A business unit encompasses a profit line and full set of value-chain elements. It usually produces a specific set of products or services, has its own profit-and-loss statement, and operates in a competitor space that can be identified most easily. Often this kind of unit is a product line or category.

At Disney, for example, individual business units such as theme parks, broadcasting, and movies are typical business units. The strategic objectives of business units are the ones discussed in Chapter 1. We might call this *competitive optimization*, and it includes building

Strategy level	Core concept	
Enterprise strategy	Disney Corporation	*Enterprise resource unit strategy* *Legal, IT, real estate*
Business unit strategy	• Theme parks • Broadcasting (ABC, ESPN) • Movies	
Value-chain process strategy	Specific functions within each of the business units (e.g., entertainment within theme parks, network operations within broadcasting, etc.)	

Figure 3.3 Strategic units at the Walt Disney Company
Source: Boudreau and Ramstad (2005); adapted with permission.

and executing compelling value propositions to generate returns in targeted markets. In a business unit, the strategy questions focus on defining the competitive domain, identifying how the unit can compete in a unique and sustainable way, and what combination of value-chain processes and resources will support that, often drawing from other parts of the organization for those processes and resources. In multi-product or multi-category organizations such as Disney, the business units consider how their strategies relate to those of other business units, but their main focus is on how to compete effectively in their own individual arenas. As John Boudreau and Peter Ramstad note, the issue facing the human resource strategy for such units is to identify how decisions about work, people, and the organization contribute to positioning the business unit in its competitive space.[22] A typical human capital strategy question in a business unit might be "Where would improving our talent and organization most enhance the brand recognition of our unit's products?"

The *enterprise*-unit level is where all the business units come together. At Disney, this is the Disney corporate level. The strategic issues for the corporate team are different from those at the business-unit level, because the corporate strategic focus is on how the full portfolio of business units comes together to create a sum that is more than the parts. Different organizations accomplish this synergy in different ways. At Disney, a key synergy factor is the ability to create value in a character across multiple platforms, such as when the lead character in the movie *Finding Nemo* became a core part of the submarine ride at the Disney theme parks, which, in turn, created demand for Nemo dolls and games in retail stores. At Apple, demand for products such as iPods, iPads, and iPhones created synergies that boosted sales of Macintosh computers. At the other extreme is Berkshire Hathaway, the company that invests under the direction of Warren Buffet, in which the processes and products of the different companies have little connection. The synergy is the investing savvy of Warren Buffet and his staff. Most organizations require their business units to produce synergy across some elements of the product line or processes. As a result, the key strategy questions are to identify what the shared "glue" is that holds things together and makes the sum more than the parts. HR strategies supporting the corporate level of the organization typically focus on questions about cross-unit coordination. As Boudreau and Ramstad note, a very typical HR strategic dilemma at the corporate level is the answer to the question "When must our individual business units give up their best leaders, and allow us to move them to other units, because the value of leadership rotation and development outweighs the cost to the unit of losing that great leader?"[23] Such questions require careful attention to the costs incurred by the units, the value created by cross-unit movement, and how to minimize the first and maximize the second.

Business units are supported by *value-chain* units, shown in the bottom row of Figures 3.2 and 3.3. Recall from Chapter 2 that the value chain was a fundamental element defining industries in the Porter strategy framework. The value chain refers to the processes that must be executed to achieve the organization's goals. At a generic level, these might include market research, product development, manufacturing, distribution, marketing, sales, and service. A value-chain unit focuses on one particular process that is a part of the larger value chain. For example, many organizations have dedicated organizational units that handle the supply chain, marketing, or research and development for the entire organization, across different business units. Of course, in some organizations value-chain units are dedicated to one business unit, so that each business unit might have its own supply-chain, marketing, and R&D group. More typically, the value-chain units actually span different business units.

Consider how differently strategy is approached in a value-chain unit compared to a business unit. The R&D functions of pharmaceutical organizations such as Pfizer, Novartis, or AstraZeneca do not ask themselves about their positioning relative to competing R&D functions. They do not directly compete with the R&D functions in their competitor companies, and for the most part their organizations would not consider moving R&D "services" to an outside company, even if it was more "competitive." It makes little sense to ask "How can we uniquely compete with another firm's R&D organization?" The same thing applies to functions such as marketing and the supply chain. Instead, the goal of value-chain units is operational optimization: building specific operations that uniquely support the competitive positions within the targeted markets.[24] This means that the strategic task of value-chain-element units is to figure out how the results of their functional area support the competitive positioning of business units and the synergies across the organization. It also means that such units focus on their operational excellence, compared to best-in-class functions in other organizations. A typical HR strategy question when dealing with value-chain units is "Where would improving our talent or organization help us better understand and target our deliverables where they most enhance competitiveness in particular business units?"

Finally, on the rightmost side of Figures 3.2 and 3.3 are what Boudreau and Ramstad term *enterprise-resource units*.[25] These are units dealing with such areas as human resources, legal, and information technology, which nurture and build resources that span the entire organization, and also span particular value-chain elements such as R&D and marketing. The objective of enterprise-resource units is to optimize their support for other corporate, business, and value-chain units, optimally to balance consistency across the organization with customization within units, and to achieve operational efficiency in their processes. Typical strategic questions at the enterprise-resource-unit level are similar to those at the *value-chain*-unit level, in that they do not focus directly on any one competitive domain but, instead, on how the unit can best contribute to the competitive success of each business unit, and how to create synergies across units to optimize the value of the resource. In the case of *enterprise-resource units*, these questions apply to a resource rather than a value-chain process element. The human resource function is usually an enterprise-resource function, which is why human resource strategy is very concerned with understanding how its focal resources – people and organizations – connect to the specific strategies of organizational business units, and to the corporate strategies of synergy between business units. In later chapters, as we describe our suggested framework connecting investments in people to strategic success, you will see how HR strategies are derived from the competitive strategies of business units and the synergy or portfolio strategies of the corporation. This is why HR strategy formulation must include a deep understanding of the vital elements of the strategies in business units, value-chain units, and the enterprise. Indeed, perhaps *the most fundamental challenge in human resource strategy is to define the connection points between the objectives of a particular organizational unit and the pivotal areas in which individuals and groups can most affect those objectives.* Chapter 5 provides a framework for understanding these connection points.

Risk management and the organizational context for human capital strategy

How might a framework for risk management inform the organizational context of human resource strategy? In Chapter 4 we provide a broader framework for integrating risk into human resource strategy and management, but it is helpful to see here how risk management can inform the different contextual elements that we have described.

Figure 3.4 (which is identical to Figure 1.3) is the enterprise risk-management "cube."[26] Recall that it depicts risk in three dimensions, with the top face of the cube reflecting the risk-management objectives:

- *strategic* – high-level goals, aligned with and supporting the company's mission;
- *operations* – effective and efficient use of its resources;
- *reporting* – reliability of reporting; and
- *compliance* – compliance with applicable laws and regulations.

The front face of the cube reflects the risk-management activities (objective setting, event identification, etc.) and the side face of the cube reflects the organizational entity or level of analysis at which the risk management occurs (subsidiary, division, etc.). The risk-management "cells" represent the intersection of each of the three dimensions, and the Committee of Sponsoring Organizations of

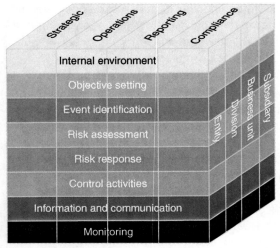

Figure 3.4 Enterprise risk-management framework
Source: COSO (2004). *Enterprise Risk Management – Integrated Framework: Executive Summary.* Chicago: COSO, 5.

the Treadway Commission suggests that this is a way to describe the domain across which opportunity, risk, and uncertainty can be managed.

Putting Figures 3.2 and 3.4 together, risk optimization would consider how the front and top faces of the ERM cube might be applied in each entity. The "entity" level in Figure 3.4 corresponds to the different types of organizational units in Figures 3.2 and 3.3. A comprehensive treatment would examine the twenty-eight cells (four types of objectives combined with seven processes, as shown in the top and front faces of Figure 3.4) for each of the four entities in Figure 3.2 (with the four entities of Figures 3.2 and 3.3 substituted for the right-hand face of Figure 3.4). Let us explore how a few of these risk-management elements would be defined in the context of a vital strategic decision at the Walt Disney Company.

Disney online gaming: the organizational-context risk-management framework in practice

In July 2010 *The New York Times* reported that the Walt Disney Company had bought Tapulous, a start-up company with successes in creating music-based games for the iPhone, iPad, and iPod Touch.

Disney said that Bart Decrem and Andrew Lacy, the co-founder and chief operating officer of Tapulous, respectively, would lead its mobile business.[27] With downloads from the Apple app store since its inception reported to have reached 25 billion by March 2012,[28] it is clearly in Disney's interest to craft its position carefully in the online gaming market. We can use this strategic initiative to illustrate how the framework for organization context and risk management can inform organization and human capital strategy. Recall the suggestion above, that organizations might apply the risk-management "cube" to the different organizational context levels to obtain a better understanding of the strategy and human capital implications.

The acquisition of Tapulous, for example, is a way not just to enhance internal development but also to reduce the risk that Tapulous would become a competitor in the future ("neutralizing competitors," in the Porter framework described in Chapter 2). With the acquisition comes the challenge of integrating this new gaming unit into Disney, and getting other Disney units to integrate and collaborate effectively with the new gaming capability.

Enterprise unit: Walt Disney Company

Table 3.1 shows examples of how Disney might address this uncertainty, focusing on the enterprise level. It shows examples of the kinds of questions and analysis that Disney might conduct, by presenting the front face of the risk-management cube applied to the online gaming analysis.

Disney would set objectives in each of the four risk types across the columns, and then objectives, assessments, control mechanisms, and communication efforts to address them. The "Risk assessment" column of Table 3.1 contains the central analysis of the situation for Disney, outlining examples of uncertainty, risk, and opportunity related to each of the risk-management types in each column. Disney's challenge at the enterprise level is to create an environment in which units across the organization develop their branded material to fit the new online gaming platform, and that Disney properly addresses the uncertainty regarding whether that platform will be developed internally or by others. The acquisition of Tapulous will do little good unless the other Disney organization units are capable of adapting their brands. It also will not be successful unless Disney functional units such as

Table 3.1 Risk-management framework applied to Disney enterprise-level online gaming

Risk type/action	Strategic	Operational	Reporting	Compliance
Objective setting	Each of the units of Disney Channel, movies, and theme parks to launch an online game featuring one of their branded products, within three years.	Disney to create the internal technical capacity to develop, build, and/or acquire access to online gaming technology platforms.	Cross-unit scorecard of online gaming "process gates" must be developed and used in strategic reporting to the executive team and board.	Balance must be retained between informing markets and retaining intellectual property and strategic first-mover advantage.
Event identification	Online gaming technology moves to a proprietary software platform.	Disney IT, legal, and product development groups work together to create an internal platform or interface with external platform.	Disney reporting and goal setting tracks and motivates platform development and cross-functional collaboration.	Disney IT, legal, and development groups ensure that alliances or Disney proprietary platform satisfy legal standards and protect IP.
Risk assessment	Uncertainty: platform is proprietary or open; Disney has access or not. Risk: platform is proprietary and Disney competitor restricts access. Opportunity: platform is open with Disney access or proprietary and controlled by Disney.	Uncertainty: Disney organization does or does not create the internal platform or interface with an external platform. Risk: Disney does not create or interface with the new platform. Opportunity: Disney creates or interfaces successfully.	Uncertainty: Disney reporting is or is not effective in tracking and motivating cross-functional collaboration. Risk: Disney fails to develop a reporting system that motivates the necessary collaboration.	Uncertainty: Disney alliances and/or platform do or do not satisfy legal standards and inform markets. Risk: Disney reporting fails to satisfy legal and market standards. Opportunity: Disney reporting succeeds in satisfying legal and market standards.

			Opportunity: Disney succeeds in developing a reporting system that motivates the necessary collaboration.	
Risk response	Develop internal cross-division project team with the goal of developing or acquiring online gaming platform. Hedge risk by developing market-scanning unit to establish alliances with promising online gaming start-ups.			
Control activities	Use rapid-prototype technology to develop and test online gaming platforms across units using small internet experiments. Establish a cross-organization team to oversee and govern these R&D efforts.			
Information and communication	Communicate to the entire Disney organization the importance of online gaming as a brand channel, and the vital importance of cross-organization collaborative teams to place brands in those channels.			
Monitoring	Track the success of different Disney divisions in launching online gaming brands.	Quarterly progress reports on alliances and software development progress.	Executive team or board reviews reporting process on a quarterly basis. Employee surveys ensure understanding and motivation.	Quarterly external auditor review reports to market and legal authorities.

IT, legal, and others can apply their expertise to the compliance and reporting elements of the acquisition.

These cross-unit organization issues are the essence of strategy at the enterprise level, and thus the essence of human capital strategy at that level as well. Table 3.1 makes clear that some of the most vital human capital and organization challenges involve getting cross-organization units to collaborate, and to adapt their traditional approaches to the new platform. They also involve specific new performance objectives for units such as IT and legal. It is apparent that each of these goals also carries clear requirements for human capital capabilities and human resource programs and practices.

The analysis shown for the *enterprise* level in Table 3.1 could also be carried through for each of the other types of organizational entities shown in Figures 3.2 and 3.3. We have not created a table for each of them, but we can briefly describe examples of the key human resource strategy and risk-management elements for each type of Disney organization unit.

Business unit: Disney theme parks   For business units such as the Disney theme parks, the challenge is to integrate this new online gaming capability at the enterprise level into their specific strategies. These units must develop and integrate their branded products into the online channel. For example, in the theme parks, the challenge is to consider which ride concept might best be adapted to online gaming. Would it be something like "Pirates of the Caribbean," which would also have the advantage of strong film audiences? Or should it be something more exclusive to the theme park arena, such as the light parade or rides such as "It's a small world"? In the theme parks, the risk analysis would include the uncertainty about whether theme park guests would identify with an online version of the experience, whether competitors would copy the online gaming approach, and whether the Disney gaming unit could successfully adapt the theme park concept. Similar considerations would be paramount for other Disney units such as ABC Television, Walt Disney Motion Pictures Group, Walt Disney Theatrical, and ESPN.

Unlike the enterprise-level analysis in Table 3.1, the individual business units will have to consider how an online gaming channel will affect their specific positioning in each of their individual competitive domains. The value and risk of an online gaming initiative will vary considerably across the business units, as will the implications for how human resources and human capital can be employed to address the uncertainty, risks, and opportunities that are uncovered.

Value-chain process unit: Disney "imagineering" Disney value-chain units that support business units will also face strategic choices and risks unique to their particular context. For example, the ride-engineering process in theme parks at Disney depends a great deal on how well engineers can embody engaging and unique songs, imagery, and characters into their rides. Boudreau and Ramstad quote an issue of *Eyes and Ears*, a Walt Disney Company internal employee magazine:

> The "Legend of the Yeti" ride has all the elements of a great adventure story. It is set in a remote mountain village at the foot of the Himalayas, home of the legendary yeti: The Abominable Snowman. Key story elements include: "The fly-by-night tour operator, Himalayan Escapes; the aging 34-passenger industrial railway struggling to reach Mount Everest; cars packed with innocent explorers; a mangled train track that causes the railway to plummet backward; and of course an encounter with the raging yeti.[29]

When Disney developed a new roller coaster ride based on the abominable snowman, it sent its engineers to the Himalayas to learn more about the myths, symbols, and imagery of the abominable snowman legend. Thus, if Disney decides, at the enterprise level, to require units such as the theme parks to migrate their branded concepts to the online gaming platform, that will place new demands on the engineering of rides and their concepts. An important element of uncertainty is whether the "imagineering" process at Disney can effectively incorporate the elements of online gaming into theme-park ride design. Should new ride features be developed specifically for their online gaming value? Alternatively, should the "imagineers" in the theme-park division simply continue to develop rides as before, and leave it up to the new gaming unit to devise ways subsequently to adapt them? Clearly, each choice carries risks and opportunities. Moreover, it is clear that the roles of "imagineer" and online gaming engineer will, in the future, depend on each other, so the human capital implications are significant. Should theme-park engineers be chosen and rewarded in part for their online gaming expertise? Should online gaming engineers spend some time working in the theme parks designing rides? Each of these human capital strategies could be seen as a way to enhance opportunities, mitigate risk, or reduce uncertainty.

Once again, the enterprise-level decision to build an online gaming presence will affect the strategy and risk-management decisions of value-chain processes such as engineering. Other value-chain processes that would be affected include television and movie production, as well as sports marketing (ESPN).

Enterprise-resource unit: Disney information technology   One of the most significant elements of the Disney decision to incorporate online gaming is the legal challenge. As Table 3.1 shows, the goals of legal and open reporting often must be balanced with the secrecy necessary to protect intellectual property. IP protection is likely to be somewhat different in traditional areas such as motion pictures and theme-park rides from what it will be in the emerging arena of online gaming. At the very least, the intellectual property will be much more defined by technology and software than by creative concepts. The Disney legal unit spans the entire corporation, and has to address such issues across business units while maintaining high corporate standards and the need to ensure compatibility and compliance across the enterprise. Some of the most significant sources of uncertainty and risk for Disney lie in the "Reporting" and "Compliance" arenas of the risk-management framework of Figure 3.4, and these risk areas are significantly affected by the quality of the human capital and the organizational effectiveness of the legal enterprise-resource unit.

From a human capital standpoint, the strategic challenges in this unit would be intriguing. Can the same type of legal capability and skills that Disney has applied to its traditional intellectual capital and reporting be applied to the online gaming arena? If not, how should Disney build up its capacity for online-gaming-related legal and reporting expertise? Even simple questions, such as how online games should be valued for financial-reporting purposes and how much of the gaming technology must be described in investor reports, may be a significant challenge for legal experts at Disney, who have not traditionally dealt with this arena. Should Disney acquire the relevant legal human capital from some of its online gaming acquisitions? Alternatively, should Disney invest in developing its existing legal group, to hedge the risk of being unprepared for future reporting and compliance risk challenges?

Conclusion The Disney example shows that combining a risk-management perspective with the context for human capital planning reveals how these issues differ across organizational units, but also how they fit together across units. Virtually every unit in any organization will face the four types of risk categories, and can consider the various actions to deal with uncertainty, risk, and opportunity. That said, certain types of units often face certain types of risks more frequently. For example, compliance and operational risk often work through value-chain and enterprise-resource units. Strategic risk is often related more closely to business units and the enterprise as a whole, because these units often formulate and are accountable for decisions about the strategic and competitive environment. That said, business units and the enterprise often bear the consequences of whether other units succeed or fail on operational and compliance risks. Financial risk pervades everyone, but in different forms. For business units, it may be more apparent in their ability to generate higher prices, volumes, and margins. For enterprise-resource units and value-chain-element units that provide services to internal customers, financial risk is often more cost-focused. By employing the risk-management framework and the organization unit categories for context, the precise nature of human capital risks can be understood better.

Human resources functional excellence (HRFE) framework

An important element of the context of human resource strategic planning is the strategy pursued by the human resource function in organizations. Indeed, one of the most significant elements of "human resource strategy," in the eyes of business leaders, is how the HR department approaches its work and its relationship with other organizational units. In fact, this element of strategy is often overemphasized at the expense of other important strategy questions, including the connection points between human capital and organizational sustainable success. This is often a mistake, which is why we provide a framework for identifying and mapping these connection points in Chapter 5. Nonetheless, the larger question of the relationship between human capital and organizational success often occurs through the context of the HR department or function. In this section, therefore, we provide a framework that describes the elements of the strategy of the human resources department or function within organizations. This framework was developed by Peter Ramstad and John Boudreau, with the assistance of colleagues at Personnel Decisions International. It is called the human resource functional excellence framework.

The search for an HR functional strategy framework   Some very valuable frameworks have been developed to guide the strategy of the HR function, and each of them serves an important particular purpose. All have a distinct "customer service" focus, and many were extrapolated from general business frameworks.

The product-line model. Perhaps the most common approach to HR strategy is to organize planning around the HR services provided, including compensation, benefits, training, staffing, performance management, industrial relations, and legal compliance. Individual programs are evaluated on efficiency and to ensure that they are being carried out according to internal standards. The HR plan is designed to deliver practices that are most in demand (staffing and compensation during tight labor markets, benefit costs and separation programs during downturns, etc.), at benchmark cost levels. This applies a product-line model to HR strategy. Product focus is a tried and true business approach, but, as any business making the transition from products to solutions knows, such a framework can overlook the need to challenge client assumptions, and may not create needed synergy across functional silos. A product-line strategy does not explicitly consider the talents in the organization as a resource, because it focuses on HR services, not the role of talent in value creation.

Profit center. In an attempt to answer demands from accounting systems for more rational resource investments, HR organizations may apply a profit-center approach, whereby the HR function charges back to its internal customers for services, and delivers only those services that clients will pay for. In this variation of the product-line model, the "invisible hand" of the market will guide the strategy and direction of the HR function, as internal customers choose which products they will support financially. Economic theory shows, however, that markets work when there is adequate information about both costs and value. Although the transaction costs of HR services are often quite visible, there are many hidden organizational costs. More importantly, the value added by HR investments is often not apparent in standard financial models, as much of what HR creates is "intangible" to the accounting system. When HR overemphasizes the profit-center perspective, it results in the creation of popular programs that may or may not adequately serve the strategic needs of the organization. One HR leader noted the popularity of Steven Covey's programs, and said, "I could use up my entire training budget delivering courses only on the Seven Habits of Highly Effective People." Of course, this would hardly serve all the organization's strategic needs, but, if left to their own devices, this is what employees would pay for.

The HR role framework. Dave Ulrich's seminal work articulates the roles of change agent, administrative expert, strategic partner, or employee champion.[30] Ulrich describes several organizational implications of these roles, but most HR organizations seem to use these roles primarily to categorize the work or competencies of HR professionals. The four-box model is a powerful way to describe HR roles and competencies, but it was not meant to reveal how roles share the design, development, deployment, and evaluation of HR systems. It can also motivate a belief that only "business partners" do HR strategy, when in fact there are deep synergies and key strategic roles for all four types of HR players.

Customer intimacy. Being "close to the business" is a popular strategic theme for many HR functions, being frequently suggested as a way HR attempts to change its inward focus to a more "outside-in" orientation. When this framework drives HR functional strategy, it often means "learning what our business-unit leader customers want and delivering on it." This assumes, of course, that business leaders have a valid logic for what they want. Evidence suggests, however, that business-unit leaders actually have few frameworks for understanding how talent investments drive strategic success. Taken to extremes, "customer intimacy" can lead to dispersing all HR into the individual business units, producing significant customization, but with significant duplication and questionable net value. Organization leaders find themselves asking questions such as "Do we really need a different performance appraisal approach for every region or product line?" Such an approach can lead to overreliance on the business-supporting professionals (e.g., "generalists") to design, deliver, deploy, and account for quality in HR programs and systems, and to try to fill every request of business leaders, including doing tasks that business leaders should do, such as performance management. Alternatively, meeting customer-driven expectations in an environment in which there is no deep understanding of the potential power of HR solutions results in a drastic reduction in HR costs, without concern for the potential consequences. This is then offset by a strong desire for HR to "sell itself" and constantly to "seek top-management support" for its initiatives.

Multiple strategy models. Some HR organizations use other strategy approaches. Business-unit-supporting HR professionals adopt a customer-intimate strategy (learn what clients want and deliver those HR services). Centers of expertise adopt a product-leadership strategy (designing ever newer programs and processes), and service centers adopt a cost-leadership strategy (driving down costs of HR programs relentlessly). Nevertheless, strategy writers routinely note the need for balance and synergy in pursuing strategies. They also note that articulating strategic goals is not the same as defining the organizational capabilities necessary to achieve them.

The HR scorecard. Some HR organization designs rely on an HR scorecard based on the categories in the balanced scorecard framework of Robert Kaplan and David Norton: financial, operations, customers, and learning and growth.[31] Scorecards are useful for organizing HR and business measures, and connecting them to strategy.[32] Measures can be valuable in demonstrating the tangibility of HR outcomes, and HR's willingness to be accountable. Even the best measurement systems are dominated by measures of HR's efficiency, however, rather than by its contribution to improved decisions and competitive success.[33] More importantly, because they often reflect a traditional activity-based focus, they are not designed to guide decisions about how to combine HR elements to achieve such outcomes as cost reduction, customer awareness, etc.

Benchmarks and best practices. As an alternative to more generic measurement frameworks, such as the balanced scorecard, HR organizations often design to benchmarks. Benchmarks can be excellent starting points for considering where practices can be improved. Nevertheless, a collection of even the best HR practices is not an organizational strategy that defines the synergies between the practices and identifies the talent areas to which they should be applied. Benchmarking as a strategic approach presumes that those practices that are most frequent, used by the most financially successful firms, or are most efficient must have survived the market test and be the best. The implicit assumption is that "there is one best answer" that all organizations should strive to achieve. This presumes that there is little value in being unique and that little value is placed on the unique strategic context of each organization in developing an HR strategy. In the extreme, the best that a benchmarking approach can ever produce is a perfect copy of someone else. Where is the differentiation in that?

Making HR unique and protectable. Realizing that the best-practice approach leads to copying others, HR leaders discovered the powerful ideas in the "resource-based view" of organizational success.[34] This view suggests that success is based in part on acquiring and exploiting resources that are unique and hard to copy. A common interpretation is that HR practices should be distinctive and hard to copy. HR practices should contribute to acquiring, exploiting, and protecting key organization resources, however, and this may or may not involve creating unique HR practices. One HR leader put it well: "My organization is competing through unique digitization of customer information, but strategic HR doesn't mean merely that we digitize our HR information."

The need for a new framework. Just as with the traditional focus on HR professional services, each of these frameworks can be useful and is potentially powerful. They were not designed to build HR functional strategies, however. Rather, they were adapted to meet particular elements of that need. They all offer insight, but fall more into the "better than nothing" category, than "the right tool for the right job" one. As with the evolution to extend the HR paradigm from services to decisions, this is not a symptom of poor HR but a symptom of a choice point in the maturity of human capital management. Many organizations have adapted one or more of these approaches to their own strategy development, discovering both the value and the limits over time. Organizations with the most well-developed approaches to strategy have moved toward more comprehensive, dynamic, and integrated methodologies. The HR profession can do this too, but it requires developing a new point of view on HR strategy.

The Boudreau–Ramstad HRFE framework   The context of the HR function requires an integrated framework – one based on sound principles of strategy, organizational design, and measurement, but also specific to the unique issues facing HR functions. Figure 3.5 shows

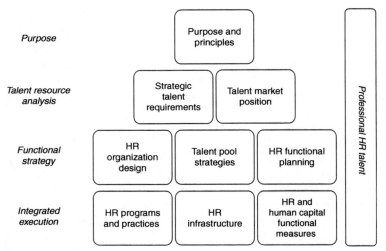

Figure 3.5 Boudreau–Ramstad HR functional excellence (HRFE) framework
Source: Copyright © 2005 John W. Boudreau and Peter M. Ramstad.

a ten-element framework to address this need. The ten elements are based on research and field experience, and reflect not HR activities but the components of a strategically excellent HR organization. For HR leaders, this framework provides a set of criteria against which to evaluate the completeness and depth of the strategy for the HR organization and function. For leaders outside HR, the framework provides a guide to the elements of HR strategy that should be present in order for the function to support the strategic initiatives and processes that prepare the organization and its talent to contribute to the broader strategy.

- *Purpose* consists of clearly defining why the HR function exists, such as the relative emphasis placed on compliance with rules, delivering services, counseling leaders, and educating leaders to make better talent decisions. It also includes the values and principles that guide HR decisions within the organization.
- *Talent resource analysis* is about segmentation in two ways. First, it is about strategic talent requirements, or how talent contributes to organizational success (where talent needs to be better than competitors to win). Second, it is about talent market position, or knowing how best to compete for the strategically needed talent (what motivates and attracts pivotal groups). Segmentation of the

workforce on these two dimensions is fundamental to developing a unique and focused HR strategy.[35] Chapter 5 discusses in detail a logical framework for identifying how different organizational roles contribute to strategic success, and the idea of creating a unique value proposition in the talent market.

- *Functional strategy* is about how the HR organization uses its resources and where it fits within the broader organizational planning and strategy processes. It includes HR organization design, which encompasses decisions about the design of the formal and informal HR organization, the service delivery model, and governance of the HR organization. It includes talent pool strategies, which involve identifying which areas of talent require distinctive approaches and how they will be integrated across the HR organization. It includes HR functional planning, which determines the resource requirements and budget for the function, how resources will be allocated and managed, and where changes in the HR function will most affect organizational success.

- *Integrated execution* includes the tangible actions of the HR organization, including its programs and practices, its infrastructure, its internal interactions, and its interactions with its stakeholders. It includes HR programs and practices, which is how individual HR specialties (such as staffing, development, leadership, rewards, and performance management) are designed, and the evidence-based principles that guide them. This includes the design and implementation of HR programs and practices, and how they integrate with each other and across the organization. It also includes HR infrastructure, which is the platforms that enable the HR organization to function, such as information, legal, and other systems. Finally, it includes human capital (HC) and human resource measures, which are the metrics, analysis processes, reports, and communication systems that evaluate and track the contributions and progress of the HR organization.

- *Professional HR talent* applies the best principles of talent development to those in the HR profession itself, such as a strategy to predict and anticipate talent needs, as well as HR competencies, career development paths, rewards, etc.

HR functional excellence and risk management   When the elements of the HR functional strategy are understood more clearly, it is also clearer that each element of the HR functional strategy can help address various types of risk in the risk-management framework. Referring to the risk-management framework of Figure 3.4, we can think of the HR department as an "entity." In the framework of Figure 3.2, HR is an "enterprise-resource unit," because it focuses on a particular resource – human capital and its organization – that spans virtually every organization unit. This means that strategic, operational, reporting, and compliance risk are all relevant to the HR organization strategy.

Strategic risk for the HR organization involves considering where uncertainty might affect the organizational objectives of the HR department itself. Such uncertainty may arise from changes in the surrounding organizational structure, but more typically it arises because of changes in the broader organizational strategy or mission. Operational risk for the HR organization typically focuses on uncertainty regarding the success of HR programs and practices such as staffing, development, rewards, and career management. Again, a good deal of uncertainty arises from how such practices will be received and implemented by the other organizational units and leaders, but this type of risk is also a function of larger organizational changes. A merger, for example, can entail significant operational requirements to reconcile and integrate the human resource systems from each of the merging organizations.

Reporting risk is perhaps one of the most significant drivers of HR department design and organization. Reducing inaccuracy in reports of workforce characteristics such as headcount, cost, and diversity is often a primary request of organizational leaders. The reports that the HR function produces are also often essential to meeting regulatory or investor requirements. In many ways, getting the necessary reporting correct is a basic requirement for HR organizations to have the "license to operate" and to participate in other elements of strategy.

Compliance risk also often receives a large amount of attention when it comes to the HR function. It is fundamental that the HR organization ensure that human capital areas such as employment contracts, labor negotiations, separation and severance arrangements, and benefits comply with legal, investor, and industry requirements. Much of the evolution of HR infrastructure has been devoted to ensuring that compliance and reporting are at acceptable levels. Because compliance and reporting risk are so tangible, it is important that leaders not fixate exclusively on these elements of HR risk. As we have seen, the context for human resource strategy is much broader, and the contribution of the different elements of HR functional excellence can extend far beyond these areas of risk.

Conclusion

Human resource strategy deals with human capital and how it is organized. Human capital is a resource that spans every element of organization life, and many of the organization's relationships with its environment and constituents. Perhaps more than any other resource, the strategies that are formulated for human capital, and the human resource department or function, must have a clear and synergistic fit with the context of other organizational units and those outside the organization that influence it or are affected by it. This chapter has emphasized the need to understand the position of the HR organization within the larger context in order to clarify how HR strategy can best be crafted to optimize the contribution of human capital to the goals of the larger enterprise. We have seen how the strategic perspective of different types of organizational units varies, and we have begun to recognize how these contextual differences define how human resource strategy addresses risk, opportunity, and uncertainty. We have also seen how important it is for senior leaders not simply to assume that the design of the HR organization will take care of itself, or that the HR organization deals mainly with risks associated with compliance and reporting. While this is not uncommon, we have seen significant opportunities revealed when senior leaders clearly recognize how different units are served differently by HC strategy, and how HC strategy reaches from the HR department to the broader organization and its environment.

What is also apparent from recognizing the context for HR strategy is that important organizational strategy issues may increasingly require much greater consideration of the issues and disciplines that have long been the domain of HR strategy. Look again at Figure 3.1. If organizations need increasingly to consider the uncertainty, risk, and opportunity created by issues such as geopolitics, technologically enabled democracy, cultural values, emerging new social institutions, and sustainability, then senior leaders will need to become more adept at the strategic disciplines that can address them. These issues may often be determined more by social processes than by operational ones. They may hinge more on psychology, politics, and social perceptions than on economics. In sum, the underpinnings of strategy and organizational risk management may increasingly draw on disciplines that have long been the domain of human capital strategy. Our next chapter considers more explicitly how the concepts of uncertainty, risk, and opportunity may be incorporated into that strategy.

Notes

1 This section is excerpted from Boudreau, J. W., and Ziskin, I. (2011). The future of HR. *Organization Dynamics*, 40(4): 255–66.
2 Boudreau and Ziskin (2011).
3 Boudreau and Ziskin (2011).
4 See Lawler, E. E., and Mohrman, S. A. (2003). HR as a strategic partner: what does it take to make it happen? *Human Resources Planning Journal*, 26(3): 15–29.
5 Boudreau and Ziskin (2011).
6 See, for example, Brockbank, W. (1999). If HR were really strategically proactive: present and future directions in HR's contribution to competitive advantage. *Human Resource Management*, 38(4): 337–52; Hughes, E. A. (2006). HR professionals struggling to shake off "pen pusher" image. *Personnel Today*, October 24: 4–5; Meisinger, S. (2004). Assessing HR: the view from the C-suites. *HR Magazine*, 49(1): 10; and Zhonghai, Z. (2005). Overcoming the system-first mentality in China HR. *China Staff*, 11(6): 15–16.
7 Cohen, E. (2010). *CSR for HR: A Necessary Partnership for Advancing Responsible Business Practices.* Sheffield: Greenleaf Publishing; Mirvis, P., Googins, B., and Kinnicutt, S. (2010). Vision, mission, values: guideposts to sustainability. *Organizational Dynamics*, 39(4): 316–24; Wehrmeyer, W. (1996). *Greening People: Human Resources and Environmental Management.* Sheffield: Greenleaf Publishing.
8 Boudreau and Ziskin (2011).
9 McIlvaine, A. R. (2010). The innovator. Human Resource Executive Online, July 1, www.hreonline.com/HRE/story.jsp?storyId=461233863 (accessed April 28, 2011); University of Washington (2009). People analytics, PhD intern: Mountain View. University of Washington, February 25, http://depts.washington.edu/hcde/2009/02/25/people-analytics-phd-intern-mountain-view (accessed April 28, 2011).
10 Boudreau, J. W. (2010). IBM's global workforce initiative, case study. Alexandria, VA: SHRM (available at www.shrm.org/Education/hreducation/Documents/Boudreau_Modify%20IBM%20Case%20Study_PDF%20Only-CS5-partA-FINAL%20TO%20POST.pdf).
11 HR Analytics Summit (2010). Interview with Melissa Graves, www.hranalyticssummit.nl/interview-melissa-graves.

12 Coleman, M. (2011). Most important function of the future = HR. HRN Europe Blog, www.hrneurope.com/blog/?p=3086 (accessed April 28, 2011).
13 Boudreau and Ziskin (2011).
14 See, for example, chapters in Mohrman, S. A., and Shani, A. B. (eds.) (2011). *Organizing for Sustainability.* Bingley: Emerald Group Publishing.
15 Boudreau and Ziskin (2011).
16 Marshall, C., and Rossman, G. B. (1999). *Designing Qualitative Research,* 3rd edn. London: Sage.
17 L. A. Kidstuff (2011). Mattel imagination toy testing center testers. L. A. Kidstuff, http://lakidstuff.com/02/19/mattel-imagine-toy-testing-center-testers/programs-classes-kids-families (accessed May 9, 2011).
18 Ulrich, D. (1997). *Human Resource Champions: The Next Agenda for Adding Value and Delivering Results.* Boston: Harvard Business School Press.
19 Conaty, B., and Charan, R. (2010). *The Talent Masters: Why Smart Leaders Put People before Numbers.* New York: Random House.
20 GE (2011). GE in Africa. GE, www.ge.com/gh/company/africa.html (accessed April 28, 2011).
21 Ernst & Young (2008). *Global HR Risk: From the Danger Zone to the Value Zone,* webcast. London: Ernst & Young.
22 Boudreau, J. W., and Ramstad, P. M. (2005a). *HR Functional Excellence Workbook.* Los Angeles: Boudreau–Ramstad Partnership.
23 Boudreau, J. W., and Ramstad, P. M. (2005b). Strategic partnership with impact, executive education seminar. Center for Effective Organizations, Los Angeles.
24 Boudreau and Ramstad (2005b).
25 Boudreau and Ramstad (2005b).
26 COSO (2004). *Enterprise Risk Management – Integrated Framework: Executive Summary.* Chicago: COSO, 5.
27 Wortham, J. (2010). Disney buys Tapulous, maker of music game applications. *New York Times,* July 2.
28 See www.ft.com/cms/s/0/4934647e-65c5-11e1-979e-00144feabdc0.html#axzz1ov1V0r31.
29 Boudreau, J. W., and Ramstad, P. M. (2007). *Beyond HR: The New Science of Human Capital.* Boston: Harvard Business School Press, 66.
30 Ulrich (1997).
31 Kaplan, R. S., and Norton, D. P. (1996). *The Balanced Scorecard: Translating Strategy into Action.* Boston: Harvard Business School Press.
32 Becker, B. E., Huselid, M. A., and Ulrich, D. (2001). *The HR Scorecard: Linking People, Strategy, and Performance.* Boston: Harvard Business School Press.
33 Boudreau and Ramstad (2007).
34 Barney, J. B., and Clark, D. N. (2007). *Resource-Based Theory: Creating and Sustaining Competitive Advantage.* New York: Oxford University Press.

35 Boudreau and Ramstad (2007); Boudreau (2010); Cascio, W. F., and Boudreau, J. W. (2011). *Investing in People: Financial Impact of Human Resource Initiatives*, 2nd edn. Upper Saddle River, NJ: Pearson Education/ FT Press; Boudreau, J. W., and Jesuthasan, R. (2011). *Transformative HR: How Great Companies Use Evidence-Based Change for Sustainable Advantage*. New York: Wiley.

4

HR strategy through a risk-optimization framework

Previous chapters have explored fundamental issues associated with strategy in general, and HR strategy in particular (Chapter 1), features of the external environment that underpin business and HR strategies (Chapter 2), and the multiple levels of HR strategy and its connections to the organization and to the surrounding environment (Chapter 3). This chapter focuses more explicitly on mitigating, managing, and optimizing human capital risks, and then incorporating these considerations into HR strategy. The risks associated with managing talent are becoming more and more obvious to decision makers, as the following sections illustrate. We begin our treatment by considering a 2011 report from the Boston Consulting Group and the World Economic Forum that focuses on global talent risks.[1]

These risks comprise looming talent and skills scarcities that threaten the strategic initiatives of companies and governments everywhere. The report proposes seven responses to global talent risks – blueprints for action on how to attract, move, develop, diversify, and retain talent. They are as follows.

(1) *Introduce strategic workforce planning:* model the labor supply and demand for different job families to understand current and future imbalances and to develop strategies for addressing them.
(2) *Ease migration:* innovative, points-based migration systems and "migration-friendly" branding by governments and companies are necessary to attract the right talent globally.
(3) *Foster brain circulation:* develop strategies to turn brain drains into brain gains as students and professionals come home to apply skills learned abroad.
(4) *Increase employability:* increase employability – of the current as well as the future workforce – through education systems that include practical and theoretical skills, lifelong learning, and upskilling.

(5) *Develop a talent "trellis":* talent development is key to ensuring a sustainable pool of highly skilled people. Focus on evolving from career tracks to a trellis, building the skills required for the jobs of tomorrow and offering vertical and horizontal career and education paths.

(6) *Encourage temporary and virtual mobility:* do this through short-term work or study in another location (temporary mobility). A networked world enables virtual mobility, allowing individuals to carry out their professions regardless of their locations.

(7) *Extend the pool:* this can be done by tapping into the skill sets of women, older professionals, the disadvantaged, and immigrants. Easily available childcare, flexible work schemes, mentoring and advisory roles, together with improved options for licensing and recognizing credentials, are solutions to the barriers that these groups face.

Organizations are beginning to hire professionals specifically for human capital or HR risk management. Here is an example.

---

http://www.robertwalters.com/en-gb/vacancy/436536/HR-Risk-Manager-United-Kingdom – London.do

Working for a leading global financial services organisation.

An excellent and challenging opportunity has arisen for an experienced HR Risk professional.

The role in summary requires the successful applicant to represent the HR Director and the global HR function ensuring that you are managing the identification of HR and people risks and audit issues globally and ensuring effective management, mitigation and control.

The role will form a large emphasis on identifying an effective action plan for all HR issues, ensuring that relevant FSA regulatory requirements which fall into HR are being met.

The successful candidate must hold a proven track record across areas such as governance, operational risk and controls, regulatory risk and business continuity.

Applicants must hold a proven track record of working in a risk management environment.

Hold strong knowledge and experience of the FSA regulatory regimes.

Have managed cross functional projects, having managed people matters and risk into business plans and process.

Human capital strategy as risk mitigation

When risk is seen only as the possibility of uncertain events creating a bad outcome, organizations focus on ways to minimize or insure against the worst case. This can lead to human capital strategies that are built largely upon the idea of reducing uncertainty, eliminating bad outcomes, or insuring against the worst outcomes.

This approach to mitigating uncertainty, risk or its consequences is quite common in strategic workforce planning. Many human resource strategies and practices strive to eliminate uncertainty by making more precise predictions about future supply and demand for skills, headcount or capabilities. Often such systems involve elaborate HR planning models that incorporate information from labor markets, organizational product demand, engineering-process efficiency information, etc. The objective is to increase the precision of the projections of workforce supply and demand, the gaps between them, and the potential remedies.

The focus on mitigating risk also arises when dealing with the activities and processes of the HR department itself. This is because it is important that processes such as administering pay and benefits, hiring, and termination be "low-risk" so that they run consistently, deliver reliable results, and minimize the chances of mistakes. Traditional quality-control tools are often applied to such HR processes to achieve the same "low-defect" rigor that is often the hallmark of engineering or production processes. Indeed, many HR leaders believe that zero-defect rigor in HR processes is the "license to operate" that allows further innovation and strategic influence. Quotes such as "No one wants to hear your ideas on strategy if the paychecks are wrong" are quite typical of this perspective.

Human capital risk is seen as important, but it is still the case that it is often defined and approached in many different ways, or not at all. Andrew Lambert and David Cooper report that 53 percent of HR directors responding to a Credit Research Foundation survey agreed strongly that people represent a significant element in assessing organizational risks.[2] Only 7 percent, however, agreed strongly that senior managers understand how people risk can affect business performance.

Most planning and forecasting is concerned with risk as defined as a bad outcome in the future. When applied to HR, risk is often defined as in Table 4.1, from the HR Council of Canada.

Notice how the risks are defined as violating laws, abusing employees, harming the environment, experiencing death or injury, etc. When defined this way, it is easy for decision makers to focus their efforts on reducing the bad outcomes. The right-hand column of Table 4.1 shows typical actions that HR leaders and their organizations can take to reduce the bad consequences from the risks in the left-hand column. The term "risk" also often reflects some element of uncertainty. If a bad outcome is certain to occur, then we may be able to prepare or insure against it, even to the point of removing the bad consequences completely, in which case it is no longer a risk. When a bad outcome or its consequences are uncertain, this is often an even more serious situation, because it requires making choices that may turn out to be wrong.

Nevertheless, unexpected future outcomes can also have positive consequences. In May 2011 the company LinkedIn went public, and its share price doubled within a day of its initial offering. This was an unexpected outcome for most LinkedIn shareholders, but one that turned out to be an opportunity. Stock prices are a good example of the difference between uncertainty, risk, and opportunity. Most of us are uncertain about the level of a future stock price, but that does not mean that our uncertainty is always a risk. If the stock price ends up below our purchase or target price when we need to sell it in the future, then that's a bad outcome, or a risk. If the price is higher than our purchase or target price when we need to sell it, however, then that's a good outcome, which we might call an opportunity.

Despite the importance of risk mitigation, it is important not to allow this perspective to dominate the way that leaders approach human resource strategy. Obviously, an exclusive focus on removing process errors can lead an organization to pursue HR strategies that are too narrowly aimed at the administrative elements of human resource management (HRM), to the exclusion of important strategic issues. An exclusive focus on improving how well an organization can predict future workforce supply

Table 4.1 Defining risk in HR as bad outcomes

HR activity	Potential risk	Potential considerations
Compensation and benefits	• Financial abuse	• Who has signing authority? • How many signatures are required? • Are there checks and balances?
Hiring	• Discriminatory practices • Hiring unsuitable or unsafe candidates • "Wrongful" hiring	• Was a complete screening completed on potential applicants? • Were provincial human rights laws observed? • Is there a set probationary period? • Were promises made to the candidate that cannot be honored? • Did the employee sign off on the policies and contract of employment before being hired?
Occupational health and safety	• Environmental • Personal injury or death	• Do we provide safe working conditions and do we conduct safety checks regularly? • Do we provide adequate training for staff? • Do we ensure the use of appropriate clothing and safety equipment? • Do we have adequate policies, procedures and committee in place?
Employee supervision	• Abuse • Reputation in the community • Release of personal information	• Do we provide sufficient orientation and training? • Do we provide adequate supervision (especially for activities that occur off-site or after hours)? • Do we have a performance management system in place? • Are personal information protection guidelines followed?
Employee conduct	• Abuse • Reputation in the community	• Do we have clearly written position descriptions for all positions? • Do we follow up when the parameters of the job description are not respected?

Table 4.1 (*cont.*)

HR activity	Potential risk	Potential considerations
		• Do we provide thorough orientation and training?
		• Do we provide an employee handbook?
		• Do we have comprehensive policies and procedures?
		• Do we provide ongoing training about our policies and procedures?
		• Do we retain written records of performance issues?
		• Do we ensure that organizational valuables are secure?
		• Do we have cash management procedures?
		• Do we have adequate harassment policies and procedures?
Exiting employees	• Property • Reputation in the community • Compensation	• Do we retrieve organizational information and equipment that a dismissed employee used (especially from home)? • Do we ensure that all access codes, passwords, etc. are de-activated? • Do we conduct an exit interview?

Source: http://hrcouncil.ca/hr-toolkit/planning-risk-assessment.cfm#_secA1.

and demand, or how accurately it can measure candidate or employee qualifications, can cause organizations to focus too narrowly on those areas that can be measured well, and miss opportunities in areas that are perhaps less predictable, but highly consequential.

For example, in many global companies it is important to achieve a top management team that has significant diversity in terms of regional background and experience. The need to draw upon familiarity with emerging markets can be particularly important. Yet, in many companies that we work with, the most predictable candidates are the ones who come from traditional career paths, often those who have grown up in the more traditional developed markets that the organization operates in. These are the candidates who most resemble the current top-management team, they are doing the "big" jobs that are most familiar to top decision makers, and they have track records that are more easily evaluated. Certainly, it is a greater "risk" to reach into newly emerging markets for leadership candidates, not so much because those markets do not have great candidates but, rather, because the organization's history and traditional approaches make it harder to identify and predict which candidates will do well. Without taking such a risk, however, the organization is likely to miss some of its most significant opportunities.

It may be best to take the risk of promoting candidates from newly emerging markets even if their performance cannot be predicted as accurately, and then "hedge" the risk by providing strong coaching and more attentive supervision, or "concentrate" the risks in areas where candidates have the chance to learn from their mistakes, rather than placing them in areas where their potential mistakes would be highly damaging and where learning is difficult.

It makes a big difference whether one views human capital strategy as about reducing uncertainty, reducing the likelihood of a bad outcome, reducing the consequences of a bad outcome, or positioning the organization to be ready for the possibility of a good outcome. Very often, however, discussions of risk management, risk mitigation, and risk strategy fail to identify clearly which of these is the most pivotal way to optimize the organization's success in an unpredictable world. Thus, before we can consider creating human resource plans and strategies, we must have a clear understanding about the "risk-management" elements that affect such strategies. This means understanding the differences between risk, opportunity, and uncertainty.

Uncertainty, risk, and opportunity

Let us start with some definitions of three important ideas in strategy in an unpredictable world – uncertainty, risk, and opportunity.

Uncertainty   This is the degree to which we are unsure about whether an outcome will occur, and/or its consequences (whether good or bad). It also includes whether we are aware of limits to our awareness of the possible outcomes, and of our ability even to estimate them. How well we predict depends on many factors, including prior knowledge or experience, how well the models we use to predict the future actually reflect future conditions, and how biased we are in our perceptions about our data, models, and about our own fallibility. In human capital strategy, as in any area of decision making, the goal is not perfect prediction, as that is generally impossible. Indeed, often the illusion of predictability is extremely harmful.[3] Leaders understand that human behavior at work is uncertain. Indeed, they are often convinced that employee behavior is so random that it is not even worth trying to make decisions using the best evidence and tools that are available. Nonetheless, even imperfect tools can often improve decisions enough to have very significant and positive consequences for the organization.[4] Even so, it is important to recognize that many areas of human capital strategy, like any strategy arena, will remain difficult to predict. Questions characterizing uncertainty include the following.

- What is the range of possible outcomes?
- How likely are deviations from our prediction?
- How confident are we in our estimation of the shape and size of the outcomes and probabilities?

Risk   As noted above, risk consists of an undesirable outcome and its consequences, usually when that outcome or its consequences are uncertain. Typically, human capital strategy focuses primarily on risks, such as those shown in Table 4.1, which is a helpful list of issues that organizations should attend to when it comes to their HR practices. Notice how the focus of this list is on the *negative* outcomes, however, and how to reduce their consequences, which is quite distinct from the question of how likely the bad outcomes are, and whether they might be offset by other *positive* outcomes. Questions characterizing risk include the following.

- What range of outcomes will produce negative consequences?
- What can be done to reduce these outcomes or mitigate their effects?
- How confident are we in our estimation of the consequences and their effect on our goals?

Opportunity   Opportunity constitutes a desirable outcome and its consequences, usually when the outcome or its consequences are uncertain. Taking advantage of an opportunity often means placing the organization in a position to benefit from an uncertain future event. For example, if the future need for engineers is uncertain, this means that the organization may need more or fewer of them than it expects. Hiring *more* engineers than forecasted can put the organization in a position in which, if demand turns out to be greater than expected, the organization will reap the benefits. Questions characterizing opportunity include the following.

- Which outcomes are desirable?
- What are the positive consequences?
- How confident are we in our estimation of the outcomes and their positive consequences?

How risk and opportunity are related   Risk and opportunity can be two sides of the same coin. Predicting the exact demand for future projects may be impossible, so the key question may not be how to improve prediction but, rather, how human resource strategy addresses this uncertainty. Having "extra" engineers on the payroll when future demand is not sufficient to employ them is a *risk*, the negative consequences being the unnecessary costs if work is not available. Having "extra" engineers on the payroll if demand proves higher than we expect is an *opportunity*, with the positive consequences that we are able to take advantage of unexpectedly greater engineering-project opportunities from customers. In the same way, you can characterize having "too few" engineers on the payroll as a *risk*, by focusing on the negative consequences of missing out on unexpectedly greater project opportunities, or as an *opportunity*, by focusing on the positive consequences of saving the payroll and other costs should the higher demand level not happen.

The Chinese idea of ji   The Chinese concept of *ji* is instructive here. Lambert and Cooper note: "John Thirlwell and Tony Blunden point out in *Mastering Operational Risk* that the Chinese have a common character – 'Ji' – in the words for both opportunity and crisis or danger." They feel this indicates that, "conceptually, the Chinese understood the twin sides of risk many centuries ago."[5]

- Crisis is *wei ji*.
- Opportunity is *ji hui*.

Note also the word *zhuan ji*, as shown in the figure, which means "turn into opportunity." Thus the Chinese link the turning of a crisis into an opportunity.

转机

John Boudreau and Ravin Jesuthasan provide this example of seeing risk and opportunity in strategic HR planning:

> When a new hire works out badly, does this failure indicate that screening needs tightening? Possibly – but HR should not automatically assume that its goal is to minimize the risk of a bad hire. It may be cheaper to accept the risk of an occasional bad hire and then mitigate that risk by weeding out mistakes more quickly. Typically, however, HR professionals do not consider this trade-off explicitly. Rather, in order to minimize the risk of a bad hire, HR professionals find someone they are certain can do the job. This is why you find so many recruiters looking for extremely specific backgrounds and skill sets. For example, if an organization needs to replace a logistics analyst for shipments of concrete on the East Coast, then HR's ideal candidate is someone who has done precisely that job before. It is a good strategy for reducing the risk of a bad hire, but restricting the pool of applicants raises costs and increases the time needed to fill the position. A more effective approach might be to take on a less qualified candidate who is available immediately and can grow into the role, or someone who lacks the ideal amount of experience but has exactly the right competencies to grow into a star performer. This is a case in which HR needs to look at the idea of risk leverage and ask, "Can we gain something by accepting a greater degree of risk?"[6]

Retooling "risk" in HR management using traditional management models

Human capital planning cannot remove all uncertainty. Instead, it must strike a balance between risk and opportunity, in a world where the key is not to create certainty but understanding and being prepared for uncertainty. What sort of frameworks might assist leaders inside and outside the HR profession to strike this balance? Does it mean that HR and non-HR leaders must develop an entirely new language and logic for risk-optimized planning when it comes to human resources?

Fortunately, the answer is "No." Many of the standard risk and planning models from business provide tools and logical frameworks to help better balance risk, opportunity, and uncertainty. These models often arise from business disciplines that have long dealt with the reality of uncertainty, and the need to optimize the level of risk, rather than simply reducing it. Table 4.2 shows examples of several HR strategy areas that have direct parallels to standard business frameworks, and how the language of these standard business frameworks can be used to rethink how organizations approach human resource planning and risk optimization.

Is risk optimized by placing top performers in every position? The first row of Table 4.2 begins with a common assumption: that, because performance in every role is important, the organization should avoid the risk of poor performance at all costs. When you think about it, though, striving for the best candidate for every organizational role makes little sense. In engineering, it is also true that every component of a product, or every product feature, is important. Nonetheless, not every component or product feature need be at the highest tolerance level. For some components it is better to strive for a moderate standard than to sacrifice feasibility on the altar of perfection. For example, the upholstery of an airplane is allowed a much wider range of deterioration than the hydraulic system, for obvious reasons. When we apply this principle to human resource strategy it means that we need to consider the implications of different performance levels in different jobs or roles. There are some jobs for which the benefits of striving for the best performance possible do not outweigh the potential costs of achieving it, nor the risks of motivating workers to constantly strive to do better. For instance, in most organizations the financial reporting/accounting processes are important, but they do not require the most advanced accounting techniques, nor the highest level of accounting-process innovation. Accordingly, most organizations should not try to compete with the large accounting firms for top accounting talent. In addition, most organizations should not set up systems that make large distinctions among well-performing accountants, because getting the financial reports done on time and accurately is what is needed. Having accountants competing to be the most innovative may actually cause a lot of harm!

Is risk optimized by hiring and promoting generally good talent that can flex to future conditions? Predicting what human capabilities will be

Table 4.2 Retooling HR involves rethinking the idea of risk in HR strategy

HR strategy area	Traditional HR risk framing	Business tool applied to HR	Retooled approach to talent risk
Work analysis	"Top performers in every position, to minimize the risk of bad performance."	Performance-tolerance analysis optimizes performance improvement against risks, costs, and benefits.	"Minimize risk in risk-averse performance situations, embrace it in risk-loving performance situations, by focusing on return on improved performance (ROIP)."
Talent planning	"Minimize the risk of talent being unprepared for the future by developing generic competencies that will apply across the board."	Portfolio analysis balances the risks of several uncertain future scenarios against their returns, combining resource investments that fit several future possibilities.	"Balance risk in talent planning, by investing in talent for several future scenarios according to their relative likelihood and risk."
Total rewards and employment deal	"Minimize the risk of employee dissatisfaction by agreeing to customized deals, or minimize the risk of inequity by doing the same thing for everyone."	Customer segmentation optimizes product and service features to customize for market segments, according to their value and cost.	"Balance the risk of dissatisfaction or inequity against the return by customizing where it achieves the greatest return and standardizing where it does not."
Employee turnover and inventory	"Minimize the risk of employee shortages by filling all requisitions as quickly as possible and keeping turnover to a minimum."	Inventory management optimizes holding costs, ordering costs, and shortage costs by planning for shortages or surpluses.	"Turnover levels and time to fill are optimized to create the level of employee shortages or surpluses that best balances the risks of surpluses and shortages against costs."
Succession and careers	"Minimize risk by having successors for every position, who have all completed the career-development path requirements."	Logistics management optimizes transport patterns to balance the risk of unavailability against the costs and returns to following various pathways.	"Optimize the risk and return to succession by balancing the costs, benefits, and timing of different career paths."

Source: Adapted from Boudreau, J. W. (2010). *Retooling HR: Using Proven Business Tools to Make Better Decisions about Talent.* Boston: Harvard Business School Press, tab. 6.1.

needed in the future is more and more difficult. Moreover, even if you knew what capabilities would be needed, it often takes a long time to build those capabilities. Even very good future forecasts are likely to be accurate only for a few years, and it takes much longer than that to build capabilities among leaders, high-level professionals, and others. Traditionally, the human resource strategy answer to such situations has been to focus on valuable but generic traits, such as intelligence, or generic competencies, such as vision, communication ability, mental agility, etc. The idea is that, if you cannot predict the future, then you should build a human resource capability on traits that will apply no matter what the future holds. Such an approach mitigates the risk that you will end up with specialized talent that is not fit to future conditions. Of course, the downside of such an approach is that your talent will not be specifically suited to any possible future situation.

If your competitors build talent that has more specific qualifications, and their "bet" turns out to be correct, they will win. How does an organization balance the risk of being wrong against the risk of being too generic? As Table 4.2 shows, the framework of financial-portfolio risk analysis may provide some insights. Just as individuals hold investments in different asset classes in order to diversify their risk, so organizations might consider building talent capabilities that are specific to several likely, but uncertain, future possibilities. Consider how to prepare a leadership group for emerging versus established economic regions. Evidence suggests that the leadership capabilities needed in emerging versus established economic regions may be quite different, and that generic leadership attributes will not fully meet the challenges. The organization might choose to "bet" on one type of leadership, such as developing leaders only for established regions, but it will bear the risk of having too many such leaders if the emerging regions develop more rapidly than anticipated, and it will miss the opportunities available in emerging regions. Portfolio theory can offer tools to suggest how to hold two different types of leadership "assets," and even the appropriate proportion of each type of leader that will maximize the return and minimize the potential risk.[7]

Is risk optimized by mass-customizing the total rewards and employment deal? The third row of Table 4.2 deals with uncertainty, risk, and opportunity in the deal that is struck with employees. It is increasingly possible to provide more customized "deals" with employees. Much has been written about the future of mass customization, in which elements as diverse as benefits, remote office support, location, schedule, and even career paths and development opportunities are customized to fit the particular wishes of those with hard-to-find skills, or certain demographic or age groups, or those in certain regions, etc. As Table 4.2 shows, mass customization is often justified because it reduces the risk of employee dissatisfaction, which can lead to turnover or other problems. On the other hand, there is a commensurate risk of hugely expensive systems to support the different employment arrangements. Faced with uncertainty about how many and what types of deals employees will want, what is an optimum approach? Optimizing the balance between uncertainty, risk, and opportunity may best be approached with tools from marketing, which have long been used to identify the optimum features of products or offerings, by customizing where it creates the greatest benefit, and standardizing where the risks are less onerous. True, not every employee will get a perfectly matched deal, nor will costs be minimized by complete standardization. The risk-optimized choice is to strike the right balance.

Is risk optimized by keeping employee turnover at a minimum?
The fourth row of Table 4.2 addresses one of the most common assumptions in human resource management. If employee turnover and vacancies are costly, then should not the HR system do everything possible to reduce employee turnover? Certainly, such a policy reduces the time and effort spent on hiring and dismissing employees, which can cost millions of dollars. Nevertheless, simply mitigating the risk of employee turnover is often not the way to optimize the balance between uncertainty, risk, and opportunity. If good-quality replacements are readily available, it may be better to allow employees to leave, and replace them, than to go to great lengths to keep them. As the table shows, the tools of inventory optimization may be well suited to reframe the typical employee turnover analysis in order to achieve a better balance between uncertainty, risk, and opportunity. For example, should vacancies be filled as quickly as possible? This certainly mitigates the disruption caused by vacant positions. If taking longer to find and select replacements significantly increases their quality, however, it may be best to absorb the risk of disruption rather than settle for a lesser candidate who can be hired quickly. Indeed, when employee "ordering costs" and "shortage costs" are high (replacements are costly to find and hire, and the disruption

caused by the vacancy is very large), it may make sense to have "extra" employees available in the organization, to step in as needed. This is a strategy being followed by oil-exploration companies today. The oil-industry project-engineering firm IMV Projects, for example, is reportedly hiring engineers for work that does not yet exist, betting that rising oil prices will create work soon enough in the future to make the bet worthwhile.[8]

Is risk optimized by having a deep "bench" for leadership positions? The last row of Table 4.2 addresses the challenge of optimizing uncertainty, risk, and opportunity in the arena of careers and succession planning. It is commonly believed that the role of talent planning and succession systems is to minimize the risk that a vacancy in a leadership position will go unfilled, by having a list of successors, and defined development and career paths for all of them. In a world of uncertainty, however, it is often not possible to predict future leadership needs early enough to be certain that any one career path will actually prepare the future leader. Moreover, the career paths that prepared today's leaders may or may not be the optimal ones to prepare future leaders. As Table 4.2 shows, the discipline of logistics may offer tools to optimize the uncertainty, risk, and opportunity that characterize leadership and succession planning. Logistics portrays the flow of information, inventory, or products as a matrix of paths between process stages. For example, a logistics model of a transportation system portrays it as a set of nodes representing different elements of sourcing, production, and storage, connected by pathways representing different modes of transportation. The cost, timing, quality, and quantity of materials from different sources vary, as do the cost and timing of moving things between the different sources. In addition, all these factors can be uncertain. Logistics tools optimize uncertainty, risk, and opportunity by making decisions about how much inventory to hold at various points in the system, how much to move along any particular pathway, and how to balance the consequences of running short with the costs of ensuring sufficient supply. The same sorts of tools may help optimize career and succession systems, by revealing the optimum "production stages" through which to build capabilities, the optimum "storage stages" at which talent should be assigned, and the optimum "pathways" through which talent should move to maximize its readiness and to minimize the costs.

Lambert and Cooper provide the following example of how organizations often consider their alternatives in dealing with risk.[9]

- *Tolerate:* no steps are taken to address the risk, with the consequences being faced in full should it occur.
- *Eliminate:* everything possible is done to eliminate the risk, as the possible outcome is considered unacceptable.
- *Minimize:* when risk elimination is not feasible, the likelihood of an outcome occurring is minimized and/or the potential impact is limited as far as possible.
- *Diversify:* the risk is spread across a number of different areas.
- *Concentrate:* all the risks are clustered into one area or theme.
- *Hedge:* additional risks are taken on so as to be able to reduce exposure, should the risk in question arise.
- *Transfer:* the risk is placed with an external party, or some form of insurance is taken out.

This is a useful list of ideas, and a good representation of how risk is typically described. When we compare this list to the examples in Table 4.2, it is clearer how each of the risk approaches can enhance strategy and success, and where the gaps may be. For instance, some of the approaches reduce the uncertainty (eliminate or minimize the risk so that its probability is zero or very small), others reduce the consequences (minimize the potential impact, diversify, hedge). One way that these approaches might be improved would be to consider explicitly the potential upside opportunity that may exist in uncertainty. They all focus on risk as a negative consequence, yet a more complete risk analysis would include attention to taking on risks in order to increase opportunities, as we have seen.

Uncertainty, risk, and opportunity applied to employee turnover

The examples in Table 4.2 often deal with employee turnover. The "risk" of employees leaving is a very frequent focus of human resource strategy, and yet its prediction and its consequences are often not well understood.[10] So, to conclude this chapter on the role of risk in human capital decisions, let us return to the ideas of *uncertainty, risk, and opportunity*, and apply them specifically to employee turnover.

Tables 4.3 and 4.4 show how this framework applies to employee turnover. Table 4.3 provides a set of general diagnostic questions to distinguish uncertainty, risk, and opportunity, and then applies them to employee turnover. Table 4.4 provides a set of general actions that

Table 4.3 Uncertainty, risk, and opportunity *questions* applied to employee turnover

Uncertainty, risk, opportunity question	Application to employee turnover
Uncertainty	
What is the range of possible outcomes?	What are the lowest and highest numbers of separations we might see?
	What are the lowest and highest probabilities that a particular person will leave?
How likely are deviations from our prediction?	What is the most likely number of separations?
	What is the most likely probability that a particular person will leave?
	What are the probabilities of higher or lower numbers of separations or a higher or lower probability?
How confident are we in our estimates of the shape and size of the outcomes and probabilities?	Have these estimates proved to be accurate in the past?
	How much disagreement is there about these ranges, likely estimates, and probabilities?
	Might individual turnover probabilities be dependent, not independent?
Risk	
Which outcomes are undesirable?	What is the number of separations that would cause significant costs or disruption?
	Who are the individuals whose departure would create significant costs or disruption?
	What are the jobs in which separations are disruptive or costly?
What are the negative consequences?	What are the costs of processing the separations and replacement?
	What productivity is lost while the position is vacant?
	What is the cost of work disruptions due to the separations?
	Have we considered ways to reduce separation costs and disruption?

Table 4.3 (*cont.*)

Uncertainty, risk, opportunity question	Application to employee turnover
How confident are we in our estimates of the outcomes and their negative consequences?	Have we had experience with separations of this type of individual or in these positions?
	Have we validated the cost estimates based on past experience and good accounting principles?
Opportunity	
Which outcomes are desirable?	What is the number of separations that would constitute healthy rejuvenation?
	Who are the individuals whose departure would be beneficial?
	What are the jobs in which separations would be beneficial?
What are the positive consequences?	What is the quality of the replacements for the separating individuals?
	What are the employment costs that would be saved after people separate?
	Have we considered ways to increase the quality of available replacements?
How confident are we in our estimates of the outcomes and their positive consequences?	Have we had experience with separations of this type of individual?
	Have we had experience with separations in this position before?
	Have we validated the estimated benefits based on past experience and good accounting principles?

can be taken to address uncertainty, risk, and opportunity, and shows specifically how they apply to employee turnover.

Addressing turnover uncertainty requires considering the range of possible outcomes and then the probability that they will occur. It also requires a careful assessment of how skilled the leaders are at understanding the range of turnover levels and their probabilities. One often-overlooked issue is the fact that individual probabilities of employee separations may be dependent on each other, rather than independent. For example, if we believe that each person's probability

Table 4.4 Uncertainty, risk, and opportunity *actions* applied to employee turnover

Uncertainty, risk, opportunity question	Application to employee turnover
Uncertainty	
Reduce the range of possible outcomes	Make work more attractive to everyone, so separations are less likely
Reduce the likelihood of deviations from the most probable predicted outcome	Develop better turnover prediction systems
Increase confidence in the shape and size of the distribution of outcomes	Ensure that turnover analysts and decision makers base their assumptions on complete and rigorous data
Recognize our inability to predict precisely	Apply scenario analysis to consider seemingly improbable turnover patterns
Risk	
Reduce the likelihood of undesirable outcomes	Make work more attractive to high performers, so that they are less likely to leave
More precisely estimate the negative consequences	Use cost-accounting systems to anticipate the full cost of employee separations
Reduce the negative consequences of undesirable outcomes	Streamline employment processes to the costs and time of separation, acquisition, and development reduce
Create insurance against the negative consequences	Create contracts with employment services to fill vacancies quickly
Hedge against negative outcomes	Buy insurance that pays out upon the loss of key executives
Diversify to reduce the exposure to any one risk factor	Have more than one employee serving key clients, so that, if one leaves, the client does not follow them
Opportunity	
Increase the likelihood of desirable outcomes	Make work less attractive to low performers, so that they are more likely to leave voluntarily
More precisely estimate the positive consequences	Treat employee turnover like inventory turnover, and identify where workforce quality can be increased through "new blood" or disrupting old patterns

Table 4.4 (*cont*.)

Uncertainty, risk, opportunity question	Application to employee turnover
Increase the positive consequences of desirable outcomes	Create a culture and work environment that is welcoming to newcomers
Hedge in favor of positive outcomes	Hire rare and talented applicants even if there is no current job vacancy
Diversify to increase exposure to more possible opportunities	Create onboarding experiences that tap the ideas from new recruits quickly

of leaving is independent of others', and if we estimate that the average probability of a person leaving in any year is 10 percent, then out of 100 people we would expect to lose ten in any year. What, however, if the probability of one employee leaving depends on the probability of others leaving? This could happen if employees work in teams, and when one team member leaves the others will follow. It could happen if the departure of some employees acts as a shock for others, making them consider their own options, etc. When this happens, the probability of separations actually rises with the number of employees leaving. Losing ten people in a year may now be a very strong signal that the organization will actually lose twenty or thirty. The separation probability may not always trend toward a stable value.

Nassim Taleb provides several examples in which the social sciences, such as economics and psychology, may mistakenly assume that things such as turnover follow a bell curve, and vastly underestimate the probability of extreme events.[11] In some organizations, the analysis of the "risk" of turnover is assessed by examining uncertainty. Google has developed a formula that predicts the probability that each employee will leave. *The Wall Street Journal* reports that Google's formula helps the company "get inside people's heads even before they know they might leave," in the words of Laszlo Bock, who runs human resources for the company.[12] Ameriprise Financial has developed similar formulas, and reports the probability for each individual who works for certain unit leaders in hopes of helping the managers target their retention efforts.[13] Much of this effort is designed to reduce uncertainty by improving how precisely employee turnover can be predicted.

Addressing turnover risk requires analyzing the range of undesirable outcomes, and their actual consequences for the organization. Wayne Cascio and John Boudreau provide formulas for calculating the costs of turnover, including the costs of separating an employee, acquiring a new employee, and developing that new employee to an acceptable performance level.[14] They note that the cost of turnover can be greater than 1.5 times the average salary and benefits in a position. As Table 4.3 notes, risk analysis also must consider the ability of decision makers to estimate the consequences of turnover accurately. Cascio and Boudreau note that the costs that are visible on accounting statements are often only a small part of the total costs, which can include losing clients, the losses of key skills or team roles, and the inability to pursue opportunities due to unavailable talent. A good deal of organizational attention is often focused on reducing turnover consequences, such as by streamlining the processes of separation, acquisition, and development, either to reduce costs or to speed up the process so that vacancies are shorter. Some organizations insure against having lengthy vacancies by having contracts with employment services to provide replacements on short notice. Others may keep a greater number of workers than the minimum needed, so that other employees will be available to step in.

Addressing turnover opportunity requires understanding and positioning for the positive outcomes of employee separations. As Cascio and Boudreau have noted, organizations are often so fixated upon the administrative costs and disruptions of turnover that they fail to consider where separations may actually be beneficial.[15] They underestimate the potential upside from employee separations. As Table 4.4 shows, this upside can occur in situations in which new employees are likely to be more valuable than existing ones. Examples would include an aging workforce that will soon retire or has obsolete skills compared to new college graduates, or when the organization can enhance the likelihood that poor performers will separate and good performers will stay, thus increasing the quality of the workforce with each separation and replacement. Trilogy created a "university" inside the company that provided its new hires with immediate opportunities to tackle some of the toughest strategic issues as a team, with the support, involvement, and oversight of the CEO. The idea was not simply to orient new hires to the organization, and bring them quickly up to the necessary performance level (which reduces risk). Rather, the idea was to get new hires to apply the fresh perspective of outsiders to company challenges *before* they became too steeped in the organization's internal culture, processes, and perspectives.[16] Boudreau notes that the upside of employee turnover is often more apparent when it is framed using traditional models of inventory turnover, in which inventory shortages and surpluses are seen as one tool for optimizing risk and return, rather than as mistakes in strategic planning.[17] Too often, employee turnover is seen only as a mistake by HR, and not as a potential opportunity.

Conclusion

Uncertainty, risk, and opportunity, and how organizations approach them, have always been a fundamental part of strategy, and the events of the early twenty-first century have conclusively reinforced the principle that ignoring them, or being arrogant about how much executives know about them or can control them, can lead to disaster. What may be less apparent is that the issue of human capital risk is also becoming a more pivotal and prominent element of strategy. Thus, frameworks for human resource strategy must incorporate risk, and the HR profession must get better at defining, measuring, and solving the thorny issues of people in an uncertain world. Recent reports on human capital risk highlight both the future importance and the emergent nature of attention to this issue. In many ways, the human resource field, and the fields of strategy and risk management, are just beginning to grasp and develop ways to approach this issue.

Chapter 1 noted that Ernst & Young, a global accounting firm, conducted a 2008 study of more than 150 global executives in *Fortune 1000* companies, and found that "HR/People risk issues" were among the top five in terms of their impact, and among the top three most likely to occur.[18] The report cited the following top five HR risks:

- talent management and succession planning;
- ethics and tone at the top;
- regulatory compliance;
- pay and performance alignment; and
- employee training and development.

Note that the executives tended to frame the risk in terms of the processes and programs that HR enacts. The report recognizes many important elements of human capital strategy, including the idea that risk can have both upsides and downsides, and that any of these (or other) HR risks can be approached from the perspectives of compliance, financial results, operational excellence, and strategic impact on the organization. The report also notes that 41 percent of the organizations said that they review their HR risk profiles on an ad hoc basis or never, despite saying that HR issues are very prominent risk factors.

HR and non-HR leaders need to approach strategic HR management with greater logical rigor and clarity. In our next chapter (Chapter 5) we provide a framework that leaders can use to connect the operational and financial elements of the programs that HR enacts (like those listed above) to their effects on the attributes of employee and leaders (such as ethics and tone), and ultimately to the pivotal processes, resources, and strategic outcomes that define organizational success. This framework provides a way not only to consider the logical connections but also to understand how to recognize and manage uncertainty, risk, and opportunity throughout the human capital strategy.

Notes

1 World Economic Forum (2011). *Global Talent Risk: Seven Responses.* Geneva: World Economic Forum.

2 Lambert, A., and Cooper, D. (2010). *Managing the People Dimension of Risk.* London: Corporate Research Forum.

3 Taleb, N. N. (2010). *The Black Swan: The Impact of the Highly Improbable,* 2nd edn. New York: Random House.

4 Cascio, W. F., and Boudreau, J. W. (2011). *Investing in People: Financial Impact of Human Resource Initiatives,* 2nd edn. Upper Saddle River, NJ: Pearson Education/FT Press.

5 Lambert and Cooper (2010); Blunden, T., and Thirlwell, J. (2010). *Mastering Operational Risk: A Practical Guide to Understanding Operational Risk and How to Manage It.* London: FT Press.

6 Boudreau, J. W., and Jesuthasan, R. (2011). *Transformative HR: How Great Companies Use Evidence-Based Change for Sustainable Advantage.* New York: Wiley.

7 Boudreau, J. W. (2010). *Retooling HR: Using Proven Business Tools to Make Better Decisions about Talent.* Boston: Harvard Business School Press, ch. 2.

8 Vanderklippe, N. (2011). No work yet in oil patch but you're hired. *The Globe and Mail,* April 13; available at www.theglobeandmail.com/report-on-business/industry-news/energy-and-resources/no-work-yet-in-oil-patch-but-youre-hired/article1984506/s.

9 Lambert and Cooper (2010: 19).

10 Cascio and Boudreau (2011).
11 Taleb (2010).
12 Morrison, S. (2009). Google searches for staffing answers. *The Wall Street Journal*, May 19: B1.
13 Boudreau and Jesuthasan (2011).
14 Cascio and Boudreau (2011).
15 Cascio and Boudreau (2011).
16 Delong, T., and Paley, M. (2002). Trilogy University, Case Study no. 403012. Boston: Harvard Business School Press.
17 Boudreau (2010).
18 Ernst & Young (2008). *Global HR Risk: From the Danger Zone to the Value Zone*, webcast. London: Ernst & Young.

5 HR strategy: linl and outcomes

108 Short Introduction to Strateg

productivity of mining
research in industri
decades, known
engagement, s
are seldom i
manageme
about th
meas
Ye

While the second author was w̶
improve its human capital planning, the ᴜᴄ
faced a shortage of mining engineers, and rising tuɪ..
existing engineers. The company was making do with the engɪɪ.
it had, which meant giving every mine the necessary engineering
attention it required, but nothing more. To do this, the company had
to rotate mining engineers across the mines at a faster rate than if
it had been fully staffed. Consequently, these mining engineers were
constantly on the move, under more pressure, seeing their families
less, and traveling far more than if the company had a full complement
of engineers.

Could talent planning address this? Should the talent strategy
be framed in terms of HR costs, activities, processes, headcount
projections, or something else? We turned to another vital asset – the
trucks that haul ore and other materials around the mine. Suppose
that a mine optimally needs four trucks, which allows each truck to be
driven at the optimal speed, keeps wear and tear at optimal levels, and
allows optimal maintenance. Truck "health" is measured relentlessly,
including real-time speeds, lubricant deterioration, tire pressure,
running hours, etc. Could a mine manager make do with only three
trucks? Yes, if he or she allows the trucks to run a little faster, allows
them to depreciate more, and delays maintenance. Indeed, this would
probably even save money – in the short run. Yet, all these measures
ensure that mine managers never do this. They are held accountable
for optimal truck usage, not short-run expedience.

So, why would a mining company tolerate a shortage of mining
engineers, with the resulting high levels of pressure, stress, health
issues, and turnover, when it would never allow that for trucks? Why
would a mining company have so many measures of truck "health
and well-being" but few or crude measures of the health, stress, and

engineers? This is even more troubling because
al/organizational psychology and HRM has, for
of high-quality measures of things such as stress,
atisfaction, and intention to leave. Such measures
the lexicons of organization leaders or even talent-
nt systems, yet they could provide the same early warning
e deterioration of the mining engineer as the maintenance
res provide for mining trucks.

, employees are tired, but hard work is not to be avoided. The key is
either to push employees beyond their limits nor to demand so little
that you cannot compete. Optimization means addressing the "fatigue
factor" analytically, with human capital planning and measures, not
just opinions or hope. Equipment optimization means finding the level
of usage and maintenance that is best for the truck and its role in the
mine. Human beings are, of course, not objects like trucks. All the
same, human talent deserves a rigorous approach to optimum health
and productivity. Properly framed, leaders can consider employee
fatigue as rigorously as they do truck depreciation.

In this chapter we provide a framework for understanding the
connections between the investments that organizations make in
"human resource management" (such as the money and time that
is spent on programs such as recruitment, training, and pay) and
the vital outcomes that the organization defines as sustainable
strategic success. Such a framework should give leaders a
language that shows them how to understand whether investments
in programs to reduce engineer fatigue might pay off in greater
organizational success. Although the precision of the analysis
might be somewhat less than the analysis of truck depreciation and
failure, the example above shows that there is often much more
available evidence and information about the workforce than most
leaders ever use. One reason is that they lack a logical framework
within which to organize the information so that it is clearly relevant
to their strategic decisions and goals. This chapter provides such a
framework.

Using the framework, the chapter describes how strategic human
resource planning is typically approached, through headcount-gap
analysis or HR activity analysis. Both are useful tools, but we shall

see that, for organization leaders, such approaches must be placed in context, and understood within a broader set of connections between investments and strategy. We show how leaders can find the "pivot points" in the strategy, to find the pivotal roles in which human capital can make the biggest difference. Sometimes those roles do not even exist in the organization's current jobs. Focusing on the pivot points in human capital allows the organization to move beyond an exclusive focus on measuring the gap between the number of people needed versus the number of people who will be available. Instead, it identifies how the workforce may need to change, and where improving the workforce can make the biggest difference.

Human capital strategy is also about how organizations invest resources to create the right array of human resource programs (compensation, staffing, training, etc.). This array of programs can often be dizzying to organization leaders, who experience it as a disjointed set of activities, each logical on its own, but not clearly integrated together. We show how the management concept of synergy can clarify how to optimize these investments.

In the end, formulating a human capital strategy means accomplishing two broad tasks: (1) finding the connections between human capital and strategic outcomes for the organization, to identify the "pivot points" where human capital makes the biggest difference to sustainable strategic success; and (2) making the investments to create a portfolio of human resource programs that fit together synergistically, to maintain the broader workforce, but also to enhance human capital at the pivot points.

Impact, effectiveness, and efficiency

Boudreau and Ramstad note that, in all areas of organization management, there is an important distinction in strategy between three types of objectives: impact, effectiveness, and efficiency.[1] They may not always be named the same in every discipline, but they are hallmarks of most organization planning systems, and they also apply to human capital and human resource planning. Table 5.1 shows the definition and planning focus associated with each of these three "anchor points" of human resource planning.

Table 5.1 Three anchor points in HR planning

Anchor point	Definition	Planning focus
Impact	Describes the relationship between sustainable strategic success and the performance of organization and talent.	Where should we target talent and organization performance improvements so they have the biggest effect on sustainable strategic success?
Effectiveness	Describes the relationship between organization and talent performance and the portfolio of policies and practices.	Where should we target policy and practice portfolio improvements so they have the biggest effect on talent and organization performance?
Efficiency	Describes the relationship between the portfolio of policies and practices and the level of investments.	Where should we target resource investment improvements so they have the biggest effect on the policy and practice portfolio?

Source: Adapted from Boudreau, J. W., and Ramstad, P. M. (2007). *Beyond HR: The New Science of Human Capital.* Boston: Harvard Business School Press.

Expanding the strategic connections using the HC BRidge framework

Expanding the three broad strategic categories of impact, effectiveness, and efficiency provides a more detailed and explicit language for leaders to understand and analyze the connection points between strategy and human capital.

Figure 5.1 shows the three strategic categories as anchor points, the linking elements that comprise each one, and then the analytical questions that reveal the strategic connections. The framework is called "HC BRidge" because it depicts the bridging elements between human capital (HC) investments and strategic outcomes. The word "bridge" starts with two upper-case letters because the "B" stands for Boudreau and the "R" for Ramstad. Consider how well the leaders in your organization can answer these questions.

In our work, we often find that within HR there are good answers to the questions in the bottom two to three boxes, regarding the effects of HR programs, but the tangible connections get fainter as you move toward

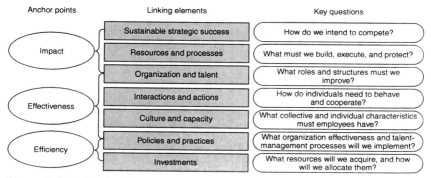

Figure 5.1 HC BRidge framework: seven key questions
Source: Boudreau, J. W., and Ramstad, P. M. (2007). *Beyond HR: The New Science of Human Capital.* Boston: Harvard Business School Press, ch. 3.

the strategic outcomes at the top of the figure. We also find that, among organizational strategists and top leaders, there is often a great deal of attention to the top two boxes, focusing on where and how to compete, and the vital processes and resources that have to be executed well, but that the connection to human capital, talent, and organization structure is much less clear. When organizations properly use these questions, they reveal new insights about how to compete for and with talent and about the role and structure of strategic HR management. When it comes to talent and organization resources, *alignment* requires understanding where differences in the quality or quantity of talent and organization have the greatest strategic effect, *execution* requires knowing what decisions are most pivotal to enhancing those vital talent and organization elements, and *agility* requires having a consistent logic that spans many situations and identifies where change must occur.[2] Now, let us look at an example that will show how the framework of Figure 5.1 can clarify and reveal vital human resource and human capital elements, and how they connect to strategy.

Disneyland sweepers more pivotal than Mickey Mouse?

Which talent pools at a Disney theme park make the biggest difference to strategic success? Would it be the characters (such as Mickey Mouse), the ride designers, the cast members on the street, the executive-leadership team, or a host of other roles that Disney employees play every day? As we saw above, the answer requires thinking about strategy at a much deeper level than simply asking

"Which talent pools help make Disney theme parks 'the happiest place on earth'?" Clearly, everyone's job contributes to that. When we ask questions such as this in any organization, the answers vary widely, and the reasons for the answers vary even more!

Becoming clearer and more consistent about the answers is vital to strategic success. Suppose we ask the question the usual way: "What is the important talent for theme park success?" What would you say? There are always a variety of answers, and they always include the characters. Indeed, characters and the talented people inside the Mickey Mouse costumes are very important. A decision science, however, focuses on pivot points. Consider what happens when we frame the question differently, in terms of pivotal impact: "Where would an improvement in the quality of talent and organization make the biggest difference in our strategic success?" Answering this question requires looking further, to find the strategy pivot points that illuminate the talent and organization pivot points. Figure 5.1 shows that this requires defining strategic success and what most affects it.

Sustainable strategic success: the competitive space defines pivotal differentiators Beginning with sustainable strategic success, what might that look like for Disneyland? Although Disneyland has many competitors, let us compare it to just one: Cedar Point, in Sandusky, Ohio. The websites for Disneyland and Cedar Point are instructive. Disneyland's visual imagery shows well-known places, such as Sleeping Beauty's castle, often with famous characters in the foreground. Cedar Point shows towering steel and wooden roller coasters. Disneyland's claim is to be "the happiest place on earth," and Cedar Point's is "the roller coaster capital of the world" (or, one might say, "the most thrilling place on earth"). Disneyland emphasizes family fun, while Cedar Point emphasizes thrills. Even these simple comparisons begin to reveal important strategic differences.

Strategic execution: resources, processes, and "waiting in line" The next element of the HC BRidge framework – resources and processes – describes what an organization must create to achieve and defend the strategic position or its mission. Figure 5.1 mentions two important categories. The first is the "resources" that need to be obtained, deployed, exploited, and protected. For theme parks, resources include brands, real estate, and relationships with key regulators or local authorities. The second is "processes," which are the transformations that the organization must accomplish to create its unique value. For theme parks, this process involves transporting people to the park, orienting them within the park, providing services and experiences while they are on the park grounds, ensuring their safety and comfort, and transporting them from the park. The "transformation" in this process is to make guests happier, more delighted, eager to return, and so pleased that they will tell stories to their friends and family, creating new Disneyland guests. The next challenge in impact analysis is to find the pivot point in the process at which improvement would make the biggest difference to Disney's strategic objective of delighting customers. One way to find the pivot points in processes is to look for constraints. These are like bottlenecks in a pipeline: if you relieve a constraint, the entire process works better. If we were to map the Disneyland experience, it might include these steps as shown in the figure.

All these process elements are important, but where would *improving* the process make the biggest difference to the Disneyland experience? Almost everyone would say that it is "waiting in line." At Disneyland, a key constraint is the number of minutes a guest spends in the park. Disneyland needs to maximize the number of "delightful" minutes. Disneyland in Anaheim, California, has eighty-five acres of public areas, many different "lands," and hundreds of attractions, small and large. Helping guests navigate, even delighting them as they navigate, defines how Disney deals with this constraint. Notice how this takes the strategy and makes it much more specific by identifying a pivotal process that supports it. This is not to say that other elements of the Disneyland process will go unsupported but, rather, that, when it comes to strategic choices, this pivot point is promising.

Organization and talent: sweepers more pivotal than Mickey Mouse? The linking element of organization and talent focuses on the work that must be accomplished and how it should be organized. Here we look for talent and organization areas in which alignment and performance improvements would make big differences in the strategic pivot points of processes and resources. In engineering, this is sometimes called performance yield, because it asks how much

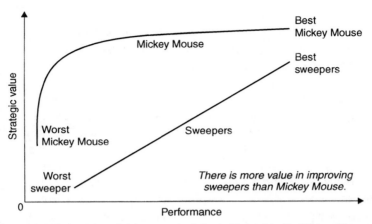

Figure 5.2 Applying yield curves to talent: Disneyland's Mickey Mouse versus the sweeper
Source: Boudreau and Ramstad (2007); reprinted with permission.

strategic value is yielded by an improvement in the performance of something. In this case, we apply it to the performance of human capital in a certain role. Identifying pivotal resources and processes now allows us to see the talent question more clearly. Instead of asking "What talent is important?" the impact question becomes "Where would improvements in talent make the biggest difference in the number of delightful minutes for guests?" Is the answer still "Mickey Mouse and other characters"? Figure 5.2 takes the performance-yield concept and applies it to two talent pools in the Disney theme park: Mickey Mouse and the park sweeper.

The graph plots the "yield curve" for performance in the two jobs of Mickey Mouse and the sweeper. The vertical axis shows the strategic value of performance, the horizontal axis shows the level of job performance. The top line represents the performance of the talent in the Mickey Mouse role. The curve is very high in the diagram because performance by Mickey Mouse is very valuable. Mickey is vitally important to Disneyland. Nonetheless, the variation in value between the best-performing Mickey Mouse and the worst-performing Mickey Mouse is not that large. In the extreme, where the curve falls off on the left of Figure 5.2, if the person in the Mickey Mouse costume engaged in harmful customer interactions the consequences would be strategically devastating. This is shown by the very steep downward slope at the left. This is why the Mickey Mouse role has been engineered to make such errors virtually impossible. The person in the Mickey Mouse costume is never seen, never talks, and is always accompanied by a supervisor who manages the guest encounters and ensures that Mickey does not fall down, get lost, or take an unauthorized break. Because the position is so well engineered, there is also little payoff to investing in improving the performance of Mickey Mouse. There is great value in investments that ensure Mickey Mouse's performance is up to the very high necessary standard, but, beyond that standard, differences in talent pool performance are not as crucial.

The role of Mickey Mouse is so important that it cannot be left to improvising by cast members. If you watch carefully, Mickey Mouse manages to interact with a lot of guests per hour. Each one gets great attention, but the interaction with Mickey does not last long. This allows more customers to see Mickey within a short time span, maximizing the number of delighted guests per minute. The Mickey Mouse role is aligned to the process constraint (number of minutes in the theme park) that is pivotal for the unique strategic position ("the happiest place on earth"). Finally, Disney characters are known and expected to be excellent, so park guests may be less likely to be delightfully surprised by characters that are friendly, attentive, and so forth. Disney executives report that, when guests write letters to share their enjoyable experiences at Disney parks, they often begin with descriptions of unexpected encounters with cast members other than characters. For example, *Eyes and Ears* (the internal publication for cast members at Walt Disney World) publishes "Fan mail," a column containing letters from guests. One guest wrote about how impressed he was with a hearing-impaired housekeeping cast member who "clearly communicated with our family and was terrific with the kids." That is not to say that guests do not write about the characters, but characters may not be the vital pivot point for surprise and delight.

If the talent pivot point for the guest experience process is not characters, what is it? When a guest has a problem, it is people such as park sweepers and store clerks who are most likely to be nearby in accessible roles, and so guests approach them. People seldom ask Cinderella where to buy a disposable camera, but hundreds a day will ask the street sweeper! The lower curve in Figure 5.2 represents sweepers. The sweeper curve has a much steeper slope than Mickey

Mouse, because variation in sweeper performance creates a greater change in value. Disney sweepers have the opportunity to make adjustments to the customer-service process on the fly, reacting to variations in customer demands, unforeseen circumstances, and changes in the customer experience. These are things that make pivotal differences in the "happiest place on earth" differentiators. To be sure, these pivot points are embedded in architecture, creative settings, and the brand of Disney magic. Alignment is key. In fact, it is precisely because of this holistic alignment that interacting with guests in the park is a pivotal role – and the sweeper plays a big part in that role.

At Disneyland, sweepers are actually front-line customer representatives with brooms in their hands. Interestingly, interacting with guests encompasses other jobs as well. Store clerks, for example, have similar opportunities to assist guests in surprisingly delightful ways. We hear stories about harried guests who grab several bottles of water from a bin, pay for them, and take them back to their table, only to realize that in their haste they purchased only three bottles of water for their four children. The store clerk comes over to say: "Here's a fourth bottle of water, no charge." When store clerks and sweepers cooperate, the possibilities for delighting customers increase exponentially. For decades at Disney, store clerks have been carefully cast for precisely these moments.

Again, this does not imply that the Mickey Mouse role is unimportant. To the contrary, the yield-curve diagram in Figure 5.2 shows that the Mickey Mouse line is higher than the sweeper line at all points. Even the best sweeper probably creates less value than the lowest-performing Mickey Mouse. In any well-run organization, everyone contributes to the mission in different ways. The key is to understand those differences systematically. The question that reveals these differences is often "What is most pivotal where improving talent and organization matter most?" Once we understand the talent and organization pivot points, we are much closer to targeting our talent investments to make a significant strategic difference. We still need to go one level deeper, however, to uncover the specific talent and organization elements and the programs and practices that will optimally affect them.

Interactions and actions: what do sweepers do that is strategic?   Interactions and actions describe how individuals'

behavior and cooperation affect the pivotal roles. What key constituents will be encountered? What will be the key role challenges and aligned responses? What will distinguish effective from ineffective behavior? For Disneyland, the pivotal actions and interactions of sweepers are probably not improving performance on sweeping! Our favorite illustration comes from an executive in one of our classes who recalled the time his hot, cranky, and sunburned child was sitting on the sunny curb waiting to watch the parade. A sweeper happened by, noticed the sunburned child, and stopped sweeping. He told the family that there was a shady spot up the hill where they could watch the parade, and he accompanied the family to that spot.

Although a clean park is incredibly important to Disneyland, the sweeping part of the sweepers' job has a flat slope for maximizing the number of delightful minutes for guests. Meeting the standard of cleanliness is essential for sweepers, but improving cleanliness beyond that standard does not surprise or delight guests. For example, there are no radioactive materials or hazardous waste products at Disney. Thus, while a clean park is very important, the level of custodial performance is not as high as might be required by facilities such as hospital operating rooms or nuclear plants. Creative cleaning is less likely to delight guests than creative customer interaction. Like the performance of Mickey Mouse, guests expect cleanliness, so it may be harder to surprise guests with cleanliness beyond the standard. Like Mickey Mouse, Disney has engineered away most of the variation in the quality of sweeping through clever park design, and even culture. Thus, if a sweeper fails to clean something, another Disneyland cast member will probably catch it before it affects a guest.

The pivotal role challenge for Disney sweepers is when a guest needs help or information, and the pivotal aligned action is providing it in a pleasantly surprising, accurate, and appropriate way. The aligned action for sweepers is not to be entertaining (singing and juggling), even though that would also fit the general description of "delighting guests." Sweepers who are busy singing and juggling will not be approached by guests with questions about ride locations, which lines are shortest, and so on. Guests feel more comfortable asking their mundane but very important questions of those in what Disney calls "accessible" roles, and they take advice from such roles more readily. So the people in the sweeper role make the pivotal difference through

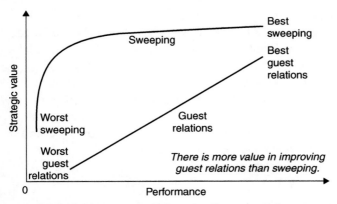

Figure 5.3 Yield curves and aligned actions: sweeping versus guest relations
Source: Boudreau and Ramstad (2007); reprinted with permission.

the quality of guest assistance they offer, and they need to be in the sweeper role to be most effective.

Therefore, a pivotal individual action for Disneyland sweepers is assisting guests with problems, particularly when those problems make them wait in line or distract them from the park features. The interactions element of the HC BRidge framework focuses on how individuals cooperate. Interactions can be the formal information sharing of profit and cost allocations between business units, or they can be more subtle, in the form of informal networks, communication patterns, and mutual trust and respect. Disney includes sweeper supervisors in planning meetings with park designers. The interaction of sweeper supervisors and high-level park designers and architects is pivotal because sweepers are constantly learning things, such as where the park needs more shady spots to watch the parade, and that information is vital to park design. Sweeper supervisors need to get that information, and park designers need to listen to sweeper supervisors. This is cooperation at its most pivotal.

Figure 5.3 shows how the concept of yield applies to the actions of sweeping versus helping guests. The same logic that helped us see more clearly where pivot points existed in the strategy and what talent pools were pivotal now applies here, revealing pivot points within the role.

Quality pivotalness versus quantity pivotalness   What about labor shortages and turnover? So far, we have focused on the pivotalness of differences in the performance of sweepers or Mickey Mouse. Boudreau and Ramstad refer to this as "quality pivotalness."[3] A different kind of pivotalness focuses on not quality but quantity. Quantity-pivotal roles exist where strategic value pivots on finding enough talent, finding it more quickly, or reducing turnover. For Cedar Point, one can imagine that the job of sweeper is mostly quantity-pivotal, because it primarily reflects the role of sweeping, which is more flat-sloped. If Cedar Point runs short on sweepers, however, its strategy suffers. The Cedar Point website aggressively encourages kids to apply for summer jobs, many of which are probably quantity-pivotal.

Talent can be purely quality-pivotal (there is plenty available, but differences in quality matter a lot), or purely quantity-pivotal (having more available matters a lot, but differences in quality do not have a large impact). Typically, however, talent is a combination of both quantity and quality pivotalness. It is important in strategic planning to keep the distinction clear. Organizations often use turnover rates (the percentage of those in a job who leave in a certain time period) as an index of workforce health. Turnover rates are one element in estimating the gaps between the number of people who will be needed in the future and the number who will be available. This is a quantity focus, and it is often quite an appropriate way to express human capital risk – the risk of running short of talent. In a job such as the Disneyland sweeper, however, it is not enough simply to fill the jobs. A significant element of the uncertainty, risk, and opportunity at Disneyland is not only whether someone will be available for the sweeper job, but will he or she know when to stop sweeping and help guests? Hence, the analysis of turnover at Disneyland must also examine whether the pattern of departures and replacements is enhancing or reducing the quality of this pivotal role.

Disneyland knows now that its strategy depends on sweepers who act as guest ambassadors, and can be agile about switching between sweeping and helping guests, but how can Disneyland create these behaviors?

Culture and capacity   The linking element of culture and capacity describes the collective and individual characteristics that employees must have to execute the vital actions and interactions. This element translates the actions and interactions into things such as skills, knowledge, engagement, and opportunities. In actual organizations, insights about culture and capacity often emerge from questions such as "What shared values, beliefs, and norms will support or inhibit execution?" and "How will success depend on individual capability, opportunity, and/or motivation?"

Organizational leaders often jump too quickly to one particular solution. Some may like capability ("Can employees do it?") and will suggest: "Increase knowledge by giving sweepers ten hours of training on park information." Some may focus on opportunity ("Do employees get the chance?"), suggesting: "Let's put sweepers near the ride lines, where all the guests are." Still others may emphasize motivation ("Do employees want to do it?"), suggesting: "Let's give a bonus for the number of times sweepers help a guest." These ideas may all be good ones, but sound strategic planning demands a logical way to evaluate and assess them. Careful consideration of which element – capability, opportunity, or motivation – is most pivotal is one way to do that.

Disneyland provides a good example of a culture that treats all customers as guests and all employees as cast members. Everyone, from sweepers to executives, goes through an eight-hour training and orientation program called "Traditions." Every month the Disneyland internal newsletter *Eyes and Ears* reports on unique examples of guest service, and Disney leaders are often in the park watching for such examples so that they can reward employees. Every Disney cast member knows the four core pillars of the Disney experience: show, safety, courtesy, and efficiency. Disney cast members carry a small card entitled "Guest-Service Guidelines" (illustrated with pictures of the seven dwarfs from *Snow White*):

> Be Happy ... make eye contact and smile!
> Be like Sneezy ... greet and welcome each guest. Spread the spirit of Hospitality ... It's contagious!
> Don't be Bashful ... seek out Guest contact!
> Be like Doc ... provide immediate Service recovery!
> Don't be Grumpy ... always display appropriate body language at all times!
> Be like Sleepy ... create DREAMS and preserve the "MAGICAL" Guest experience!
> Don't be Dopey ... thank each and every Guest!

This makes culture directly relevant to the most pivotal actions and interactions. Often the pivotal moments when individual employee judgments will make big differences occur when no one is there to supervise or direct the employee, and culture helps ensure that the person will make good choices.

Disney also provides innovative opportunities for sweepers by designing its park trash collection so that sweepers do not have to walk a long way to discard trash. Even the most capable and motivated sweeper cannot do much if he or she spends all day walking between the park and the trash receptacles. The key is to balance capability, opportunity, and motivation within a collective culture.

This approach to capacity and culture suggests a different approach to employee engagement. Every Disney employee understands the mission to create "the happiest place on earth" by delighting guests. Virtually any employee action that improves the guest experience might be seen as aligned with this goal. Thousands of times a day, Disney sweepers have to decide whether to sweep or help guests. Truly aligned execution occurs when the sweepers make those decisions correctly.

Organizations that use their human capital strategy to guide employee engagement will ask questions such as the following.

- Do sweepers understand the relative pivotalness of sweeping versus helping guests?
- Do sweepers say that they have the capability, opportunity, or motivation actually to stop sweeping and talk to guests?
- Does the culture of customer service enable them to take the initiative to provide the specific service that makes the pivotal difference?

Strategy execution also requires decisions about how to make the aligned actions and interactions happen. Next, we show how to identify the pivot points where supporting policies and practices must work together to do this.

Policies and practices   If sweepers are pivotal at Disney for their customer interactions, then should we enhance those actions by rewarding sweepers, by investing more in their training, or both? Figure 5.1 shows that the linking element "Policies and practices" in the HC BRidge decision framework describes the programs and activities that will create the pivotal capacity and culture. Such practices need to work individually, but it is more important that they work as a portfolio. Insights into policies and practices are often revealed by questions such as the following. How will our practices distinguish us in the talent market? How will our practices work together? What are the conditions for success?

In Florida, Disney's sweepers are unionized, which limits Disney's ability to differentiate pay based on individual performance ratings. That does not stop Disney from creating a portfolio of programs and practices that enhance sweeper capacity and culture. Performance policies include asking guests to rate or describe something that a sweeper did that delighted them. Disneyland provides "Great Service Fanatic" cards for guests to write down the name of a cast member and what that person did that was so special. "Great Service Fanatics" are eligible for special drawings for prizes; in addition, they receive a special notation on their employment record. Sweepers at Disney know that their career path can lead to positions in which they will be working with park designers or imagineers (the engineers and architects who design the rides) – a developmental reward that other theme parks may not be able to offer.

All Disney cast members go through the famous "Traditions" orientation and training program, but there is also a formalized on-the-job training program for Disney sweepers. Trainers include former sweepers, who are selected for their ability to train and their job knowledge and experience. A detailed training outline goes well beyond the custodial basics and includes specific guest service elements. In staffing and sourcing, sweepers are selected not just for their experience or capability at cleaning but for their orientation and passion for providing one-on-one service, and for their emotional and verbal capabilities. With such a professional approach to the sweeper role, it may not surprise you to learn that Disney even renamed the job from sweeper to "showkeeper," to capture the pivotal nature of the role.

Notice how the portfolio of practices is directly connected to the pivotal interactions and actions. Disneyland would not provide the same customer-service training or incentives to everyone. Just as with well-executed marketing or financial decisions, Disney's talent investments are targeted to where they will have the greatest effect. Disneyland is competing with and for its sweeper talent in a way that is very different from competitors, which see the sweeper job solely in terms of sweeping the park, or which provide the same kind of customer-service training to everyone. Disney will not only create more of the pivotal capacity and culture; it will also present a unique position in the talent market for the customer-oriented sweeper candidates. For those individuals who are motivated by the opportunity to provide great customer service, Disney becomes a uniquely appropriate place to work. Disney begins to attract the best of the candidate pool because it offers an integrated employment proposition that also exploits its unique business model.

Talent alignment changes the competitive game   We have seen how the logic of the linking elements helps to clarify the relationships between sustainable strategic success and decisions about where and how to invest in human capital. Disney will compete more effectively and achieve strategic success more readily by recognizing that sweepers are pivotal, and that sweepers are pivotal because they are customer ambassadors with brooms in their hands. Disney will also compete better for sweeper talent. It has changed the market for customer-oriented sweepers by identifying, attracting, rewarding, developing, and retaining precisely the kind of customer-focused sweeper it needs. Before Disney changed the game, other theme parks might have attracted their share of customer-focused sweepers. Now, as applicants learn what Disney wants and that Disney can provide very distinct rewards and development, the company will attract more of the sweeper applicants who want the customer ambassador role. Disney can refine the supply further by developing tests that reveal which candidates have a passion for customer service, helping it identify characteristics that others may miss. When Disney provides training and incentives that further increase the quality of its sweepers as customer ambassadors, it increases the internal supply of such talent.

Strategic talent investments: beyond efficiency benchmarks   Every organization must determine a budget for its talent practices, and many human resource strategies focus mostly on reporting program costs, budget variances, or the planned savings from redesigning or outsourcing HR processes. Nonetheless, any good strategy will include more than budget levels. Effective human capital planning goes beyond simply looking at budgets and costs. There are also specific questions about the investments themselves, including the following. What resources will we consider (money, HR staff time, participant time, leadership time)? What will be the resource trade-offs? How much will we invest, and where will we invest it?

Typical efficiency measures in the Disney example might include the cost per hire for sweepers, the cost per training hour delivered to sweepers, the time to fill vacancies, or the average sweeper pay compared to sweepers in other theme parks. HR leaders often diligently benchmark such numbers, attempting to match or exceed the efficiency levels of their competitors. Lacking a framework that includes effectiveness and impact, organizations often maximize cost or time savings by making HR programs more efficient. When efficiency is the sole focus, it can motivate attempts to increase the yield of programs and processes per unit of resource expended. This can lead to trying to "shrink to success."[4]

Disneyland provides very detailed and intensive on-the-job training for new sweepers. The training lasts forty-six hours (in addition to the eight-hour "Traditions" program). Although statistics are not available on the amount of on-the-job training offered by other theme parks, it seems likely that Disney probably spends more time and money than competitors to attract, select, and train its sweepers. Disneyland looks inefficient on benchmarks such as cost per new hire. Of course, the investment is well worth it, as we have seen, because Disneyland makes the most of that investment. In fact, when other theme parks focus exclusively on efficiency, it actually lowers Disneyland's costs! Why? Because the other sweeper employers attract those who meet the minimal standards, who will sweep minimally well. This leaves a wide open market for Disney to attract and retain sweepers who provide great customer care. The sweepers who are less skilled at customer care and are willing to work with less on-the-job training in a job that is defined exclusively in terms of sweeping end up at other theme parks, while those with great customer-care potential end up at Disney. Disney does not have to get into a bidding war, because others are too busy cutting costs to understand the value Disney creates from its sweepers.

A risk-based perspective on talent and strategy connections

Recall the enterprise risk-management framework from earlier chapters, shown again in Figure 5.4. The HC BRidge framework for connecting talent investments to strategic success, and the notion of searching for pivot points throughout the strategy, provide a useful framework for understanding and managing strategic risk through human capital.

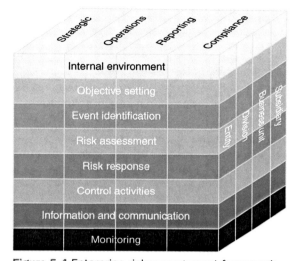

Figure 5.4 Enterprise risk-management framework
Source: COSO (2004). *Enterprise Risk Management – Integrated Framework: Executive Summary.* Chicago: COSO, 5.

Recall in Chapter 1 that we noted that one way HR strategy affects the risk elements in Figure 5.4 is by connecting human capital to those risk factors. The HC BRidge framework can be used, for any cell of the matrix in Figure 5.4, to examine where changes in the quantity or quality of talent are most pivotal to reducing uncertainty, exploiting opportunities, or mitigating risks. There are talent and organization pivot points throughout the matrix.

Operational risk mitigation in the job of Mickey Mouse For example, recall the performance-yield curve for Mickey Mouse in Figure 5.2. Disneyland is a subsidiary of the Walt Disney Company (in the right-hand face of the cube), and the performance of Mickey Mouse significantly affects operations (in the top face of the cube). Across the front face of the cube, we can see that Disneyland sets objectives for Mickey to be available to guests at specific places and times, and identifies the risky events as being when Mickey is out of place or not behaving in the standard and expected way. The risk response is to create a Mickey Mouse role that is characterized by strong control activities, including having a handler at all times, not having the person in the Mickey costume talk, etc. As Figure 5.2

shows, this type of control is appropriate to minimize the substantial downside risk if Mickey is not precisely up to standard at all times.

The downward-sloping curve of Figure 5.2 is a classic example of a job in which the important strategic issue is to minimize the risk of poor performance, much like pilots in a commercial airline.[5] Boudreau notes the similarity between the performance-yield curves such as those in Figures 5.3 and 5.4 and similar curves that are often drawn for returns to improving production elements, consumer advertising, or product features.[6] Deep strategy connections in areas such as operations management, marketing, and finance often produce such yield curves for other resources.

The second way to use an enterprise risk-planning framework like the one in Figure 5.4 is to apply some of the ideas to the HRM function and its practices. For example, it will be important to ensure that the staffing programs for sweepers are reliable and consistent, and avoid the temptation simply to select solely on the ability and willingness to sweep well. Thus, operational risk control may require monitoring and risk assessment to be certain that hiring managers consider the full array of necessary characteristics. In terms of finding opportunities, not just mitigating risks, leaders might be encouraged to "take a chance" by allowing some of the most observant sweepers to jump to the theme-park-design career path. Park design would be a stretch for most sweepers, but the opportunity to bring new insights into the park-design process could outweigh the risks. Deep analysis of human capital strategy should also look for such insights when it comes to human resource programs, job performance, and organization design.

Strategic opportunity at the entity level for PepsiCo Inc. An item in *The New Yorker* magazine of May 16, 2011, described PepsiCo's efforts to position itself to benefit from future demand for foods that are not only tasty but healthy as well. For PepsiCo, traditional talent such as manufacturing, supply chain, marketing, and branding will of course be important for this, or any, strategy. Nevertheless, the greatest *improvement* in PepsiCo's future readiness to achieve this strategy will come from human capital that has never existed in the company beforehand. A key talent acquisition for PepsiCo was Derek Yach, PepsiCo's director of global health policy. In 2002, as a leader at the World Health Organization (WHO), he drafted new dietary guidelines, which were circulated among United Nations member states. They were resisted by food industry and government leaders, and little progress was made. By 2006 he had already left the WHO when the CEO of PepsiCo, Indra Nooyi, asked Yach to join PepsiCo and "do exactly what you were doing at the WHO here at PepsiCo." The *pivotal* talent for PepsiCo's future strategy lay in a job that had not existed previously and in a person, Derek Yach, who might seem an unlikely member of a snack-food-leadership team.

The PepsiCo example of hiring the former head of the World Health Organization is at the entity level (right-hand side of the cube), and involves a strategic uncertainty (top face of the cube) about the future demand for snacks that are good for you. The CEO of PepsiCo set out to capitalize on this new uncertainty and the opportunity it created for a global healthy food organization. This objective to enhance the healthiness of PepsiCo's products initiated a risk response (front face of the cube) that required both creating a healthier image of the organization and incorporating new knowledge about healthy food into operations. The pivot point in the talent arena was to hire from outside PepsiCo a world expert on healthy food.

There are many other examples showing how a deeper understanding of the connections between investments in human capital and strategic success can illuminate how human capital decisions can define and affect strategic uncertainties, opportunities, and risks. By combining the risk-management framework of Figure 5.4 with the HC BRidge framework of Figure 5.1, organizations can develop deeper and more precise logical connections between strategic success and their investments in talent and organization, and apply those insights to finding the pivotal human capital elements involved in dealing with uncertainty, risk, and opportunity. The Mickey Mouse and sweeper examples show how risk management can be incorporated at the operational level, into the very definition of the performance of individual jobs. The PepsiCo example shows how the same analysis can provide clarity about a key human capital strategy at the entity level.

Deciphering human resource strategy using the HC BRidge framework

For business leaders, human resource strategies can emerge in many different forms. As Chapter 3 noted, these different sorts of human resource strategy often reflect one particular perspective, such as a product-line model, a cost-efficiency model, a customer-service model, or a competency model. Using the HC BRidge framework in this chapter, it is possible to understand these different HR strategy approaches better, and for leaders within and outside of HR to see opportunities to deepen or extend them.

Resource efficiency   In organizations dominated by a financial perspective, HR strategy is often an extension of the budgeting process. In such cases, the HR strategy is often presented through the efficiency lens of the HC BRidge framework, focusing on the HR activities and programs to be delivered, and on the time, money, and headcount that will be devoted to them. Frequently, such strategies are presented with reference to available benchmarks, such as the cost per hire, the time to fill vacancies, the cost per training hour, and the ratio of HR headcount to total employee headcount. From a risk perspective, the emphasis is often on minimizing the risk of HR budget overruns, through strict cost control, or by finding less expensive ways to deliver HR programs. Large reorganizations of HR departments are often presented through the efficiency lens, emphasizing the available savings through outsourcing, shared services, etc. Leaders who receive such strategies are generally impressed by their numerical precision, but also often overwhelmed by the sheer volume of numbers describing HR costs and deliverables. Figure 5.1 shows that, while this strategic perspective is important, leaders should extend it by focusing on questions regarding the effectiveness of HR programs and practices, and ultimately whether the investments are being made at the most vital pivot points. In other words, will HR cost cutting take place where it will have the least effect on vital pivot points?

Product line and process   In organizations in which strategy is defined in terms of the products delivered or the processes accomplished, HR strategy is often an extension of process-based strategies, or product-focused analysis. Here, the emphasis is on the array of HR programs and practices, often emphasizing improvements in process delivery (such as moving some processes to the web or a shared services center for greater efficiency or accessibility), or on the degree to which HR practices represent the state of the art, or the newest ideas. Leaders who receive such strategies are often impressed with the volume of work that the HR organization is achieving, and they often find that they value the practices that HR is delivering. When strategy is presented in this way, however, it can also deliver a daunting array of programs, frequently with little connection to one another. Figure 5.1 shows that this approach is often focused on the programs and practices linking element, or perhaps some elements of effectiveness (such as when engagement, learning, or hiring levels are shown to be associated with improvements in HR programs). In terms of the risk-based framework, this kind of strategy focus is often designed to address concerns about the risks of process failure within the HR programs and practices. Alternatively, it may be used to demonstrate that HR programs are in place to address human capital risks, such as the departure of key talent or the potential lack of preparation of leaders.

Leaders facing such strategies can use the HC BRidge framework in two ways. First, they can ask how the different programs actually fit together, to produce changes in vital elements of the organization or the workforce. Boudreau and Jesuthasan refer to this as the synergy across HR programs and practices.[7] The idea is that, although it is good to have development, staffing, and compensation practices that each represent the state of the art, a key question is whether they work together or at cross-purposes. Ideally, the results of each HR practice will seamlessly reinforce other HR practices. Moreover, organizations would avoid trying to make all HR practices state of the art when, in fact, the greatest effect might be to invest more heavily in one practice and make sure the others sufficiently reinforce it. There is a common phrase: "Hire heavy and manage light, versus hire light and manage heavy." The idea is that sometimes the synergistic answer is for an organization to hire very carefully, so that those hired require less training and performance management, and can be given more freedom in their work. At other times, the synergistic answer is to take some risk when hiring, and then improve those hired through strong development or performance management. This idea of "make or buy" optimization is common in other areas of strategy, and applies as well to human capital strategy.

Second, leaders can connect the effectiveness elements of HC BRidge to the impact elements, as shown in Figure 5.1. Here, the idea is to ask where the effects of HR programs and practices will be seen, and whether those effects are directed at the most pivotal organization and talent elements. This often takes the form of a question such as "What are we solving for with our HR programs and practices?" The idea is to step back to the fundamental strategic imperatives and pivot points, use them to evaluate where workforce and organization improvements are most vital, and then connect that to the portfolio of HR practices.

Headcount-gap analysis   Some of the most sophisticated numerical human capital planning involves projecting the movement of employees through the various jobs and roles in the organization, the movement of employees out of the organization, and the movement of new employees into the organization. This is perhaps the most classic version of human capital strategy. Today, such analyses are often conducted using complex analytical tools to project workforce and skill availability in specific regions of the world, sophisticated formulas to predict the likely turnover of individuals in vital roles over several years, and the mathematical analysis of the movement of employees between different jobs or roles to project the internal supply chain of the workforce. The result is often an impressive array of predictions that can isolate those organizational positions that are likely to experience surpluses, and those likely to experience shortages. Then, where the gaps are large and pivotal, HR programs can be proposed to alleviate them. Sometimes, such strategic analyses also incorporate scenarios to build in uncertainty, risk, and opportunities on the basis of potential changes in key parameters of the forecast.

Leaders presented with such strategies justifiably find them impressive in their quantitative depth. They often find it very valuable to have the ability to change the parameters of the model and envision the effects of those changes on future headcount gaps. Questions that can be answered with this kind of strategy include the following. "What if our managers choose to continue to work longer and retire later?" "What if we could increase the number of engineering degrees in this emerging country by 10 percent over the next five years?" That said, it is important not to become fixated on the numerical projections. Such strategic analyses are very helpful in projecting the movements of employees into, through, and out of the organization, but they often depend heavily on a framework that reflects the jobs and roles of the past. We repeatedly encounter leaders who say: "I am very impressed with the analysis of future headcount gaps, but in some areas my dilemma is not whether we will have enough engineers defined in today's terms but, rather, whether we have defined the new role for tomorrow's engineers, and are building our talent to meet that new role." If the new role does not exist yet, headcount-gap analysis may overlook it, perhaps missing significant sources of opportunities or risks.

Looking at the HC BRidge framework of Figure 5.1, such headcount projections reflect the "organization and talent" linking element, in the form of the array of jobs and roles. They also reflect the "actions and interactions" linking element, in the form of the movement of individuals into, out of, and through the organization. Often it is useful to extend such analyses to include questions within the linking element of "impact." This would include questions such as "Which of the headcount gaps are likely to have the greatest effect on our most vital future processes, resource, or strategic differentiators?" and "Considering our most vital strategic goals, are there any areas where the basic nature of the jobs and work must change significantly?" These sorts of questions will ensure that impressive headcount-gap analyses are focused where they can add the most value to vital decisions, and that they reflect potential future changes in the work itself.

Conclusion

A hallmark of strategic analysis in areas such as finance, marketing, and operations is that there is an accepted logic and language about how the strategic pieces fit together. For example, financial reports at the organization level aggregate budgets at the business-unit level, which, in turn, integrate and connect specific analyses such as cash flow, inventory, and sales. A massive amount of numbers and data are included in such reporting, but it is strategically sensible, because it reflects a logical framework that leaders understand and use consistently. In this chapter, we have suggested that, for organization leaders to have a similarly strategic understanding about human capital and organization design, they must develop and use a framework that reveals the connections between the investments and the strategic outcomes they produce.

As we have seen, a framework based on the distinctions between efficiency, effectiveness, and impact provides a useful way to understand and integrate the array of potential strategic information about human capital, and does so in a way that is compatible with the strategic frameworks that are already well developed in other functions. The HC BRidge framework described here is one example of a logical approach that leaders can use to understand the pivotal elements of their human capital, to connect human capital risk to organizationally pivotal risk factors, and to make sense of the many different sorts of human resource strategies that they encounter.

In the next chapter, we continue this theme by focusing on the similarities between human capital decisions and decisions about other resources. We show how "retooling" human capital questions in similar ways to other resources can enhance understanding and communication, and provide a common language about uncertainty, risk, opportunity, and returns. We also discuss how an emerging approach to "evidence-based" management offers the potential for future leaders to tap into decades of research on employment and human capital – research that is often ignored today.

Notes

1 Boudreau, J. W., and Ramstad, P. M. (2007). *Beyond HR: The New Science of Human Capital*. Boston: Harvard Business School Press.
2 Boudreau and Ramstad (2007).
3 Boudreau and Ramstad (2007).
4 Cascio, W. F., and Boudreau, J. W. (2011). *Investing in People: Financial Impact of Human Resource Initiatives*, 2nd edn. Upper Saddle River, NJ: Pearson Education/FT Press.
5 Boudreau and Ramstad (2007).
6 Boudreau, J. W. (2010). *Retooling HR: Using Proven Business Tools to Make Better Decisions about Talent*. Boston: Harvard Business School Press.
7 Boudreau, J. W., and Jesuthasan, R. (2011). *Transformative HR: How Great Companies Use Evidence-Based Change for Sustainable Advantage*. New York: Wiley.

HR strategy: communication and engagement

Can you use standard dimensions of risk management to determine and evaluate the pivotal elements of an organization's talent strategy? Terry Gray and Matt Hankes, two human resource and organization effectiveness leaders at Cargill, have done just that.[1] Recall from earlier chapters the dimensions of risk that were described by the Committee of Sponsoring Organizations, shown here as Figure 6.1.

Notice the front face of the cube, and its list of elements for addressing risk: objective setting; event identification; risk assessment; risk response; control activities; information and communication; and monitoring. At Cargill, decisions about human resource management strategy, programs, and policies are framed in terms of their impact on strategic risk factors, particularly when it comes to internal controls. Cargill already used the COSO framework for its risk management, so the framework provided a natural way to connect human capital strategy and decisions to the larger organizational risk objectives. Cargill HR leaders used several elements of the COSO framework to help their non-HR leaders better understand the impact of HR.

For example, regarding the "control environment," the Cargill HR audit process notes that it depends on integrity and ethical values, commitment to competence, management philosophy and operating style, organization structure, and authority and responsibility assignments. Leaders consider that these things are directly affected by factors such as unrealistic performance targets, the bonus structure, poor segregation of duties, excessive decentralization, and insignificant or unpublicized penalties for improper behavior. The process asks a simple question: "Is HR involved in any of the above?" The answer is "Of course," and this sets the tone for a deeper dialogue about how investments in people can create organization and talent outcomes that are pivotal to Cargill's most vital risk issues. Here

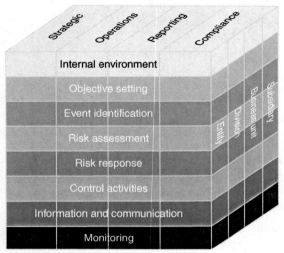

Figure 6.1 Enterprise risk-management framework
Source: COSO (2004). *Enterprise Risk Management – Integrated Framework: Executive Summary.* Chicago: COSO, 5.

is how Cargill's HR team summarizes the relationships between the COSO risk control components and HR activities.

Risk assessment:
* objective setting;
* change management.

Control activities:
* performance management;
* compliance.

Information and communication:
* HR communication;
* employee relations;
* employee advocacy.

Monitoring:
* self-assessment;
* measurement.

As we have seen, human resource strategy has elements and implications that go well beyond the domain of the human resources function. Choices made about human capital and human resource programs affect virtually all elements of organizational strategic success, so there should be a clear understanding of the human resource strategy and how it supports strategic success, as well as how organization strategy should be influenced by the nature of the organization's human capital and how it is organized. Nevertheless, evidence suggests that communication and understanding of the HR strategy are typically not very clear.

Communicating strategic HR management – and its impact on risk and strategic success – is different from formulating and constructing the strategic workforce plans themselves. Accordingly, this chapter focuses on how organizations can use principles from communication and persuasion to increase the chances that strategic workforce planning will actually get used. First, let us explore the extent of the need for communication by considering the evidence about how investors and boards of directors do or do not use human resource strategic information.

Human capital reporting to investors

One review of the financial statements of the Fortune 50 organizations for the treatment of "human capital intangibles" found that the leading organization (IBM) devotes 15,000 words to the topic of human capital, while Chevron, Kroger, and Dow all devote 6,000 to 7,000 words to the topic, with the average Fortune 50 firm devoting only 2,500 words, and none of the firms uses "a well-thought-out framework."[2] The authors note how IBM reports on diversity. IBM gives a rationale on why diversity should be of interest to shareholders, explaining that it seeks to grow revenue in midmarket businesses and that its market research shows many of these businesses are led by women. The company then goes on to describe its diversity practices, such as holding managers accountable for various diversity initiatives and outcomes. IBM also reports metrics, breaking down the numbers of women and ethnic groups by management level. Similarly, Dow publishes graphs showing trends in the percentage of female managers. The authors conclude that companies are "taking baby steps."

Human capital reporting to boards of directors

Another key constituency for human capital strategy information is the board of directors. Edward Lawler and John Boudreau surveyed

North American HR leaders in 2004, 2007, and 2010, and found the following results, shown in Table 6.1, regarding the type of help HR gives to boards.[3]

The average results in the right-hand columns show that only two issues, executive compensation and executive succession, consistently emerge as areas in which the extent to which HR helps the board is rated to a great or very great extent by more than 50 percent of those surveyed, though the condition and capability of the workforce is somewhat strongly rated. Issues such as risk assessment and strategic readiness are seldom areas in which HR is seen to provide boards with assistance, despite the importance of human capital to these issues.

Opportunities to communicate about human capital strategy may vary a great deal with the sort of strategy that organizations pursue. Lawler and Boudreau found, for example, that the more an organization's strategy emphasized a bureaucratic or low-cost-operator approach, the less extensive was HR's help to the board in all areas. In contrast, the more that organizations pursued strategies that relied on high involvement from workers or sustainable practices, the greater was the extent of HR help with all the areas listed in Table 6.1. They conclude that organizations pursuing high-involvement or sustainability strategies may offer more promising avenues for communicating and engaging boards with HR strategies and plans, because such strategies may rely more heavily on engaged and flexible human capital. The good news is that it does appear that HR has an opportunity to communicate about human capital strategy through executive compensation and executive succession. The less good news is that there appears to be little opportunity for broad strategic conversations beyond the focus on the executive team.

As we have seen in many of the examples in this book, however, the pivotal strategic human capital issues often arise in talent pools that are not limited to the executive team. David Creelman and Andrew Lambert reach a similar conclusion after examining how boards address human capital issues:

> Traditionally, many boards concentrated primarily on the selection, performance and reward of the top executives and their potential successors. In the last 10 years, boards have devoted increasing

Table 6.1 Areas of HR help to corporate boards

HR helps the board with... (1 = little or no extent; 3 = moderate extent; 5 = very great extent)	Percentages					Means		
	Little or no extent	Some extent	Moderate extent	Great extent	Very great extent	2004	2007	2010
Executive compensation	8.6	8.6	9.2	30.5	43.1	4.2	4.1	3.9
Addressing strategic readiness	16.3	19.8	34.3	24.4	5.2	2.8	2.8	2.8
Executive succession	6.9	10.3	19.5	35.6	27.6	3.8	3.8	3.7
Change consulting	23.3	24.4	24.4	20.3	7.6	2.6	2.7	2.6
Developing board effectiveness/corporate governance	38.8	19.4	23.5	16.5	1.8	2.5	2.5	2.2
Risk assessment	19.7	32.9	20.2	23.1	4.0	2.4	2.6	2.6
Information about the condition/capability of the workforce	9.9	16.9	29.7	32.0	11.6	3.3	3.3	3.2
Board compensation	31.4	13.6	16.6	24.3	14.2	3.4	3.0	2.8

Source: Lawler, E. E., and Boudreau, J. W. (2012). *Effective Human Resource Management: A Global Perspective*. Palo Alto, CA: Stanford University Press, ch. 4.

attention to a wider talent pool. However, we found that boards exercising full responsibility for human capital ensure they understand and monitor the way the entire workforce is managed. Only then can they have a feel for the fundamental factors influencing performance, capability, and reputation – now and in the future – and also for what executive management is doing. The people lens discussion depends entirely on the nature of the business issues and the sophistication of the board about HR matters. While set-piece yearly or twice-yearly examinations of people strategy are the norm, a people-focused board considers the human dimension in every business discussion. Some boards, however, are less alert to how people factors can undermine strategy, making the mistake of considering them to be "operational" detail.[4]

Creelman and Lambert include the following quote from Randall MacDonald, IBM's senior vice president of human resources: "Board oversight of people issues is not some special event, it's almost continuous. In the executive compensation and management development committee, yes, we are talking about reward, but always in the context of how do we retain the best talent, what is the best talent, and what areas we should be most concerned about. In IBM, developing leaders is a way of life; it is part of the DNA of both the management system and the board systems."

Creelman and Lambert offer suggestions about the topics that boards should address when they oversee human capital, including:

- people strategy – as a part of organizational strategy;
- people-related risk;
- succession and talent;
- reward and pensions;
- legal requirements and codes of behavior;
- vision and values;
- employee relations and employer reputation;
- change initiatives;
- diversity and inclusion; and
- the capability of the HR function.

The models in this book provide logical frameworks for organizing the discussion of these topics.

Table 6.2 Human capital information that boards get and want

	Should and do get	Should not get but do	Should get but do not	Should not and do not get
Succession planning data for most management positions	73.1	0	24.4	2.6
Succession planning data for key technical positions	46.8	1.3	32.5	19.5
Metrics on turnover	59.0	3.8	33.3	3.8
Metrics on recruiting success	49.4	5.2	36.4	9.1
Attitude survey data	51.9	1.3	42.9	3.9

Source: Lawler, E. E., and Worley, C. (2011). *Management Reset: Organizing for Sustainable Effectiveness*. San Francisco: Jossey-Bass, tab. 5.1.

Finally, Edward Lawler and Christopher Worley report research that suggests that boards may desire to receive more information about human capital strategy than they currently receive.[5] Table 6.2 shows the results of their survey of board members.

The data suggest that boards often receive succession planning data for management positions, and that they strongly desire it when they do not get it. In none of the categories did boards that get information feel that they should not get it. Boards that do not get these categories of information usually believe that they should. Thus, it appears that boards may be interested in receiving a wider variety of human capital information than they currently receive. Simply providing the information is not enough, however. Boards, and other constituencies, must have the means to understand and interpret the information in ways that help them see the connections between human capital and strategic success, and make better decisions.

When it comes to strategic human capital planning, the evidence is pretty clear that today's organizations are typically at only a very early stage of using such information at the investor and board levels.

There is very little systematic reporting. What is reported is mostly ad hoc, and not so much about connecting human capital decisions and investments to strategy as about reporting on the most prominent HR activities, particularly when they affect the top executive team or the leadership pipeline. It would seem that the HR profession often leaves it to investors and boards, and even to organization leaders and employees, to make sense of the HR strategy, using whatever frameworks that investors, employees, managers, and leaders can muster.

This is a missed opportunity. As earlier chapters have shown, there are frameworks for organizing and reporting how investments in human capital are logically connected through the outcomes they produce, and their ultimate connection to pivotal strategic objectives, risks, and opportunities.

Principles of persuasion and human resource strategy communication

There is a large research literature on persuasion and communication with many approaches and frameworks. Jay Conger offers an actionable framework for increasing the persuasiveness of communication, in four elements.[6] They are a useful reminder of some of the principles of effective communication, and of the idea that such communication often goes beyond just information, numbers, or evidence. Conger suggests that persuasive communication must do the following.

Establish credibility, by showing the audience why they should believe in the message or information. Credibility may arise from expertise, such as ensuring that the HR strategic plan reflects the best thinking on the part of the organization's strategists, marketers, finance professionals, and others, and that those who formulated the plan were sufficiently expert in the necessary principles. Credibility may also arise from relationships, including a history of integrity and reliability, and a demonstrated capacity to be inclusive and share credit. In the world of human resource strategy and planning, this often means that HR leaders must find allies in other functional areas, or among leaders who are responsible for business units, and find ways to engage them in formulating and then communicating the connections between human capital and talent.

Frame for common ground, which means understanding the concerns of the audience, and making sure that they can see advantages in what is being suggested. When it comes to human capital planning and strategy, this means battling the perception that, when employees, managers, and leaders are asked to make investments of time or money in HR programs, it is just more work for them. It is not unusual for HR organizations to restructure activities such as enrolling in benefits programs, making changes to employment status, and even completing performance reviews to rely more on "self-service" by employees and managers. This is often seen as code for "You do the work that HR used to do for you." Not very persuasive! Instead, HR should consider how to frame such restructuring in terms of benefits. For example, the savings gained from self-service may actually flow to the bottom line of the manager who is running a business unit. Equally, the ability to make changes to benefits enrollment online may mean that employees spend far less time on such tasks than they did beforehand, when they had to meet with or call up an HR administrator.

Use vivid language and compelling evidence. As we have seen, there is great opportunity for human capital planning and risk optimization to make more use of analytics and numbers. Human capital strategy need not be relegated to something that is "intangible," "soft," or "unmeasurable." That said, it is also important to make sure that the compelling evidence is framed in language that is engaging and actionable for those outside HR, who are often the ultimate audience for human capital planning. General managers are justified in demanding that human resource plans go beyond just providing lots of numbers about things such as turnover, performance, engagement, labor costs, etc., and provide frameworks that help employees and managers understand them. As we saw earlier in the book, this may be accomplished by actually embedding human resource information within management models that focus on pivot points, such as operations, supply chain, marketing, or finance. It may also be accomplished by organizing and describing the strategy in terms of the connections between the investments in human capital and the vital strategic outcomes that the organization must achieve, perhaps using a model such as HC BRidge, described earlier and below.

In their book *Investing in People*, Cascio and Boudreau summarize the research showing associations between employee attitudes, engagement, and the production, sales, and financial outcomes of organizations.[7] They also show how reporting the costs of employee turnover can often make employee turnover rates much more vivid for financially oriented business leaders. Leading organizations have frequently used the association between employee attitudes and organizational outcomes as one of the first ways they make HR numbers more vivid.

For example, Boudreau and Jesuthasan describe how HR leaders at the Royal Bank of Scotland Group noticed that there was wide performance variation in its retail locations (bank branches), even after taking into account traditional factors such as location, customer base, and product offerings.[8] They found that a significant amount of such unexplained variation was associated with employee attitudes and whether employees felt they had high-quality supervision. As one HR leader put it, "We reached the important but not new conclusion that two lead indicators, in terms of superior sustainable business value in customer service, are great leaders and highly engaged staff. Underneath those two measures are the hundreds of activities that contribute to it."[9] The key was to see how persuasive it was to report the two lead indicators, and their association with branch performance, rather than being tempted to report on the hundreds of activities. Once engaged with the leading indicators, Royal Bank of Scotland leaders had greater motivation to learn more about how to improve them.

Connect emotionally, which means keeping in mind that, even in organizations, it is often emotions that matter. This means that HR leaders must be willing to show their own emotional and personal commitment to their positions, and that their hearts are in it. It also means understanding the audiences' own emotional states, and knowing when to come on forcefully or gently. Sometimes, it is the emotional commitment to a personal vignette that is key.

For instance, in a large global consumer goods organization, an emotional connection was key to improving leadership diversity. In this case, the organization was privately owned, with headquarters in the United States but many global operations. The company's dilemma was not that its top leadership had too many members from the United States but, rather, too few. The reason was that, because the US operations were by far the largest, no one wanted to promote great leaders out of them, and rotate them through global assignments to prepare them for top positions. Thus, whenever a global rotation assignment arose, it was generally a non-US leader who was chosen. Every year the top leaders would meet and agree to work hard to increase US leader representation, but their heart apparently was not in it, because every year, when they looked at the results, they saw they had made little progress. The HR leader of this organization took a creative approach, by getting beyond the numbers, gap analysis, flow statistics, etc. Instead, at the next leadership meeting, she brought forward the names of three US leaders who had been overlooked for global assignments for several years, despite everyone's good intentions. She asked, "How do you feel knowing that these three people are consistently overlooked for the global assignments that would make them ready for top positions? Are you prepared to take the risk of moving them?" When the top leaders were confronted with the "human face" of the issue, they quickly found ways to create the global opportunities for US leaders.

These four elements of persuasion will turn up in many of the examples and principles we describe next, as we discuss specific ways to enhance the effectiveness of human capital strategy and risk communication.

Finding the "trust territory"

Often, one of the most difficult elements of communicating a human resource strategy is that general managers and leaders are not accustomed to having HR leaders involved in discussions of competitive assumptions, financial performance, process improvement, or other traditional strategic issues. As Boudreau and Ramstad note, human resources are often seen through the value proposition either of "compliance" (keeping the organization out of trouble by ensuring that the rules are followed) or of "services" (waiting for requests for HR programs, from their "internal customers," and then delivering those services in a customer-focused way).[10] When seen through these perspectives, it is no surprise that it may seem strange to have talent and human capital issues at the forefront of strategy and risk management. Nevertheless, this is often what is needed for strategic success and agility. Boudreau and Ramstad advise HR leaders and their constituents to consider the HC BRidge framework, shown here again as Figure 6.2.[11]

Boudreau and Ramstad suggest that this framework is not just a way to convey the logical connections between human capital investments

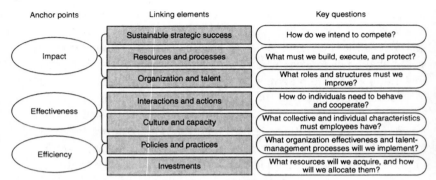

Figure 6.2 HC BRidge framework: seven key questions
Source: Boudreau, J. W., and Ramstad, P. M. (2007). *Beyond HR: The New Science of Human Capital.* Boston: Harvard Business School Press, ch. 3.

and strategic success, but also can be used to analyze where the HR function is trusted to engage in discussions about performance and strategy. The "trust territory" can be expressed in terms of the different boxes in the model. For example, in the most extreme case, HR leaders have permission only to engage in discussions about the HR programs and practices they implement, and the necessary budget. This is the bottom two boxes in Figure 6.1. If this is where the HR function has trust, then it does little good to try to engage in a discussion about strategic success, business processes, or resources at the top of the figure. Rather, a better strategy is to start with the questions about HR programs and practices, and try to move "up" the diagram by one or two boxes. For example, HR leaders might say "I understand you want me to implement a more aggressive system in which the good performers get more pay and the poor performers get less. We'll do that, but can you tell me what you hope will happen if this program is successful?" This guides the discussion toward the "Interactions and actions" box, and prompts a dialogue about what sorts of culture and employee capacity will be necessary for employees to respond to the new incentive system. The "trust territory" has been expanded.

Eventually, over time, as leaders see the connections in the nearby boxes, they will begin to appreciate the value of considering the full range of connections. Rather than try to make the jump all at once, however, it may be more persuasive and more feasible to advance sequentially. Moreover, even a slight expansion of the discussion may yield important insights about where and how to make human capital investments more effective, even if the discussion never actually reaches the top levels of strategy.

For example, Corning Incorporated was an early adopter of the ideas in Figure 6.2, and encouraged its HR business partners supporting its product divisions simply to ask "What action or interaction among our employees would most improve our unit's success?" This question was asked as part of the strategy discussions across businesses as diverse as fiber optics, medical instruments, consumer flat panel displays, etc. Each business had a different version of the answer, but the patter was similar. They all described the need for their technical professionals (engineers, R&D scientists, medical doctors, process designers, etc.) to acquire a better understanding of the evolving needs of customers. This prompted a useful discussion about how greater "customer centricity" would enhance the technical professional role, improve specific processes and resources, and eventually contribute to Corning's innovation strategy.

Communicating human capital strategy to employees: impressions matter

Much attention in human capital and human resource strategy is paid to the quality of the programs, processes, and investments that are made. Far less attention is paid to the impressions or messages that employees take away from the array of HR programs, practices, and communication. Nonetheless, an emerging stream of research in human resource management suggests that these impressions may matter a great deal.

This view emphasizes the importance of the psychological processes through which employees attach meaning to HR practices. The same HR practices may result in different individual or organizational outcomes if employees find it difficult to attach only one kind of meaning. For example, a performance rating system that requires leaders specifically to identify which employees are in the bottom 10 percent of performers might be seen either as a positive signal that the organization wants to help poor performers develop or as a harsh attempt to identify those with performance problems so that they can be punished or laid off.

David Bowen and Cheri Ostroff have argued that the virtue of HR practices is achieved only if they are delivered so that employees perceive the HR practices as they were intended.[12] They suggest that, for a company's HR strategy to be effective, employees should be able to perceive HRM as distinctive, consistent, and consensual.

Being "distinct" refers to whether the HR elements stand out, capturing attention and arousing interest. Distinctiveness is achieved through making HR practices highly visible, helping employees understand their purpose and how they operate and are based on a legitimate authority, and showing how they are relevant to an important goal.

Being "consistent" means that the effects of HR practices are similar over time and situations, regardless of whether the process is encountered online, interpersonally, or through the HR department or call center. Consistency is achieved by making sure that HR practices have similar consequences for all employees, that the HR practices actually do what they say, and that the messaging is consistent across all different communication methods and encounters. This may be easier said than done, as it is not uncommon for well-meaning leaders to implement HR practices differently. In our work with organizations, we often encounter situations in which there is a policy of being flexible in terms of allowing workers to attend to family or other activities outside work, with some supervisors being quite diligent about implementing the policy, while others see it as a "nice to have" option only when it is convenient. The point is that it is not just the policy itself that must be consistent but how it is implemented, and how it is seen by employees.

Consensus results when there is agreement among organization members about the cause and effect of HR strategy and practices. When this exists, it is likely that employees will be more accurate in understanding how their behaviors are evaluated, how they lead to outcomes for themselves, and how their work affects organizational goals. This is achieved by ensuring that HR decision makers understand and agree on the messages of the HR strategy. It also depends on justice. This means that the practices are implemented in a way that is trusted, and that the interactions that employees experience at work are seen as positive.

When human resource management is implemented in a way that satisfies these three conditions, employees can clearly understand what behaviors are expected and will be rewarded by employers. Recent research has supported the view that organizational members interpret HR strategy through the impressions they form about how it is implemented.[13]

Starbucks aprons and the power of trust   A good example of the power and importance of employee perceptions to human capital strategy was seen when Starbucks introduced a program to reduce theft by employees. The coffeehouse chain decided to remove the pockets from baristas' aprons, which made it all too easy for a barista to pocket a few dollars that should have gone into the till. We can readily imagine the argument that was made for this program, and how reasonable it sounded. Unfortunately, however, this effort was completely at odds with the Starbucks employment brand, which emphasized treating baristas as valued talent. The theft-reduction program was fine, and the employment brand was fine, but together they sent a message that was in conflict, and the net result was negative synergy. Starbucks, realizing that its employment brand mattered more than any potential loss due to theft, reinstated the pockets.[14] The head of HR at Starbucks at the time, David Pace, observed that, when Starbucks made the decision to reinstate the pockets, "you would have thought we had given everybody a $50,000-a-year raise because it was that important for our frontline partners."[15] Nonetheless, the same theft-reduction program might make sense in a different company with a different employment brand. The issue is not that it was a dumb idea but that it was at odds with an important part of Starbucks' HR strategy.

Pace saw the importance of employee communication in HR strategy this way:

> I describe this as like playing the world's largest telephone game where one person tells something to the person next to them, they have to tell the person next to them. They have to tell the person next to them and you work your way around the table and you see what comes out at the other end as to what was actually said. And there's usually quite a bit of distortion. The challenge for us is, in order to build and sustain the culture that we have in the organization, we have to take somewhat of a similar approach where we tell the people that are here and we try to help them understand and relate to the kind of culture that we're trying to create. They have to tell others and those others have to tell new people and then suddenly the new people are the ones that have to tell other new people.[16]

How to communicate human capital strategy with managers and leaders

We showed in Chapter 1 how HR issues such as staffing, rewards, leadership, and development can be framed within the more familiar mental models that leaders already use, such as supply chains, inventory models, financial portfolios, and product designs. This idea of "retooling HR" is one illustration of the search for ways to communicate strategic workforce planning so that it is more understandable, accessible, persuasive, and engaging for general managers and leaders outside the HR profession.[17] Indeed, many of the chapters in this book are intended to provide frameworks and examples to help HR and non-HR leaders reach a more complete and mutual understanding of the connections between human capital decisions, human resource strategy, and organizational strategic success. Here we briefly provide a few additional examples that deal very directly with some pivotal issues when it comes to communicating HR strategy to non-HR leaders.

Consider the concept of workforce diversity. Increasing numbers of organizational mission statements and strategies tout diversity as a vital organizational goal. In many cases, however, the meaning of diversity is not consistently understood. For some, it may mean simply avoiding the violation of laws that require treating people in an unbiased way with regard to gender, sexual orientation, color, race, ethnicity, etc. For others, it may mean welcoming and nurturing all manner of individual differences at work, as a basic tenet of fairness and humanistic behavior. Unfortunately, such definitions may fail to connect the concept of diversity to specific elements of organizational success. Moreover, such vast divergence can often create inconsistency and even conflict at the workplace. This is particularly true when the objective of workforce diversity is prominently stated in organizational communication, and endorsed by organization leaders.

Royal Bank of Canada makes diversity a strategic pillar   At Royal Bank of Canada (RBC), HR and business leaders found a way to communicate the strategic and employment implications of their diversity commitment more clearly.[18] Imagine that a family emigrates from Mumbai to Montreal, and one of the first things it does is go to a bank to open a savings account. In what way is this story about HR? At RBC it most definitely is. RBC's success at winning the business of newcomers to Canada is a natural consequence of its internal diversity programs – although one could just as easily say that RBC's internal diversity programs are a natural consequence of its aim to serve customers.

The focus on diversity fits within a much broader strategic vision of always earning the right to be clients' first choice, and a goal of being a high-performing, customer-centric organization. Among the customers RBC wishes to serve are newcomers to Canada; it wants to be the financial institution of choice for newcomers and the cultural markets they represent. The bank works on making it easier for newcomers to get over the hurdles of becoming established financially after they arrive. To inform people about RBC's attention to newcomers, even before they immigrate, the bank has introduced a website aimed at potential immigrants and created a "Welcome to Canada" banking package in fourteen languages.

At this point diversity sounds like a marketing initiative, but human resource management is deeply involved in driving the success of the program. The HR function assessed the languages spoken by the bank's staff and proactively recruited to fill any gaps, and helped create a telephone service that can serve clients in over 150 languages. When immigrants arrive from Mumbai, chances are the RBC employees can serve them in the Marathi language. RBC clients, using an online tool, can also find the nearest of 1,200 branches in Canada at which employees speak their preferred language. The workforce strategy and the marketing strategy are neatly aligned. Notice how the RBC example shows how to communicate a clear connection between the somewhat "soft" idea of workforce diversity and the "hard" organizational outcomes of customer attraction and retention.

Notice as well how the result of making this connection leads to a different way of thinking about human capital risk. Should RBC take a risk of not asking prospective employees to name their educational institutions? One "out-of-the-box" move HR made to smooth the hiring of a diverse workforce was to refrain from asking prospective employees to name the institution at which they received their education during the preliminary employment screenings. This helped avoid inadvertent bias. Instead, credentials and education were verified much later in the hiring process. RBC sees the question of educational background as no longer about inadvertent bias and more about knowing the best schools internationally in order to secure the best candidates. From a business perspective this is human resource management supporting the newcomer initiative, but from an HR perspective it can be seen as simply one facet of creating a diverse workforce and an inclusive culture. It was worth the risk of not knowing the educational institution in the interview, to get the payoff of avoiding even inadvertent bias among interviewers.

PNC Bank and the risk analysis of compensation programs   PNC is a rare banking company that not only weathered the financial crisis of 2007/8 but actually doubled in size during that time, and was named "Bank of the year" in the United States by *The Banker* magazine.[19] PNC chairman and chief executive officer James E. Rohr believes and reinforces the principle that risk management is "everyone's business." The commitment to a moderate risk profile is closely incorporated in the company's HR practices.

PNC's commitment to risk management influenced key decisions during the acquisition of National City. As part of that acquisition, PNC inherited hundreds of incentive plans, many of them with complicated design features and some reflecting a different compensation philosophy from PNC's. Administering these incentive plans created an enormous administrative challenge, and it presented significant risks to the organization. HR needed to develop a thoughtful process to evaluate these plan designs using objective assessment criteria that would enable business leaders and HR to make informed decisions quickly. HR partnered with the business, finance, and risk professionals to bring a new sophistication to how HR understands and manages risk.

PNC HR leaders worked with the company's risk-management professionals to develop a series of questions that would help categorize incentive plans based on the probability of risky behavior and its likely impact on the organization. This two-dimensional framework was precisely the same one that the risk-management function at PNC used for other investments and decisions. This analysis considered the following questions.

- Does the plan incorporate balanced metrics and multiple measures? That is, does the plan avoid an overreliance on a single measure that might not fully reflect the business results?
- Are the metrics based on individual, team, or corporate performance? Metrics based on individual performance can create a higher level of risk for the organization.
- Are the metrics based on top-line or bottom-line measures? Undue emphasis on top-line measures can generate problems.
- What is the nature of the payout curves? Are they steep? Are there cliffs? Are payoffs uncapped? All these features impact how an individual will behave.
- Is there management discretion in the amount awarded? Management discretion can act as a brake on risky behavior.

The second set of criteria targeted business-specific questions.

- Does the plan cover individuals or functions that take principal risk and/or commit capital?
- What is the level of residual risk?
- How well collateralized is the principal risk or commitment to capital?
- Is the business primarily, or exclusively, fee-based or advisory?

Once the assessment process had been completed, the path to implementation also became clearer. In partnership with business leaders, the HR team launched the communication effort. In addition to informing employees about what incentive plans would change and how, they also focused on the "Why?," thus providing employees with a better understanding of PNC's risk-management decision making.

"Typically, we would spend a lot of time and energy on the what, but not enough time on the why," says Bei Ling, PNC senior vice president of total rewards. "In this process, we learned that if employees understand and relate to the rationale for change, it is easier for them to accept it, even if the change negatively impacts them."[20]

Cascading goals and learning maps as strategic communication at PepsiCo

There is a classic management case study about PepsiCo Inc. in the 1980s.[21] After the company had acquired a large portion of its bottling organization, PepsiCo's leaders realized that fundamental elements of the corporate culture would have to change. Process excellence, long seen as dull and uninteresting, would need to become paramount. The customer base had shifted from a relatively small number of bottlers, to which the company sold drink concentrate, to thousands of grocery stores, restaurants, bars, and other purveyors of the final product to customers. How could PepsiCo leaders formulate a strategy and its human capital implications that would invigorate their employees and leaders to rethink their roles in light of this new definition of customers and markets? How could an organization as large as PepsiCo communicate such a fundamental strategic shift, and have all its employees understand its implications for them? The full array of management techniques to communicate the strategy and its human capital implications is beyond the scope of this chapter, but two elements are notable, because they vividly show how strategy communication can get very personal, and because they are often used in leading organizations.

Cascading goals to communicate but also to teach   Strategy communication is often less about telling than engaging. At PepsiCo in the 1990s, the process started by asking the top leadership to develop a shared vision of the future. The top leaders were divided into task forces, with each task force dedicated to things such as "customer focus," "employee empowerment," and "bottling profit and loss." The result of this first step was the realization that none of the suggested approaches was correct, because they failed to integrate across the different goals. The vision that emerged was simple yet elegant: "We realized that we had a 'wrong-side-up' organization…where the front-line performers catered to managers at the top, instead of worrying about how to support customers." The team converged on the image of the "right-side-up" company, which placed customers at the top, those who directly faced customers in the next tier, and so on, with top leadership supporting at the bottom.

The enrollment process to carry out and engage with the strategy involved a series of meetings and cascading goals. Starting at the top, each set of leaders would conduct enrollment meetings and brainstorming sessions with their direct reports (those employees who reported directly to them). Then the individuals in those meetings would conduct similar meetings with their direct reports, and so on.

While this was an efficient way to train the organization in the new strategy, it had a much more fundamental purpose: to force leaders to learn the strategy thoroughly because they knew they would be teaching it to their reports. As one leader put it, "It was hell, because we couldn't map out everything in advance. We didn't know what we were going to do tomorrow until we'd lived it today."[22]

To translate the "right-side-up" vision for employees, the HR group at PepsiCo gathered detailed examples illustrating the tenets of customer focus, employee empowerment, and shared values in action. Outstanding performers shared their experiences and rationale for performing as they did. These behaviors were translated into competencies, which became the building blocks of human resource investments. Again, all this was couched within the cascading communication process, with HR leaders as key facilitators and drivers of the process.

The enrollment process culminated in "Team 20,000," a one-day session in which every front-line employee saw a series of presentations from top management and then broke into small groups locally to discuss the vision. At these meetings, PepsiCo's strategy communication process used learning maps not just to depict the strategy and its elements but also to engage employees in creative ways. A learning map is a graphical depiction of organizational goals and the factors that affect them. An example of a learning map for PepsiCo is shown in Figure 6.3.

PepsiCo has produced such learning maps to illustrate how certain processes (such as bottling or delivery) contribute to strategic outcomes, as well as those that show the foundations and competitive challenges that the company faces. Notice in the learning map shown in Figure 6.3 that the emphasis is on how the values form the main branches of the tree that supports PepsiCo's brands, and that the foundation or roots of the tree are the specific actions that employees take when they interact with the different stakeholders shown around the periphery. This is an example of communicating a values-based strategy, as discussed in Chapter 2.

The learning map is produced in card-table-sized sheets that can be laid atop a table with employees surrounding it. The strategy communication session proceeds by asking each table to consider a series of questions about PepsiCo operations, strategy, or customers,

Figure 6.3 PepsiCo's "Living our values" learning map
Source: PepsiCo Inc.; personal communication with Allan Church, January 2012; used with permission.

and then to find the answer on the map. For example, one question might be "How much of every dollar that a customer spends on Pepsi shows up as profit for PepsiCo?" In one session, the estimates by employees were three times the actual amount. This led to a much greater understanding about the importance and significance of even small changes in cost or price.

The PepsiCo example illustrates not just the importance of strategy communication, but the importance of adopting a communication process that conveys more than just information. The process should engage and involve leaders, managers, and employees. For PepsiCo, this was accomplished by having managers teach the strategy, and by using vivid graphical metaphors to explain it.

Conclusion: strategy communication and transformative HR

Boudreau and Jesuthasan suggest that the future of organization effectiveness will rely upon an approach to human capital and HR

Table 6.3 Transformation of HR toward evidence-based change

Typical HR today	Transformative HR future
• Evidence of HR value added is rare	• Evidence of HR value is routinely provided
• HR data and analysis do not engage action	• HR data and analysis motivate strategically vital actions
• HR constituents do not routinely use HR evidence in change efforts	• HR constituents routinely demand and use HR evidence to direct strategic change
• HR is valued for its perspective on functional processes and outcomes	• HR is valued for its unique perspective on how to achieve strategic success

Source: Boudreau, J. W., and Jesuthasan, R. (2011). *Transformative HR: How Great Companies Use Evidence-Based Change for Sustainable Advantage.* New York: Wiley, xxv.

strategy that takes "evidence-based change" as a fundamental premise, the evolution of which is summarized in Table 6.3.[23]

They also suggest that five principles will underlie this transformation:

(1) logic-driven analytics;
(2) segmentation;
(3) risk leverage;
(4) integration and synergy; and
(5) optimization.

These five principles and their implications for the transformation of HR are shown in Table 6.4.

These principles have significant implications for how HR strategy and strategic workforce planning are communicated. These principles are reflected in the examples and frameworks of this chapter, encouraging organization leaders to go beyond simply preparing or reporting strategies, and instead to strive for strategies and communication processes that truly engage and motivate transformation. These principles are also reflected throughout the book, in the emphasis on using evidence skillfully combined with logic, to unearth the most pivotal human capital elements, and the synergistic approaches necessary to optimize risk and return.

Table 6.4 Five principles that support transformative HR and evidence-based change

Logic-driven analytics	
Typical HR today	**Transformative HR future**
• Information overload	• Information optimization
• Data reflect IT system priorities	• Data reflect HR's needs for decision making
• Lots of numbers, but no "story"	• Data and analysis focused on the vital issues
• Analysis fails to engage constituents	• Analysis is that demanded by key constituents
• Logic models for HR issues are ad hoc	• Logic models for HR issues are common and widely understood
Segmentation	
Typical HR today	**Transformative HR future**
• Organization reluctant to treat different segments differently	• Organization naturally treats different segments differently when it makes sense
• Employment customization versus standardization decisions are ad hoc	• Employment customization versus standardization decisions based on common logical frameworks
• How strategic value of different employee groups varies is poorly understood	• How strategic value of different employee groups varies is routinely analyzed and reported
• "More is better" is assumed for performance, engagement, and so on	• "Return on improved performance" is routinely considered for investments in performance, engagement, and so on
Risk leverage	
Typical HR today	**Transformative HR future**
• HR risk rarely receives attention	• HR risk is routinely analyzed and considered
• Risk reduction	• Risk optimization
• HR risk is ill-defined	• HR risk elements are well understood
• HR risk analysis is ad hoc	• HR risk analysis follows common logical rules

Table 6.4 (*cont.*)

Integration and synergy	
Typical HR today	**Transformative HR future**
• Individual HR processes operate in silos	• HR processes operate as interconnected systems
• HR programs implemented and evaluated independently	• HR programs implemented and evaluated for greatest combined effect ("1 + 1 = 3")
• HR priorities established separately in different organization units	• HR priorities established jointly across multiple organization units
• HR systems focus on unit-specific performance goals	• HR systems focus on trade-offs that optimize performance across organization units
Optimization	
Typical HR today	**Transformative HR future**
• Fairness is seen as equal treatment or "peanut butter" approach, with investments spread equally across all groups	• Fairness is understood to mean strategically differentiated treatment
• Focus is on justifying investments in HR	• Focus is on HR investments with the largest strategic impact
• HR programs rarely canceled even as new programs are added	• HR investments routinely reduced in some areas and redeployed elsewhere

Source: Boudreau and Jesuthasan (2011: xxv–xxvii).

Notes

1 Terry Gray and Matt Hankes, Cargill, personal communication, 2011.
2 Creelman, D., and Lambert, A. (2011). *The Board and HR: How Board Oversight of Human Capital Works*. Toronto: Creelman Lambert Research.
3 Lawler, E. E., and Boudreau, J. W. (2012). *Effective Human Resource Management: A Global Perspective*. Palo Alto, CA: Stanford University Press, ch. 4.
4 Creelman and Lambert (2011).
5 Lawler, E. E., and Worley, C. G. (2011). *Management Reset: Organizing for Sustainable Effectiveness*. San Francisco: Jossey-Bass.
6 Conger, J. A. (1998). The necessary art of persuasion. *Harvard Business Review*, 76(3): 84–95.

7 Cascio, W. F., and Boudreau, J. W. (2011). *Investing in People: Financial Impact of Human Resource Initiatives*, 2nd edn. Upper Saddle River, NJ: Pearson Education/FT Press.

8 Boudreau, J. W., and Jesuthasan, R. (2011). *Transformative HR: How Great Companies Use Evidence-Based Change for Sustainable Advantage*. New York: Wiley, ch. 5.

9 Boudreau and Jesuthasan (2011: 109).

10 Boudreau, J. W., and Ramstad, P. M. (2007). *Beyond HR: The New Science of Human Capital*. Boston: Harvard Business School Press.

11 Boudreau and Ramstad (2007).

12 Bowen, D. E., and Ostroff, C. (2004). Understanding the HRM–firm performance linkages: the role of the "strength" of the HRM system. *Academy of Management Review*, 29(2): 203–21.

13 Li, X., Frenkel, S., and Sanders, K. (2011). How do perceptions of the HRM system affect employee attitudes? A multi level study of Chinese employees. *International Journal of HRM*, 22(8): 1823–40; Nishii, L. H., Lepak, D. P., and Schneider, B. (2008). Employee attributions of the "why" of HR practices: their effects on employee attitudes and behaviors, and customer satisfaction. *Personnel Psychology*, 61(3): 503–44; Sanders, K., Dorenbosch, L., and de Reuver, R. (2008). The impact of individual and shared employee perceptions of HRM on affective commitment. *Personnel Review*, 37(4): 412–25; Takeuchi, R., Lepak, D. P., Wang, H., and Takeuchi, K. (2007). An empirical examination of the mechanisms mediating between high performance work systems and the performance of Japanese organizations. *Journal of Applied Psychology*, 92(4): 1069–83.

14 Boudreau and Jesuthasan (2011).

15 Boudreau and Ramstad (2007: 163).

16 Boudreau and Ramstad (2007: 162).

17 Boudreau, J. W. (2010). *Retooling HR: Using Proven Business Tools to Make Better Decisions about Talent*. Boston: Harvard Business School Press.

18 Boudreau and Jesuthasan (2011: ch. 6).

19 Boudreau and Jesuthasan (2011: ch. 3).

20 Boudreau and Jesuthasan (2011: 72).

21 Sull, D. (1994). Pepsi's regeneration, 1990–1993, Case Study no. 395048. Boston: Harvard Business School Press.

22 Sull (1994: 5).

23 Boudreau and Jesuthasan (2011: ch. 1).

7 Outcomes of successful business and HR strategies

Chess is a game of strategy. Chess strategy consists of setting and achieving long-term goals during the game – for example, where to place different pieces – while tactics concentrate on immediate maneuvers. The initial phase of the game is called the *opening*, usually the first ten to twenty-five moves, when players develop their armies and set the stage for the coming battle. Opening strategies, many with colorful names such as the Bird's opening, the Benko defense, or the Sicilian defense, have been developed over many years.[1] Some of these are more aggressive than defensive, but, by the end of the game, the effectiveness of a given strategy, and the tactics used to execute it, become clear as one player captures the opponent's king and declares "Checkmate."

In business settings, a basic question about strategy is how a firm will compete and defend itself against outside threats. The effectiveness of its strategy may be measured on a number of dimensions, such as sustainability, profits, competitiveness, and growth. Does it meet the needs of multiple stakeholders, such as shareholders, customers, suppliers, employees, and communities? If not, in the extreme, the analog to "Checkmate" in the game of chess occurs when a firm declares bankruptcy, or otherwise abandons a particular product or service offering, most often due to a lack of market demand for it.

As an example, consider Friendly's – a chain of restaurants and ice cream parlors based in New England, which declared bankruptcy in October 2011. Here is a brief excerpt from *The Boston Globe* newspaper:[2]

> Yesterday, 63 of Friendly's approximately 500 locations closed without warning, including 30 in Massachusetts, leaving many without jobs and many more without lunch. In typical Gen Y fashion, we spread the news as fast as we could tweet – labeling Friendly's

as a place of fondly remembered family outings, a high school hangout and meeting spot, and the provider of a traditional New England feeling.

The down economy is considered a major factor, but how did Gen Y contribute to the fall of this timeless establishment? The answer, it seems, is a simple one: We grew up. "Happy Endings" (a Friendly's slogan) were replaced with "Happy Hour," and for reasons unknown, today's youth have neglected to take a seat in the booths we left behind.

"It's a kids' restaurant, but aside from the kids' menu, there is nothing to appeal to modern kids," said a waiter at a Shrewsbury, Mass., location that is staying open for now. "It's old-school, it's out of style – Friendly's didn't evolve with the generations."

Do you remember a popular advertisement that showed a man in a suit holding a sign that read "Change or die"? The demise of Friendly's is a good illustration of that. The important lesson is that strategies are dynamic, and have to evolve with the times. The title of this chapter demands some type of measurement system to gauge how successful a strategy is or has been. Since our primary concern is with HR strategy, we begin by presenting several broad frameworks that might prove useful for any firm to assess the outcomes of its strategy. Two such frameworks are the balanced scorecard[3] and metrics from a recent book, *Good Company: Business Success in the Worthiness Era*.[4] Then we focus on assessing the outcomes of HR strategy itself, with examples from Sysco and Universal Weather and Aviation.

The balanced scorecard: from financial to strategic reporting It is a truism that what gets measured gets done. Measures send powerful signals to managers and employees at all levels, and they clearly affect behavior. Consider firm A, which values long-term customer relationships. If a half or more of a manager's incentive pay hinges on customer satisfaction with his or her services, what do you think the manager will focus on? Alternatively, consider firm B, in which incentive pay depends on the profit margin of goods sold. Do you expect the manager or employee to push low-margin products?

At the level of the firm, traditional financial accounting measures, such as return on investment and earnings per share, can give misleading signals to managers and employees regarding continuous improvement and innovation – activities that today's competitive environment demands. In fact, no single measure can provide a clear performance target or focus attention on the critical areas of a business. Managers want a balanced presentation of financial and operational measures alike. The balanced scorecard is just that. It includes financial measures that tell the results of actions already taken, and it complements them with operational measures on customer satisfaction, internal processes, and the organization's innovation and improvement activities. These drive future financial performance. Viewed as a whole, the balanced scorecard represents strategic reporting. It makes sense primarily for business units and divisions with well-defined strategies, and is suited chiefly for internal rather than external reporting. To do otherwise might be to reveal sensitive or proprietary information to competitors.

In practice, the balanced scorecard provides answers to four basic questions:

(1) How do customers see us (the customer perspective)?
(2) What must we excel at (the internal perspective)?
(3) Can we continue to improve and create value (the innovation and learning perspective)?
(4) How do we look to shareholders (the financial perspective)?

A key objective of the balanced scorecard is to limit information overload, and it does this by limiting the number of measures in each category, typically four to five, or even fewer. Companies rarely suffer from having too few measures. Given the easy availability of comprehensive data systems, the problem is more often too many measures. It is just not realistic to expect that people might be able to track and digest fifteen to twenty measures in each of the four areas. The challenge is to identify just a few in each area that are most critical, and to focus on those. Here are some examples.

Customer perspective: how do customers see us? Customers' concerns tend to fall into four categories: time, quality, performance and service, and cost. Kaplan and Norton use the example of a fictitious semiconductor company – Electronic Circuits Inc. (ECI) – to illustrate how managers might translate these general customer concerns into specific goals and measures. Figure 7.1 shows the actual goals and measures that ECI used.

Financial perspective	
Goals	Measures
Survive	Cash flow
Succeed	Quarterly sales growth and operating income by division
Prosper	Increased market share and return on equity

Customer perspective	
Goals	Measures
New products	Percentage of sales from new products, percentage of sales from proprietary products
Responsive supply	On-time delivery (defined by customer)
Preferred suppliers	Share of key accounts' purchases
	Ranking by key accounts
Customer partnerships	Number of cooperative engineering efforts

Internal business perspective	
Goals	Measures
Technology capability	Manufacturing geometry versus competition
Manufacturing excellence	Cycle time, unit cost, yield
Design productivity	Silicon efficiency, engineering efficiency
New product introduction	Actual introduction schedule versus plan

Innovation and learning perspective	
Goals	Measures
Technology leadership	Time to develop next generation
Manufacturing learning	Process time to maturity
Product focus	Percentage of products that equal 80% of sales
Time to market	New product introduction versus competition

Figure 7.1 ECI's balanced business scorecard
Source: Kaplan, R. S., and Norton, D. P. (1992). The balanced scorecard: measures that drive performance. *Harvard Business Review*, 70(1): 71–9, 76.

To track the goal of providing innovative solutions, ECI measured the percentage of sales from new products, and also the percentage of sales from proprietary products. Such information was available internally. To assess whether the company was achieving its goal of reliable, responsive supply, however, ECI had to go outside to its customers and to see the business through their eyes. It measured on-time delivery (as defined by the customer), the share of purchases from the company by key accounts, company ranking by key accounts, and the number of cooperative engineering efforts the firm was engaged in. Other companies might define the customer perspective somewhat differently, and their scorecard measures will reflect that (e.g., ordering, paying for materials, number of returns or amount of substandard merchandise).

Internal business perspective: what must we excel at?   Customer-based measures are important, but they have to be translated into measures of the kinds of internal business processes that must be executed well in order to meet customers' expectations. This second part of the balanced scorecard provides that internal perspective to managers.

Business processes that have the greatest impact on customer satisfaction include those related to cycle time, quality, employee skills, and productivity, for example. Managers at ECI determined that submicron technology was critical to its market position. They also decided that they had to focus on manufacturing excellence, design productivity, and new-product introductions. As Figure 7.1 illustrates, the company developed operational measures for each of these four internal business goals.[5]

Innovation and learning perspective: can we continue to improve and create value?   A company's ability to innovate, improve, and learn is directly related to the company's value. In other words, only through the ability to develop and market new products, create more value for customers, and improve operating efficiencies continually can a company penetrate new markets, thereby increasing revenues and margins.[6] Growing the company, in turn, increases shareholder value and provides employment security for employees.

ECI's innovation measures, as Figure 7.1 shows, focus on the company's ability to develop and introduce standard products rapidly, those that will form the bulk of its future sales. Its manufacturing-learning measure focuses on new products, the goal being to achieve stability in the manufacture of new products. A final measure is time to market – that is, how long it takes from design to distribution for a product, relative to the time competitors require to do the same thing. As with measures of the customer's perspective, other companies may choose to measure innovation and growth by estimating specific improvement goals for existing business processes (such as time to market), or they may specify desired rates of improvement for on-time deliveries, cycle time, defect rate, and yield. Still others may require managers to demonstrate improvements within a specific time period. In all cases, the targets emphasize the role for continuous improvement in customer satisfaction and internal business processes.[7]

Financial perspective: how do we look to shareholders?   Financial performance measures indicate whether a company's strategy, implementation, and execution are contributing to bottom-line improvements. Typical financial goals have to do with profitability, growth, and shareholder value. As Figure 7.1 demonstrates, ECI's financial goals are straightforward: to survive (measured by cash flow), to succeed (measured by quarterly sales growth and operating income by division), and to prosper (measured by increased market share and return on equity).

An important qualifier is in order, however, as Kaplan and Norton, the creators of the balanced-scorecard concept, emphasize.[8] Even an excellent set of balanced-scorecard measures does not guarantee a winning strategy. The best it can do is to translate a company's strategy into specific, measurable objectives. If improved performance, as reflected in the achievement of those objectives, fails to be reflected in bottom-line outcomes, then executives should reexamine the basic assumptions of their strategy and mission. Not all strategies are profitable ones.

Perhaps the most attractive feature of the balanced-scorecard approach is that it links measurements to strategy. Beginning with mission and vision statements that describe senior executives' vision of the future, the process requires answers to questions such as "If our vision succeeds, how will we differ with respect to shareholders, customers, internal management processes, and the ability to innovate and grow?" Specifying critical success factors helps the organization identify appropriate measurements of those success factors. The result is a comprehensive, balanced view of a firm's performance, and, by extension, an assessment of the success of its strategy.

A visual representation of the cause-and-effect relationships among the components of an organization's strategy is known as a "strategy map." It is often as big a revelation to senior executives as the balanced scorecard itself, for it tells the story of an organization's strategy.[9] Figure 7.2 shows this graphically.

Private-sector organizations · Public-sector and nonprofit organizations

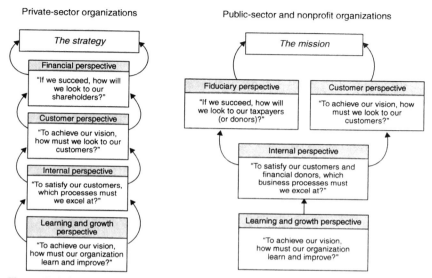

Figure 7.2 Strategy maps tell a story about how an organization creates value
Source: Kaplan, R. S., and Norton, D. P. (2006). *Strategy Maps: Converting Intangible Assets into Tangible Outcomes.* Boston: Harvard Business School Press, 6; used with permission.

In presenting the map's overall structure, it is best to say something along the lines of "We create value for our shareholders ..." (point to the financial perspective) "... by delivering value to our customers ..." (point to the customer perspective) "... through superior execution of our internal processes ..." (point to the internal process perspective) "... that are built upon our people and knowledge" (point to the learning and growth perspective). Rather than reading each objective, paraphrase it and build it into the story. After all, the audience members can read faster than you can speak.[10] Now let us consider how one company used the balanced scorecard to plan long-term performance.

Apple Inc.: the balanced scorecard in action As one might expect, Apple has put its own spin on the original balanced-scorecard concept.[11] Apple developed a balanced scorecard to focus senior management on a strategy that would expand discussions beyond gross margin, return on equity, and market share. Its purpose was to plan long-term performance; it was not a control device to drive operating changes. For the financial perspective, Apple emphasized shareholder value. For the customer perspective, it emphasized customer satisfaction and market share; for the internal process perspective, core competencies; and, for the innovation and improvement perspective, employee attitudes. Senior executives prioritized the categories in the following order.

- *Customer perspective: customer satisfaction.* Based on the results of its own independent surveys to track key market segments around the world, these metrics help orient employees toward creating a customer-driven company.
- *Internal processes: core competencies.* Apple has developed quantitative measures of hard-to-measure competencies such as user-friendly interfaces, powerful software architectures, and effective distribution systems. The purpose is to focus employees on those that are most critical to Apple's future.
- *Innovation and improvement: employee commitment and alignment.* Customized internal surveys focus on how well employees understand the company's strategy, as well as whether or not they are asked to deliver results that are consistent with that strategy. Results are displayed in terms of the actual level of responses as well as overall trends.
- *Customer perspective: market share.* This metric is important, not only for the obvious benefits in sales growth but also to attract and retain software developers to Apple platforms.
- *Financial perspective: shareholder value.* This metric helps offset the emphasis on gross margin and sales growth – measures that ignore the investments required today to generate growth for tomorrow. The shareholder-value metric quantifies the impact of proposed investments for business creation and development.

These metrics, with the exception of shareholder value, can be driven both horizontally and vertically into each functional organization. For example, when thought of horizontally, the measures can identify how design and manufacturing contribute to an area such as customer satisfaction.[12] This language of measurable outputs provides guidance on how to launch and leverage programs.

How has the company done? Measured in terms of financial returns, consider some 2011 results. It ranks number 35 on the Fortune 500, with a market value at the end of the first quarter of $324 billion. It recorded 2010 profits of $14 billion on revenues of $65.2 billion. From

January 2009, when (now deceased) CEO Steve Jobs announced the second of his three medical leaves of absence, through October 14, 2011, Apple shares soared almost 400 percent.[13]

From internal reporting to external analysis: the Good Company Index   An alternative way to assess the outcomes of organizational strategy, at least among large, publicly traded companies, is the Good Company Index.[14] It is based on a simple assumption: that now, more than ever, people are interested in and able to evaluate which companies are worthy of their business as customers, their best efforts as employees, and their capital as investors. The index combines ratings on these three dimensions. Two broad factors explain why these particular factors are critical indicators of the external success of business strategy.

One is the rise of interactive Web 2.0 technologies and a corresponding culture of participation and disclosure, whereby millions of people are publishing their experiences and opinions online. The second is a growing global consciousness of human interdependency, fueled by factors such as international trade, travel, and global climate change, that is making people care more about how companies treat workers, customers, communities, and the environment.[15]

Worthiness as an employer means treating workers decently while striking the right balance between viewing people as costs to be cut and also as assets to be developed. To optimize employees' contributions, firms need two things: smart HR management practices (underpinned by a rigorous, analytic approach to optimizing quality, quantity, and costs) and an inspiring mission.

Worthiness as a seller means seeking win-win exchanges with customers that leave both parties better off. Companies such as Zappos, L. L. Bean, and Costco are justifiably famous for their no-hassle merchandise-return policies. Their objective is clear: win-win exchanges with customers. In return, customers are more likely to return to buy more merchandise, thereby validating that aspect of their business strategy.

Worthiness as a steward means caring for the environment and the communities in which a firm operates. It has two faces. One side strives to limit ecological harm through pollution and energy consumption. The other side strives to do good in nearby communities. Thus the "Make your mark" program at Starbucks allows employees time off to work on projects that contribute to the betterment of their local communities, such as painting a school or cleaning up a park.

Data that underlie the Good Company Index[16]

(1) *Good employer rating.* The index relies on two publicly available sources: the *Fortune* magazine list of best places to work (a positive indicator) and employee ratings collected anonymously by Glassdoor.com (which may be either a positive or a negative indicator).

(2) *Good seller rating.* The market research firm wRatings provides investors with original, standardized research across almost 5,000 companies in a variety of industries. It rates how well each company meets customer expectations. It collects weekly consumer behavior and pricing-power data, thereby providing a common framework with which to evaluate the customer metrics of any stock.[17] Consumers rate companies by quality, fair price, and trust.

(3) *Good steward rating.* To capture quantitatively how well a firm cares for its community, the environment, and society as a whole, Laurie Bassi, Ed Frauenheim, and Dan McMurrer (with Larry Costello) considered four different measures.

  (a) *Environment.* Data come from the Dow Jones Sustainability United States Index and *Newsweek's* environmental ranking of the 500 largest corporations in the United States. This indicator may be positive or negative.

  (b) *Contribution.* This component captures the extent to which companies use their core capabilities to contribute to society (outside their day-to-day business operations). It is a positive indicator. Bassi *et al.* created the database for this measure by systematically collecting information from company websites, as well as by inviting every Fortune 100 company to provide information on how it uses its core capabilities to make contributions to society.

  (c) *Restraint.* This is a negative indicator of companies that maximize their profits at the direct expense of the community, and that focus disproportionately on the personal benefits derived by company executives. The index uses the following two measures:

(i) tax avoidance through offshore registration in tax havens (based on information from the US Government Accountability Office); and

(ii) excessive executive compensation (based on data from a study commissioned by *The New York Times* as well as rankings available through the American Federation of Labor and Congress of Industrial Organizations).

(d) *Penalties and fines.* Government-imposed penalties or fines are clear negative indicators of a company's behavior as a steward of the community and the environment. The authors therefore penalized any company that had been assessed total penalties or fines by US regulatory bodies totaling more than $1 million over the most recently available five-year period, with a larger penalty for those with total fines that exceeded $100 million.

The maximum possible points ranged from –2 to +2 for the "Good employer" and "Good seller" measures, and from –3 to +4 for the "Good steward" measure. The total number of possible points therefore ranged from –7 to +8. The authors then used each Fortune 100 company's numerical score to assign a grade ranging from "F" for those at the bottom (total scores of –4 or lower) through "A" (+5 points or higher).

Results Among the publicly traded Fortune 100 firms, only Disney and FedEx got a grade of "A." FedEx stood out as a good employer and steward. It made *Fortune*'s list of "Best companies to work for" from 2008 to 2010, and it is working to minimize its environmental impact through steps such as the introduction of zero-emission electric delivery vehicles in the United Kingdom. Disney earned points as an employer, seller, and steward, reflecting the way the entertainment giant has done such things as emphasize leadership training, deliver holistic experiences to customers at its theme parks, and hold "Environmentality summits" focused on sustainability issues. Disney had no negative points against it, and scored six of the maximum possible eight points in the Good Company ranking system. By any standard, that is an impressive performance.

What about performance in the stock market (changes in share price, after incorporating dividends paid)? When the authors compared pairs of Fortune 100 companies within the same industry, they found that those with higher scores on the Good Company Index outperformed their peers in the stock market over periods of one, three, and five years. Companies that outscored their peers by three points or more on the Good Company Index outperformed them, on average, by eleven percentage points annually over the previous three years. For example, Chevron and ConocoPhillips are both major oil and gas companies. Chevron earned a Good Company Index score of +1 ("C+"), while ConocoPhillips scored a –3 ("D") – a difference of four points, or more than one full grade. Over three years Chevron outperformed ConocoPhillips by nine percentage points annually. This example, combined with other industry-pair cases, suggests that the better companies are when compared to their peers, the more they will outpace them.

Holistic assessments of strategy   Like the balanced scorecard, the Good Company Index uses a collection of measures to offer a holistic assessment of company performance, and, by extension, its strategy. This is important, because it protects against over-weighting any single dimension of a company's performance. To illustrate the dangers of focusing only on financial results, for example, to the exclusion of other considerations, consider Hewlett-Packard, a company that has enjoyed a long and proud tradition of being an enlightened and forward-thinking employer. The famed "HP way" includes trust and respect for individuals as core tenets.[18] Under the leadership of recent CEOs Carly Fiorina and Mark Hurd, however, those tenets were seriously undermined. The company had laid off thousands of workers in the past decade. Indeed, after Fiorina was summarily ousted by the HP board, Hurd pulled off one of the great rescue missions in US corporate history, refocusing the strife-ridden company and leading it to five years of consistent revenue gains and a stock value that soared 130 percent. Every metric that Wall Street uses to judge companies had gone in only one direction: up. From a shareholder's perspective, therefore, the company's strategy was superbly successful.

At the same time, however, a former HP engineer told *The New York Times* that Hurd was "wrecking our image, personally demeaning us, and chopping our future."[19] As one writer noted: "The consensus in Silicon Valley is that Mr. Hurd was despised at H.P., not just by the rank and file, but even by H.P.'s top executives… He was a cost-cutter who indulged himself."[20] As an employer, therefore, HP left much to be desired. The company's employees, the very sources of innovation and renewal, were demoralized and angry.

In light of conditions inside the company, therefore, it makes little sense to claim that the company's strategy was successful just because its financial results were strikingly positive. As a postscript, Hurd was ousted in mid-2010 in a scandal involving allegedly fudged expense reports and his relationship with an HP marketing contractor. Less than one year later the HP board also ousted Hurd's replacement, Leo Apotheker.[21]

Assessing the outcomes of HR strategy

Now that we have examined two frameworks for assessing the outcomes of an organization's overall strategy, the remainder of this chapter focuses on assessing the outcomes of HR strategy per se. To do this, we highlight the approaches of two companies: Sysco Corporation, the largest food marketer and distributor in North America; and Universal Weather and Aviation, a firm that facilitates travel by private airplane.

Sysco   Sysco Corporation is a $39.3 billion company. It is the global leader in marketing and distributing food products to restaurants, healthcare and educational facilities, hotels and inns, and other food service and hospitality businesses. Although it does not grow any food or own any restaurants, it provides the path that connects these two ends of the food-service chain. Each year Sysco delivers more than 1 billion cases of food and related products to more than 400,000 customers in the United States, Canada, and around the world. It serves these customers through a network of ninety-four local operating companies that deliver products both to independent and chain-restaurant customers and other food service locations, ranging from sports arenas to healthcare and educational facilities. Its 8,000 local marketing associates work closely with customers to identify and meet their needs.[22]

Creating value from human capital   Sysco developed a chain of logical connections to help leaders inside and outside HR to understand how it creates value from its human capital. It then developed measures to assess the statistical relationships among the links in the model. Sysco's model, shown in Figure 7.3, is based on the service-profit chain,[23] although it includes a more descriptive explanation of the process of creating customer value, with a broader range than the service sector per se.

SYSCO's Value-Profit Chain

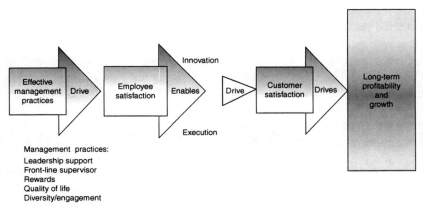

Figure 7.3 Sysco's value-profit chain
Source: SHRM Foundation (2004). *HR in Alignment: The Link to Business Results* DVD. Alexandria, VA: SHRM Foundation.

As the figure shows, effective management practices drive employee satisfaction (and engagement). A satisfied and engaged workforce, in turn, enables a company to pursue excellence in innovation and execution. Logically, higher employee satisfaction/engagement drives innovation and execution, which, in turn, enhances customer satisfaction, customer purchasing behavior, and, eventually, long-term profitability and growth. Certainly, management needs to put in place systems, people, technology, and processes that will initiate and sustain innovation and execution – the principal components of an effective value-profit chain. Competitors can easily copy technology and processes, but a highly skilled, committed, and fully engaged workforce is difficult to imitate.

Notice the management practices listed on the lower left-hand side of the model. That set of practices is known as the five-star management model, and it is based on five underlying principles:

- ensuring that leaders offer direction and support;
- strengthening front-line supervisors;
- rewarding performance;
- addressing employees' quality of life; and
- including employees by engaging them and leveraging diversity.

The five-star model is all about taking care of people, extending the same respect to employees that managers do to their external customers. The

Table 7.1 Sample items from Sysco's work climate/employee-engagement survey

Five-star principle	Work-climate survey item
Leadership support	I know what is expected of me at work.
	Upper management spends time talking with employees about our business direction.
Front-line supervisor	My supervisor treats me with dignity and respect.
	My supervisor and I review my top goals and discuss how they contribute to the company's success.
	I have received constructive feedback on my performance within the last six months.
	My supervisor removes obstacles so that I can do my job better.
Quality of life	I trust what the company tells me.
	Different departments of our company work together to get the job done.
Rewards	My pay is the same as or better than other companies in our market.
	Doing my job well leads to monetary rewards.
	Decisions made about promotions or job changes within this organization are fair.
Engagement/diversity	I am willing to work harder to make this company succeed.
	I am proud to work for Sysco.

Source: Carrig, K., and Wright, P. M. (2006). *Building Profit through Building People: Making Your Workforce the Strongest Link in the Value-Profit Chain.* Alexandria, VA: SHRM Foundation.

framework is general enough to apply to any type of company structure or business model, and it gives businesses wide discretion in actual implementation. Indeed, the logic of the model is so compelling that it is taught to every manager and employee from the first day on the job.

Measuring the effects of management practices Sysco developed a work climate/employee-engagement survey built around each of the five-star principles. All members of each Sysco operating company participate in a comprehensive, annual self-assessment, and also in impromptu and informal assessments on an as-needed basis.[24] Table 7.1 shows some of the items from that survey.

Table 7.2 Satisfied employees deliver better results

Associate satisfaction	4.00 – 5.00	3.90 – 3.99	3.75 – 3.89	3.55 – 3.74	< 3.55
Customer loyalty score	4.55	4.40	4.25	4.15	4.05
Retention, marketing associates	88%	85%	81%	75%	76%
Retention, drivers	87%	81%	81%	75%	76%

Source: Carrig and Wright (2006).

Do high scores rather than low scores on the management practices matter? Do they distinguish better-performing from worse-performing operating companies? Two types of evidence suggest that the answer is a cautious "Yes." Data in Table 7.2 show that Sysco operating companies with the most satisfied employees consistently receive the highest scores from their customers and have higher retention of marketing associates and drivers.

Retention is higher in operating companies with better associate satisfaction/engagement. At the same time, however, cause-and-effect relationships are not obvious. Does making employees more satisfied and engaged cause customers to be more loyal? Or is it more rewarding to work in operating companies with loyal customers, and, as a result, employees who work there tend to be more satisfied and engaged? The information in Table 7.2, while compelling, simply does not provide answers to these important questions.

A second analysis correlated work climate/employee-engagement scores, productivity, and retention data collected about six months earlier in the fiscal year with the percentage of operating pretax income at the end of the fiscal year. The multiple correlation (R^2) was 0.46. This is a powerful result, for it indicates that scores on these three human capital metrics serve as a leading indicator of subsequent financial performance. Fully 46 percent of the variability in pretax earnings was associated with variation in these three employee-related variables. That got management's attention.

Using the balanced scorecard to leverage best practices Sysco assesses the performance of each operating company in terms of balanced-scorecard metrics in four areas: financial, operational, human capital, and customer performance. Scores on the work climate/ employee-engagement survey comprise one element of the human capital metrics, along with measures of productivity (employees per 100,000 cases shipped) and employee retention (among marketing associates, drivers, and night warehouse employees).

We noted earlier that Sysco has a decentralized organizational structure consisting of ninety-four autonomous operating companies. It employs an organization-wide rewards system to encourage managers of the autonomous operating companies to share information with each other and to transfer best practices within the organization. Sysco built a "best business practices" web portal on its intranet to provide a platform for organization-wide improvement. The web architecture offered a framework for managers to do two things: to share information on their own operating company's successful practices; and to learn from the best practices of other Sysco operating companies. Indeed, managers of operating companies can use the "best business practices" portal to identify and learn from operating companies in the top quartile of performance on any of the metrics in the balanced scorecard.

The financial impact of HR strategy Sysco took its analysis of the retention of marketing associates and drivers to another level when it developed estimates of the fully loaded costs of turnover (separation, replacement, and training) for these groups of employees. In 2000 retention rates for the groups were 75 percent and 65 percent, respectively. By 2005 the retention rates had improved to 88 percent and 87 percent, respectively. Sysco then estimated the replacement and training costs of these two groups of employees as $50,000 per marketing associate and $35,000 per driver. Assuming 100 employees per business unit, from 2000 to 2005 each business unit saved (in terms of costs that were not incurred) $650,000 among marketing associates and $770,000 among drivers, for a total savings of $1.42 million. Corporate-wide savings in retention over all categories of employees from 2000 to 2005, assuming 10,000 employees, totaled $156.5 million.

Those numbers are impressive, but Sysco's then chief administrative officer, Ken Carrig, did not stop there. According to the chief financial officer, every $5 million in savings at Sysco represents a cent per share.

A total savings in turnover costs of $156.5 million represents 31.3 cents per share. When was the last time you saw an HR program assessed in terms of its payoff for investors?

HR at Sysco   By determining what management practices and processes drive its human capital indices, and how these influence financial outcomes over time, executives at Sysco's operating companies can assess the impact of their HR strategies. These strategies are key to leveraging the chain of relationships in the business model shown in Figure 7.2. By demonstrating clearly how the company creates value from its human capital, and then measuring the various links in its business model, HR is not only a business partner, but also a driver of business success at Sysco.

Universal Weather and Aviation[25]   Since 1959 privately held and Houston-based Universal Weather and Aviation Inc. has been providing complete global resources to company-based flight departments, all coordinated and executed by team members around the world. Its purpose is to facilitate private aviation trips, domestically and internationally. It also operates its own business aircraft and flight department, giving it an owner's perspective, as well as an opportunity to test product and service enhancements. To date, it has facilitated more than 2.5 million global trip segments. Currently the company employs more than 1,700 employees (more than 900 in the United States), located in more than twenty countries, and aligned to one mission: successful trips. To illustrate what the company does (that is, trip support), consider the three phases of just one segment of a trip.

Pre-planning. Trip-itinerary consulting; permits – clearances and over-flights; ground handling: customs and immigration, credit, catering, security, ground transportation, hotels, flight planning, weather briefings, fuel arrangements.

In flight. Weather updates, schedule-change management, flight following.

Aircraft lands. Ensure all pre-planning arrangements are executed, fuel the aircraft, prepare for the next flight segment.

Aligning HR goals to the company's vision   Delivering profitable growth is a key corporate objective, but from the customer's perspective a successful trip depends on two interrelated factors: employees who are equipped to succeed, and superior global service. This results in delighted and loyal customers and vendors. These factors are shown in Figure 7.4.

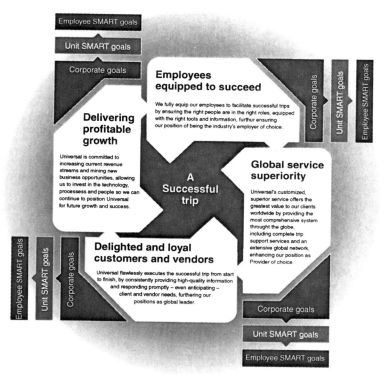

Figure 7.4 Aligning goals to Universal Weather and Aviation's vision
Source: Ginsburgh, S. (2011). Creating competitive advantage through strategic talent management. Presentation at preconference workshop "Creating strong links: connecting strategy, talent management, and organizational outcomes," annual meeting of Society for Industrial and Organizational Psychology, Chicago, April 13.

The company's vision is to be the provider (of trip support) of choice, employer of choice, and the global leader in its field. The human resources aspect aligns with the vision's key element of "Employees equipped to succeed." Notice how the corporate goals cascade to unit (in this case, HR) and each employee's SMART goals (Specific, Measurable, Appropriate, Realistic, and Timely).

Let us turn the clock back to 2006. In July of that year the company's HR issues were legion. Here are some of the most serious ones: no compensation structure, no HR processes

Figure 7.5 How Universal Weather and Aviation creates value from its human capital
Source: Ginsburgh, S. (2011). Talent/talent risk-management process and client retention: Universal Weather and Aviation case study. Presentation at SHRM Foundation "Thought leaders" retreat, Chicago, October 5.

other than payroll (recently audited with more than fifty problem areas), no staffing plan, no succession plan or talent inventory, no development-based training, underutilized HR information system self-service, a cumbersome and non-aligned appraisal process, all new HR staff, low credibility with employees and executives, a lack of meaningful metrics or an employee survey, and no HR strategy. Whew! Where would you begin?

Over time, the new chief HR officer focused on three key building blocks: alignment, capabilities, and engagement (ACE).[26] "Alignment" refers to the strength of employees' connection to corporate goals and strategy. "Capabilities" refer to the strength of company talent and HR systems designed to deliver strategic value to the business. "Engagement" refers to the strength of employees' willingness to go beyond the minimum for the customer or to advocate for the company as a great place to work. The chief HR officer used these building blocks to show how the company creates value from its human capital (see Figure 7.5).

With respect to the links in Figure 7.5 labeled "Talent process" and "Talent risk management," here are the major initiatives the chief HR officer undertook.

Talent process – staff planning, a valid selection process, strategically focused performance management, a talent inventory/review, individual development plans, and career-building assignments.
Talent risk management – competitive total rewards, recognition, career advancement, an employee survey and metrics, a coaching approach to leadership, team structures, institution of systematic HR processes, and change management.

Now consider how some specific initiatives within each of the above areas link to the next set of blocks in Figure 7.5, namely "Alignment," "Capabilities," and "Engagement."

Alignment – talent process
- Competencies for positions
- Top-down SMART goals linked to corporate goals
- Employee-accountable monthly progress meetings
- Year-end summary – rating the year the employee had
- Talent inventory linked to succession and compensation

Capabilities – talent process
- Upgrade and globalize core-competency training
- Collaborative leadership training (customer teams)
- All training has end-of-program performance standards and post-training assessments (business impact)
- Customer-service training formalized
- Client education yields better performance for client
- New systems projects with change management integrated
- Developmental team-lead positions created
- Tracking of individual-development-plan progress (high-potential individuals)
- Highlight capabilities to clients with employee profiles and pictures

Engagement – talent risk management
- Competitive total rewards with variable compensation for all employees
- Transparent career progression – career ladders
- New employees – mentoring and several early-career steps
- Retention of best employees as a corporate goal – counts toward bonus
- Employee barometer (ACE) assessments (three times a year)
- Talent-inventory integration with bonus-award guidelines
- Family-based activities: holiday events for kids, "We care," chili cook-off
- Multiple tools for recognition – spot awards, service, employee "corporate art"
- Promote a culture of inclusion and access

What have been the results of these efforts? Many of them are reflected in the metrics the company uses to assess the outcomes of its strategy. At the level of the executive committee, HR shares the following metrics: retention of A-level talent, readiness of successors for key positions, the employee barometer scores (ACE assessments), and data on healthcare cost sharing. In addition, the chief HR officer oversees the preparation of an HR annual report. The report highlights key accomplishments for the current year, and also identifies "must-win" battles (initiatives) for the next year, along with the name of the HR staff member who is responsible for each initiative (to promote accountability).

In terms of accomplishments, Universal Weather and Aviation has come a long way since July 2006. Here are just a few of its more notable recent achievements.

- Year-on-year company earnings (before interest, taxes, depreciation, and amortization) increased by more than 20 percent in 2010.
- The retention of most valuable clients stands at 99.6 percent.
- Revenue from client-education efforts grew by more than 80 percent in 2010.
- The company has dramatically reduced the turnover of key employees – a metric for the annual bonus program.
- The human capital score (employee barometer) averaged 70 to 80 percent positive responses from 2007 to 2011 on alignment, capabilities, and engagement; the goal is 80 percent of divisions over 80 percent.
- The company has achieved an average of more than $500,000 in HR cost avoidance annually.
- It was named one of the "Best places to work in Houston" every year from 2006 to 2011.
- Its HR function received the Organizational Excellence award in 2010.
- HR contributions are now included in all the company's grant proposals because they are seen as a competitive advantage.

In addition to engineering a massive turnaround in the state of HR systems and processes since 2006, HR strategy at Universal Weather and Aviation stands out for several reasons. First, it is closely intertwined with other elements of the business strategy, and also with the company's mission and vision. Second, it uses a systematic process and overarching framework (ACE) to demonstrate how the company creates value from its human capital strategy. Third, it explicitly links elements of the talent process to alignment and capability, and elements of talent risk management to engagement. Finally, in terms of Figure 7.4, we know from several research studies,[27] as well as Sysco's experience with the service-profit chain, that satisfied customers do two things. One, they come back, and thereby generate more business for your company. Two, they tell others about their positive experiences, and that leads to revenue growth – a key financial metric for the company as a whole.

HR strategy and risk management

Human capital risk refers to the uncertainty arising from changes in a wide variety of workforce and people-management issues that affect a company's ability to meet its strategic and operating objectives.[28] Identifying and optimizing human capital risks is important, if for no other reason than the fact that, in many companies, human capital accounts for at least a half of all operating costs.

At the top of the list of potential human capital risks is the linkage of HR strategy and plans with business strategy and plans, short- and long-term alike. In the two examples we presented earlier, both Sysco and Universal Weather and Aviation explicitly link their HR strategies to their overall business strategies as a way to mitigate HR risk. In fact, at Sysco human capital metrics are an explicit component of the balanced scorecard that the company uses to assess the success of its business strategy.

Two recent findings, however, should be a wake-up call for the need to pay more careful attention to human capital risk as an enterprise risk. (1) Human capital risk ranks fourth (behind regulatory, operational, and strategic risks) in terms of its impact on business results. It is ranked higher than financial, reputational, supply chain, and the risks associated with information technology. (2) At the same time, however, it ranks *tenth* in terms of how effectively it is now managed.[29] There is reason for hope, however, because risk-management language is already familiar to most boards of directors and senior executives, and it may offer a useful way to reframe human capital issues. For example, consider raising issues such as the following.[30]

- What is the risk that we do not attract or retain the right talent to achieve our strategic targets?
- What are the underlying assumptions about human capital in our business forecasts (are we assuming adequate internal and external supplies)?

- What is the risk that our company culture does not support our strategic intent?
- Which HR policies, programs, and practices pose potential risks? How do we manage them?
- How do we ensure that assessing and managing human capital risk is not an HR-only exercise?

While there are many potential human capital risks, here are the top five, as reported in a recent study: (1) a shortage of critical skills within a company's workforce; (2) compliance/regulatory issues; (3) succession planning/leadership pipeline questions; (4) the gap between current talent capabilities and business goals; and (5) a shortage of critical skills in the external labor force.[31]

Conclusion

We began this chapter by presenting several broad frameworks that might prove useful for any firm to assess the outcomes of its strategy. The first relied on strategic reporting using the balanced scorecard, and the second relied on three metrics from a recent book, *Good Company: Business Success in the Worthiness Era*. These metrics can help interested parties to evaluate which companies are worthy of their business as customers, their best efforts as employees, and their capital as investors. Then we focused on assessing the outcomes of HR strategy itself, with examples from Sysco (based on the value-profit chain) and Universal Weather and Aviation (based on the ACE model of alignment, capabilities, and engagement). Our final section focused on identifying and optimizing human capital risks – an ongoing challenge that the frameworks presented in this chapter may help to address in a systematic manner.

Notes

1 See http://chess.about.com/od/reference/g/bldefini.htm; see also http://en.wikipedia.org/wiki/Encyclopaedia_of_Chess_Openings (both accessed September 29, 2011).

2 Amorello, A. (2011). A "friendly" farewell: Mass. chain declares bankruptcy, closes stores. *Boston Globe*, October 6 (available at www.boston.com/lifestyle/blogs/thenextgreatgeneration/2011/10/a_friendly_farewell_mass_chain.html; accessed October 7, 2011).

3 Kaplan, R. S., and Norton, D. P. (1992). The balanced scorecard: measures that drive performance. *Harvard Business Review*, 70(1): 71–9; Kaplan, R. S.,

and Norton, D. P. (1993). Putting the balanced scorecard to work. *Harvard Business Review*, 71(5): 134–47; Kaplan, R. S., and Norton, D. P. (1996). Using the balanced scorecard as a strategic management system. *Harvard Business Review*, 74(1): 75–9.

4 Bassi, L., Frauenheim, E., and McMurrer, D., with Costello, L. (2011). *Good Company: Business Success in the Worthiness Era*. San Francisco: Berrett-Kohler.

5 Kaplan and Norton (1992).

6 Kaplan and Norton (1992).

7 Kaplan and Norton (1992).

8 Kaplan and Norton (1992).

9 Gold, R. S. (2004). Presenting the balanced scorecard strategy map, newsletter B0407D. Harvard Business School, Boston.

10 Gold (2004).

11 Kaplan and Norton (1993).

12 Kaplan and Norton (1993).

13 Lashinsky, A. (2011). Inside Apple. *Fortune*, May 23: 125–34. See also http://uk.finance.yahoo.com/q/hp?s=AAPL&a=8&b=7&c=1984&d=9&e=17&f=2011&g=d&z=66&y=660 (accessed October 17, 2011).

14 Bassi *et al.* (2011).

15 Bassi *et al.* (2011: 5).

16 Bassi *et al.* (2011: 92, 93).

17 See www.wratings.com/about.php?s=2 (accessed October 17, 2011).

18 Packard, D. (1996). *The HP Way: How Bill Hewlett and I Built Our Company*. New York: HarperCollins.

19 Nocera, J. (2010). Real reason for ousting HP's chief. *The New York Times*, August 13 (available at www.nytimes.com/2010/08/14/business/14nocera.html?pagewanted=all; accessed October 2, 2010).

20 Nocera (2010).

21 *International Herald Tribune* (2011). H-P doomed by slapdash CEO transition. *International Herald Tribune*, September 23 (available at http://asq.org/qualitynews/qnt/execute/displaySetup?newsID=12163; accessed October 17, 2011).

22 Sysco Corporation (2011). *2011 Annual Report*. Houston: Sysco Corporation (available at www.sysco.com/investor/annual-reports.html; accessed October 17, 2011).

23 Heskett, J. L., Jones, T. O., Loveman, G. W., Sasser, W. E., and Schlesinger, L. A. (1994). Putting the service-profit chain to work. *Harvard Business Review*, 72(2): 164–74.

24 Carrig, K., and Wright, P. M. (2006). *Building Profit through Building People: Making Your Workforce the Strongest Link in the Value-Profit Chain*. Alexandria, VA: SHRM Foundation.

25 The authors would like to acknowledge the extremely helpful input of Universal Weather and Aviation's senior vice president, HR and workforce development, Steve Ginsburgh, throughout this section.

26 Schiemann, W. A. (2009). *Reinventing Talent Management: How to Maximize Performance in the New Marketplace*. New York: Wiley.

27 Rucci, A. J., Kirn, S. P., and Quinn, R. T. (1998). The employee-customer-profit chain at Sears. *Harvard Business Review*, 76(1): 82–97; Heskett *et al.* (1994).

28 Young, M. B., and Hexter, E. S. (2011). *Managing Human Capital Risk*. New York: Conference Board.

29 Young and Hexter (2011).

30 Young and Hexter (2011).

31 Young and Hexter (2011).

8 | Future forces and trends driving HR strategy

Consider a recent newspaper headline: "Most companies lose top talent." Fully 75 percent of employers in a Manpower Group survey reported that they voluntarily lost at least some of their most high-performing employees between 2010 and 2011.[1] Is this a cause for concern? Certainly. The risk of losing key talent, especially members of talent pools in which investments in the quantity or quality of people can have a major impact on an organization's ability to achieve sustainable strategic success, is one of the highest-ranked HR risks.[2] These are known as pivotal talent pools.[3]

A critically important question that senior leaders must address with respect to strategy is "How will we compete and defend?"[4] This implies two things, symbolized by the Chinese characters for the word "risk": crisis and opportunity (as we noted in Chapter 4). Just to refresh your memory, "risk" refers to an undesirable outcome and its consequences, while "opportunity" refers to a desirable outcome and its consequences. A danger is that firms focus their HR strategies only on "defending" against undesirable outcomes, such as the loss of key talent, regulatory/compliance issues, or shortages of critical talent within an organization's workforce. Do not allow this perspective to dominate the way that leaders approach human resource strategy! Doing so might blindside the organization to important opportunities. Taking advantage of opportunity, in turn, means placing your organization in a position to benefit from an uncertain future event. In this chapter, we present examples of firms that attempted to focus on both of these two faces of risk: crisis and opportunity.

This synergy between crisis and opportunity will be a key theme in the future of human resource strategy, so it has been a central idea throughout this book. Treating human resource strategy in this way is a relatively new idea, but one that we think must become a foundation for future leaders both inside and outside the HR profession.

To reinforce this important point, the next section recaps the major lessons of the previous chapters, as a reminder about the elements of HR strategy, how they fit together, and how they reflect the importance of a balanced approach to risk. After that, we summarize future global forces that are just emerging but promise to shape human resource strategy for decades to come. Finally, we conclude with examples of organizations that illustrate the future of HR strategy in the ways that they are driving innovation, using talent (HR) analytics, and emphasizing values-based human capital approaches.

The elements of HR strategy and a balanced approach to uncertainty and opportunity

Chapter 1 focused on competitive strategy – the decisions, processes, and choices that organizations make to position themselves for sustainable success. These elements define a firm's competitive position in the marketplace. In general, therefore, strategy is about choices and trade-offs that firms make. More specifically, HR strategy refers to the decisions, processes, and choices that organizations make about managing people. We examined strategy formulation ("How should we compete?") in the context of examining the internal and external environments, as well as from the perspective of building defenses against competitive forces or finding a position in the industry where the forces are weakest.

Strategy analysis, on the other hand, defines the crucial (or pivotal) elements for the strategy's success. It answers the question "What must we execute well?" Overall business strategy, through its hierarchy of goals – vision, mission, and strategic objectives – provides helpful guidance about the type of talent that will be necessary to fulfill the organization's strategic objectives, and to move toward its mission and vision. This is where HR strategy comes into play. It parallels and facilitates the implementation of the strategic business plan. When carried out well, HR strategies align with the organization's strategy by creating the capacity in the workforce to achieve the organization's strategic objectives. Finally, we noted that senior leaders increasingly see the levels of risk and the metrics of risk as inherent components of developing and executing strategies, and in evaluating the appropriate tolerance for risk.

Chapter 2 examined the external environment that underpins decisions about business and HR strategies. Two mega-trends that define that external environment are globalization and technology. Others include global labor markets, legal and regulatory requirements, political developments, virtual mobility, and disruptive technology, such as new business models that no one saw coming. Consider the Tata Nano in automobiles, or the iPhone. They reinforce the idea that change is discontinuous, abrupt, and distinctly non-linear. Whether a firm adopts a conventional or a values-based approach to developing its competitive strategy, HR strategy is central to the process of building a company and a culture that leverages these trends to the benefit of all stakeholders.

We noted in Chapter 3 that human capital permeates every aspect of organizations. Hence, understanding the context of HR strategy is essential for leaders to formulate and evaluate their HR strategy. To be sure, the nature of human capital strategy also varies depending on the type of organizational unit in question, such as customer-facing versus a support unit in the value chain. Moreover, faced with challenges such as diversity, sustainability and socio-economic disparities, HR strategy welcomes inputs from a variety of perspectives and academic disciplines, including I/O psychology, labor economics, operations management, and marketing, among others. In addition to crossing disciplinary and functional boundaries, boundaries also will be more permeable among the HR function, the organization, and the environment.

Executives outside the HR profession recognize that vital issues such as the following must be addressed in HR strategy, for they clearly impact their organizations' exposure to HR risks: globalization, the aging workforce, the changing demographics of the workforce, scarcities of skilled labor, regulatory and compliance issues, and vendor management and sourcing. Indeed, the most fundamental challenge in HR strategy is to define the connection points between the objectives of a particular organizational unit and the pivotal areas in which individuals and groups can most affect those objectives. The key "takeaway" from this chapter is that HR strategy must support the context of the organization.

The broad theme of Chapter 4 was HR strategy through a risk-management framework. We emphasized that, when risk is seen only as the possibility of uncertain events creating a bad outcome, organizations focus on ways to minimize or insure against the worst case. This can lead to human capital strategies that are built largely upon the idea of reducing uncertainty, eliminating bad outcomes, or insuring against the bad outcomes. Unexpected future outcomes can also have positive consequences, however. Despite the importance of risk mitigation, do not allow this perspective to dominate the way that leaders approach human resource strategy. Doing so may well cause organizations to miss some of their most significant opportunities. Two important lessons are that frameworks for human resource strategy must incorporate risk, and that the HR profession must get better at defining, measuring, and solving the thorny issues of people in an uncertain world.

We addressed HR strategy formulation, as well as its linkages, anchor points and outcomes, in Chapter 5. To do so, we provided a framework for understanding the connections between the investments that organizations make in HR programs and the vital outcomes that they define as sustainable strategic success. We stressed that formulating a human capital strategy means accomplishing two broad tasks: (1) finding the connections between human capital and the strategic outcomes for the organization, to identify the "pivot points" where human capital makes the biggest difference to sustainable strategic success; and (2) making the investments to create a portfolio of human resource programs that fit together synergistically, both to maintain the broader workforce and to enhance human capital at the pivot points.

The concepts of efficiency, effectiveness, and impact illuminate how the issues that confront strategic leaders in human capital strategy can be analyzed and conceived with the same logic that would be used for other vital resources, such as money or customers. These three ideas show how leaders can conceive of the logical connections between investments, programs, effects, and strategic outcomes regarding human capital. They also illustrate how valuable it can be to "look for the pivot points" all along these strategic connections, to identify where risk, return, and uncertainty are likely to be most significant.

Chapter 6 focused on HR strategy communication and engagement. It showed how organizations can use principles from communication and persuasion to increase the chances that strategic initiatives will actually be implemented. Four such principles are: (1) show the audience why it should believe in the message or information; (2) understand the concerns of the audience, and make sure that they can see advantages in what is being suggested; (3) use vivid terminology and compelling evidence, framed in language that is engaging and actionable for those outside HR; and (4) connect emotionally. Using these four principles within the broader HC BRidge framework conveys the logical connections between human capital investments and strategic success, and it also illustrates where HR is trusted to engage in discussions about performance and strategy. Finally, employees perceive an effective HR strategy as being distinctive, consistent, and consensual (decision makers understand and agree on the messages of the HR strategy). When HR practices are implemented in a way that is trusted, and when the interactions that employees experience at work are seen as positive, HR strategy is working as intended.

Finally, Chapter 7 addressed the outcomes of successful business and HR strategies. In other words, how do you know if they worked? To do this, we presented two broad frameworks that might prove useful for any firm to assess the outcomes of its strategy. The first was the balanced scorecard, and the second was a set of metrics from a recent book, *Good Company: Business Success in the Worthiness Era*. The balanced scorecard is a constellation of measures that address four broad questions. (1) How do customers see us (the customer perspective)? (2) What must we excel at (the internal perspective)? (3) Can we continue to improve and create value (the innovation and learning perspective)? (4) How do we look to shareholders (the financial perspective)? We recommend that leaders identify just a few measures in each area that are most critical, and focus on those.

Like the balanced scorecard, the Good Company Index uses a collection of measures to offer a holistic assessment of company performance, and, by extension, its strategy. This is important, because it protects against over-weighting any single dimension of a company's performance. The Good Company Index assesses publicly traded firms on three dimensions of worthiness: (1) as an employer (treating workers decently while striking the right balance between viewing people as costs to be cut and assets to be developed); (2) as a seller (seeking win-win exchanges with customers that leave both parties better off); and (3) as a steward (caring for the environment and the communities in which a firm operates).

To assess the outcomes of HR strategy per se, it is important to be able to explain how your organization creates value from its human capital. A logical model, such as the service-profit-chain approach, can be particularly valuable in this context. Then develop metrics that assess each of the key links in the model. Doing so ties management practices to employee behaviors, employee behaviors to impacts on customers, and, finally, customer behaviors to financial outcomes. Now let us examine some current trends and future forces that will define future HR strategy.

Global forces that will define future HR strategy

The context in which business takes place is changing dramatically as the world experiences a period of profound change. As the context changes, so must HR strategy, in order to defend against the many human capital risks. As a framework for discussion, therefore, consider the following seven key contextual factors that are affecting the climate for business.[5]

(1) *The economy, and the need to retain pivotal talent.* Many sectors and companies have not recovered from the recession and are struggling to survive. Turbulence, volatility, and tremendous uncertainty characterize economies in North America, Europe, and the Asia-Pacific region. As a result, a serious competitive threat is the loss of pivotal talent. To defend against that threat, some firms have developed talent-retention programs, many of which have been described in the book *Love 'Em or Lose 'Em*.[6] At the same time, however, management actions such as downsizing employee numbers can undermine the best of such programs. Why? Because employee morale is the first casualty in a downsizing. When a firm institutes its first round of downsizing, employees' initial reaction is usually a sense of betrayal. Longer-term consequences of altering the work environment include increased voluntary turnover and decreased innovation. This is one of the reasons why firms such as Aflac, SC Johnson, Synovus Financial, and Southwest Airlines have never downsized. In fact, the shock of changing from a non-downsizing organization to a downsizer is a major reason why rates of voluntary turnover increase among remaining workers. Empirical

research has demonstrated that an organization that lays off 10 percent of its workforce can expect to see a 15.5 percent rate of voluntary turnover among surviving employees, compared with a 10.4 percent turnover rate among companies with no layoffs.[7]

(2) *Globalization*. Knowledge, trade, technology, capital, goods, and services are more globally connected than ever. Coupled with the rise of emerging markets, and the constant focus on finding new revenue streams, these trends have created global labor markets, workforces, supply chains, customer bases, and fierce global competitors.

(3) *Technology*. New technologies such as social media, mobile technologies, cloud computing, and automation are changing how people live and work, and how businesses operate. Consider social media. It already accounts for one of every six minutes spent online.[8] As examples, consider the four most dominant social networks. Facebook and Twitter are the most popular sites for personal networking, while LinkedIn and BranchOut are the two most popular sites for professionals.[9]

(a) *Facebook*. Facebook has 800 million monthly users, and 500 million people visit the site on a daily basis. Every day 20 million Facebook applications are downloaded. Facebook has become the most engaging place on the internet. The average age of Facebook users today is thirty-eight.

(b) *Twitter*. Twitter has 100 million monthly users and it generates 230 million tweets per day. Since the beginning of 2011 there has been a 110 percent increase in the number of tweets. Twitter is a platform for one-to-many communication.

(c) *LinkedIn*. LinkedIn has 94 million monthly users, but fewer than 1 million use it daily. LinkedIn usage accounts for a small amount of total time spent on the internet. Its focus is white-collar professional workers.

(d) *BranchOut*. BranchOut is the largest professional network and the largest job board on Facebook. It has millions of users in sixty countries, supports fifteen languages, and has 3 million jobs posted. BranchOut leverages Facebook's 800 million members.

(4) *Demographics*. Society is becoming older and more diverse. In most countries, by 2020 half the workforce will be over fifty (except in China). These demographic shifts are changing the nature of retirement. People will work longer, but the amount and type of work they do will change. The challenge for companies

will be to find new ways for older employees to contribute. At the same time, members of generation Y (born between 1977 through 1997) will account for nearly half the employees in the entire world by 2014,[10] and they are looking for different things from employers. These employees will have many more employers than "baby boomers" have had. They will stay longer, however, at companies they feel are good places to work. This trend affects how organizations craft their employee-value propositions. Younger employees want to be treated as equals. Research suggests they will sacrifice as much as 15 percent of their salary to work for a socially responsible company.[11]

(5) *The nature of work.* All aspects of work are changing, including where, when, and why people work.

    (a) *Where.* Technology allows people to work from anywhere, and more people are working remotely from home. In 2011, for example, 63 percent of US organizations offered some form of telework arrangements to their employees.[12]

    (b) *When.* Technology means that people can and often do work 24/7.

    (c) *Why.* Members of generation Y, especially, do not work purely for money; they work for purpose and meaning, and they want to work for organizations whose values are aligned with their own. For example, consider the top five characteristics that "millennials" want in a boss:[13]

        (i) will help me navigate my career path;

        (ii) will give me straight feedback;

        (iii) will mentor and coach me;

        (iv) will sponsor me for formal development programs; and

        (v) is comfortable with flexible schedules.

(6) *The evolving nature of leadership.* Command-and-control leadership structures are fading away. More authentic servant-leadership models are replacing them.[14] Robert Greenleaf developed the concept of servant leadership in 1970. The servant-leader serves the people he or she leads. To do that, servant-leaders remove obstacles that limit employees' maximum productivity, they develop employees to bring out the best they have to offer, coach them and encourage their self-expression, facilitate personal growth in all who work with them, and listen well, in order to build a sense of community and joint ownership. In theory, servant-leaders are effective because the needs of followers are so well looked after

that they reach their full potential, and hence perform at their best. If adopted, this way of looking at leadership forces executives away from self-serving, domineering leadership, and makes those in charge think harder about how to respect, value, and motivate the people reporting to them. As a result, despite significant work-related pressures, effective leaders can help employees and organizations become stronger.

(7) *Cross-cultural leadership skills.* These are more important than ever, particularly because major cultural differences exist between the East and West. These considerations become more important as firms do business across international boundaries. Leaders need to recognize how cultural differences affect interactions with employees. To illustrate, consider the experience of a senior Western manager with the Chinese division of a major bank. One branch reported the loss of $50,000, and the bank's local managers suspected a teller of theft. Since the police were unable to identify the guilty party with certainty, the Western manager had to choose between dropping the inquiry and having the police arbitrarily select a suspect, whose punishment would be execution. The Western manager dropped the inquiry, but, in retrospect, he wished he had taken an approach that reconciled the Eastern and Western value systems. In the West people rely on values, while in the East people rely on relationships. Chinese employees trust family and friends but often do not trust authority figures such as the police, judges, or company executives. The Western manager said he should have spoken to the informal Chinese employee leader and said that, if the money was returned, it would be held in trust for the branch employees over five years. If no additional thefts occurred, the bank would add $5,000 to the trust each year. Looking ahead, the reconciliation of different value systems will be a major challenge for global companies that want to survive and thrive.[15]

Each of the seven contextual factors discussed above creates internal as well as external human capital risks for organizations. Here are examples of five of them.[16]

(1) *Loss of key talent.* We noted at the beginning of this chapter that many organizations have lost "A" players recently. Others that damaged the employee-value proposition, as a result of massive downsizing, for example, or permanently suspending contributions

to employee-retirement programs, are concerned that when the economy improves they will be at significant risk of losing top people.

(2) *Not investing in the future.* During tight economic times many organizations have focused on survival and on maximizing short-term cash flow. They have decreased their focus on and investments in leadership development and succession planning. This trend poses an enormous longer-term human capital risk.

(3) *Lack of innovation.* In today's rapidly changing world, having cultures and management systems that encourage innovation in products, services, and ways of managing people is essential, yet many organizations lack these key ingredients. Indeed, their singular focus on avoiding undesirable outcomes blinds them to opportunities for innovation that will make their organizations more competitive.

(4) *Lack of emphasis on values.* The financial crisis showed that many organizations either lack core values or fail to live them. Ironically, while many firms view their values as sources of long-term sustainability, many failed to emphasize them as they struggled to survive during the recent global economic recession.

(5) *Ignoring social media.* Ignoring or underinvesting in social media is a risk that could put a company at a competitive disadvantage. At the other end of the spectrum, excessive openness can lead to employees potentially sharing critical information with outsiders.

In the following sections we consider what some progressive organizations are doing to address several of these risks: driving innovation, using talent (HR) analytics, and emphasizing values.

Driving innovation

Consider how HR leaders at a more than 100-year-old packaging company used the company's strategic business plan to identify progressive HR practices that promoted innovation.[17] Wisconsin-based Menasha Packaging is a family-owned, privately held, 162-year-old packaging company with 3,570 employees and $1 billion in sales. It specializes in creating high-end graphic packaging and merchandising products for retail, food, and pharmaceutical applications.[18] Since the packaging industry is highly competitive and consolidating rapidly, Menasha wanted to enhance its existing businesses and to enter new markets. To attain these goals, Menasha focused on two focal points for innovation: "outside-in" and "inside-in."

Outside-in activities. Menasha interviewed its customers and engaged with its customers' customers. Then it used the insights gained from these perspectives to drive internal discussions about growing sales. These conversations led Menasha to shift away from durable-goods customers, who were moving overseas, to focus instead on food, personal care, and household products.

Inside-in activities. The HR team played a major role in cultivating an innovative culture in the company. The HR emphasis united people from diverse functional areas and developed tools to manage innovation. According to HR manager Sharon Swatscheno, "HR had the role of driving the innovation culture, and it really was the right place for this to be. HR is responsible for culture." Menasha's human resource team focused on five key areas to develop a culture of innovation.

- The company's strategic plan was the starting point. All innovation had to fit with the strategy, and that strategy had to be clear enough to identify the company's next growth platform. From that platform, the HR team sought to identify the major implications for talent.
- The HR team built on the company's existing core strengths, such as lean manufacturing, and its talent-management system (TMS). The innovation initiative then leveraged existing lean tools and used TMS to hold people accountable for the completion of projects. According to Mike Riegsecker, vice president corrugated businesses, "We brought innovation in as part of what we were doing already. If innovation was a bolt-on program, it wouldn't work."
- The HR team introduced new tools. To help prioritize ideas, for example, a "stage-gate" system was introduced. Such a system provides a conceptual and operational road map for moving a new-product project from idea to launch. Stage-gate divides the effort into distinct stages separated by management-decision gates (gatekeeping). Cross-functional teams must successfully complete a prescribed set of related cross-functional activities in each stage prior to obtaining management approval to proceed to the next stage of product development.[19]
- The HR team ensured that every functional area was part of the new culture by leading cross-functional teams from finance, sales,

and marketing to change the culture. To engage as many people as possible, the team held thirteen cross-functional events over a twelve-month period.

• To focus employees on innovation throughout the year, Menasha relies on a leadership-planning process. The process starts in December, with a TMS-alignment meeting for the upcoming year. In January TMS goals are finalized, and in April a TMS-progress meeting is held. In July the team begins identifying key initiatives for the next December planning meeting.

Menasha's innovation program has generated excellent results. The company experienced record performance during the 2007–9 economic downturn. In addition, lean teams created a new manufacturing method that led to $20 million in new business in the grocery channel. After another team had researched European trends, the company purchased a new technology to lead the industry in "retail-ready packaging."

Notice several important features of Menasha's drive for innovation. First, the process began with the requirement that all innovation had to fit the company's strategy, and that strategy had to identify the company's next growth platform. Second, the HR team took a leadership role, rather than a "followership" role, for it recognized that HR leaders are keepers of the organization's culture. Third, the company's leadership-planning process ensures that employees stay focused on innovation initiatives throughout the year. That is an effective HR strategy in action.

A second example of HR leaders driving the process of innovation comes from India.[20] Coromandel International Limited manufactures fertilizers, specialty nutrients, crop-protection products, and retail products. It is India's third-fastest-growing company, with revenues of about $2 billion and more than 7,000 employees in 509 locations. Coromandel is ranked among the top twenty best companies to work for by *Business Today* and it has been recognized as one of the ten greenest companies in India, reflecting its commitment to the environment and to society. Coromandel is a part of the $3.8 billion Murugappa Group.[21]

Three initiatives drove the company to adopt an innovation program. The first was to grow revenue. The company sought to double its revenues every three years, but did not have sufficient new business ideas to meet that goal. Second, innovation can help deal with extreme volatility in commodity prices. The world economy was slowing, and commodities were experiencing inflation and wide swings in prices. Third, the company was trying to manage its business amid changing rules. India is in the process of revising its laws, so business rules are changing.

In the midst of this environment, the company engaged in an innovation-readiness assessment to determine how prepared it was for innovation. The senior leaders participated in an innovation-roadmap workshop and a venturing process, facilitated by an outside expert. This work prepared the company to implement an innovation program with the following attributes:

- *Leadership support.* The firm's innovation council comprises top management representatives from each division.
- *Employee involvement.* Innovative employees are called "i-leads." People meet with an i-lead to discuss new ideas. If the i-lead likes an idea, he or she finds people from different divisions/functions to work on it.
- *i-Sponsors.* Once teams develop ideas, they bring them to i-sponsors, who are divisional heads. Ideas approved by i-sponsors go to the i-council. Alternatively, an i-sponsor may direct a team to rework an idea.
- *i-Pitch day.* On i-pitch day, teams present ninety-day plans for their ideas to the i-council. Teams with approved plans engage in a ninety-day deep dive into their ideas. Employees view this ninety-day time frame as challenging, but achievable.
- *Business-plan evaluation.* At the end of the deep dive, ideas may be dropped or may move to the business-plan level. Once a business plan is approved, a new business is launched within the company.

Coromandel International's HR team played several important roles in promoting innovation. First, *it set the context.* HR pushed the need for an innovation program, identified potential program partners, changed organizational mindsets, and implemented extensive communication and training for the company. Second, the HR team took a lead role in *building the culture.* Coromandel's HR group developed a systematic way to assess employees for innovation, and it added innovation to the recruitment process. In addition, employees are rewarded and recognized for innovation, even when they fail, which reduces the fear of failure. Third, the HR team took a lead role in *aligning innovation with business goals*. The HR emphasis facilitated collaboration, deployed the right process and structure, and added innovation to the balanced scorecard and incentives. As Arun Leslie George, Coromandel's chief HR officer, noted, "Do not be satisfied with supporting innovation. HR has to drive it. Unless we stand up and do it, it is not going to happen."

The results? Coromandel's innovation initiatives are impressive. Ideas that have made it through Coromandel's rigorous evaluation process have demonstrated a net present value of nearly $1 billion. Innovation-team participants are enthusiastic and unafraid of "fruitful failures." In addition, the company enjoys strong employer branding thanks to its employer-value proposition, which includes innovation as a key component.

Using talent analytics

Do you *think* you know how to get the best from your people? Or do you *know*? How do investments in your employees actually affect the performance of your workforce? Who are your top performers, and how can you empower and motivate other employees to excel?

These were the opening questions in a recent article in the *Harvard Business Review*.[22] Talent analytics is an important force that is driving HR strategy because the insights that it provides can be profound. As an example, consider Wawa Inc., a Pennsylvania-based food service and convenience company. Leaders had suspected that hourly wages were the biggest factor in turnover among clerks, but careful analysis found that the most significant predictor of employee turnover was hours worked. Those working more than thirty hours per week were classified as full-time and separated less. This discovery opened the door to moving from 30 percent part-time to 50 percent full-time, reducing turnover rates by 60 percent.[23]

More and more leading companies are using sophisticated methods of analyzing employee data in order to enhance their competitive advantage – how to ensure the highest productivity, engagement, and retention of top talent, for example. Talent or HR analytics at Best Buy demonstrated that a 0.1 percent increase in engagement among employees at a particular store translated into more than $100,000 in the store's operating income.

OK, so now you are interested. Where should you begin? At the outset it is important to note that HR analytics is fact-based decision making, and that analytics varies on a scale from purely descriptive data, such as turnover rates for various segments of the workforce, to highly sophisticated, such as insights about the talent supply chain. To illustrate the various levels of sophistication that talent analytics can take, consider an example used by Google's people analytics group: counting, clever counting, insight, and influence.[24] Each higher level requires mastery of the lower levels.

(1) *Counting*. All relevant data about the workforce are tracked, organized, and accessible. Getting this basic step right can be difficult. HR technology solutions – both off the shelf and internally built – can be clunky. The challenges of continually updating the database and ensuring that all end users, from line managers to HR generalists, are getting the data they need are unceasing. Google's current solution is a hybrid external vendor/internal customization model. It allows users to display headcount, attrition, promotion, and other data through customizable dashboards that have the ability to filter the data and display it according to hierarchy, employee location, and cost center, for example.

(2) *Clever counting*. Extrapolating from descriptive data yields new insights. For example, consider workforce planning. Using basic data on promotions, attrition, headcount by level, and anticipated organizational growth rate makes it possible to project the "shape" of your organization (the percentage of employees at each level) at the end of a year, at the end of two years, or after three-plus years. With the proper formulas in place, users can input anticipated future attrition/promotion and organizational growth rates to model different scenarios. By assigning salaries to employees at each level, one can see the financial impact of having an organizational shape that looks like a typical pyramid (with fewer employees at each level as one moves up the organization) or a more uniform distribution across levels, which would occur if the organization is not hiring but employees continue to receive promotions.

(3) *Insight*. What drivers of the trends do you find through clever counting? The preceding example of modeling organizational shape is most useful if we can understand what is driving each component of the model. For example, we may find that the

organization's projected shape in five years is top heavy. Why? Close investigation might show that promotion rates are too high, combined with attrition that is higher at lower levels than it is at higher levels. This process of inquiry provides the insight needed to understand the results of more sophisticated analyses.

(4) *Influence*. The results of counting, clever counting, and insight can help make a difference. At this level, the relevant question is "How can we shape outcomes rather than just measure them?" Insight from the organizational-shape models described can lead to change if you partner with the right people in your organization. The overall objective is to ensure that managers have a shared understanding of the goals (for example, sustaining a pyramidal organizational structure) and the levers they can pull to achieve those goals. For example, if analysis shows that the current or projected future shape of the organization is top heavy, the levers include these:

(a) decrease yearly promotion rates;

(b) launch attrition-prevention programs if insight has revealed that the highest-performing employees are most likely to terminate; and

(c) backfill vacant positions at lower levels.

The four steps to analytical sophistication do not apply solely to workforce planning. Instead, they apply to any data-collection and analysis activity, such as employee opinion surveys, employee selection research, or employee diversity analyses. Your goal should always be to get to the last step: influence. Here is an example of how Google did that with respect to an age-old question: what makes a good boss?[25]

"Project oxygen"   Google's effort, code-named "project oxygen," started with some basic assumptions.

People typically leave a company for one of three reasons, or a combination of them. The first is that they do not feel a connection to the mission of the company, or sense that their work matters. The second is that they do not really like or respect their co-workers. The third is that they have a terrible boss – and this was the biggest variable. Google, where performance reviews are done quarterly, rather than annually, saw huge variability in the ratings that employees gave to their bosses. Google also found that managers had a much greater impact on employees' performance and how they felt about their jobs than any other factor.

In "project oxygen," the statisticians gathered more than 10,000 observations about managers – across more than 100 variables, from various performance reviews, feedback surveys, and other reports. Then they spent time coding the comments in order to look for patterns. They also interviewed managers to gather more data, and to look for evidence that supported their working hypotheses. The final step was to code and synthesize all these results – more than 400 pages of interview notes. The process of reading and coding all that information was time-consuming, but necessary.

The result was a list of eight qualities that Google started teaching in training programs, as well as in coaching and performance-review sessions with individual employees. Surprisingly, technical expertise – the ability, say, to write computer code in your sleep – ranked dead last among the eight key qualities. What employees valued most were even-keeled bosses who made time for one-on-one meetings, who helped people puzzle through problems by asking questions, not dictating answers, and who took an interest in employees' lives and careers.

"In the Google context, we'd always believed that to be a manager, particularly on the engineering side, you need to be as deep or deeper a technical expert than the people who work for you." That is the view of Laszlo Bock, Google's vice president for people operations (HR). "It turns out that that's absolutely the least important thing. It's important, but pales in comparison. Much more important is just making that connection and being accessible."

The company's laser-like focus on teaching bosses, particularly problem bosses, the kinds of characteristics that really matter paid off quickly. "We were able to have a statistically significant improvement in manager quality for 75 percent of our worst-performing managers," according to Bock.

He tells the story of one manager whose employees seemed to despise him. He was driving them too hard. They found him bossy, arrogant, political, secretive. They wanted to quit his team. "He's brilliant, but he did everything wrong when it came to leading a team," Bock recalls. Because of that heavy hand, this manager was denied a promotion he wanted, and was told that his style was the reason. Google offered him one-on-one coaching – and he accepted it. Six months later team members were grudgingly acknowledging in surveys that the manager had improved. "And a year later, it's actually quite a bit better," Bock says. "It's still not great. He's nowhere near one of our best managers, but he's not our worst anymore. And he got promoted."

Perhaps what is most striking about what this example of talent analytics demonstrates is the simplicity of the rules, and the fact that applying them does not require a complete makeover of a manager's personality. "You don't actually need to change who the person is," Bock says. "What it means is, if I'm a manager and I want to get better, and I want more out of my people and I want them to be happier, two of the most important things I can do is just make sure I have some time for them and to be consistent."[26]

As this example illustrates, leading-edge companies are using sophisticated methods of analyzing employee data in order to drive decisions about HR strategy based on evidence. These efforts are helping them to enhance competitive advantage through their people – improving their productivity, raising their levels of engagement, and increasing the retention of pivotal talent.

There are some key mistakes to avoid, though, with respect to metrics and talent analytics. Here are four of the most common ones.[27] (1) Keeping a metric alive when it has no clear business reason for existing. (2) Relying on just a few metrics to evaluate employee performance, enabling smart employees to game the system. (3) Ignoring aspects of performance that cannot easily be translated into quantifiable metrics (such as helping fellow team members reach their goals). (4) Analyzing only metrics that focus on efficiency, such as time to fill vacancies or cost per hire – with no link to the performance of the business.

Now, in our penultimate section, we examine how some firms are emphasizing values as sources of long-term sustainability, and as drivers of HR strategy.

Focusing on values

Defining an organization's values is the first step in building a culture of employee engagement (see Figure 2.3, "A values-based view of strategy"). At the same time, values are so much more than this. They become an integral part of a company's DNA. They determine the minimum behaviors for which people are accountable. These desired behaviors, in turn, influence how organizations make decisions, such as hiring decisions, and they greatly impact customer satisfaction and brand credibility. As an example, consider Starbucks Coffee. Here are its mission statement and guiding principles:[28]

> Establish Starbucks as the premier purveyor of the finest coffee in the world while maintaining our uncompromising principles as we grow.
>
> The following six guiding principles will help us measure the appropriateness of our decisions:
>
> Provide a great work environment and treat each other with respect and dignity.
>
> Embrace diversity as an essential component in the way we do business.
>
> Apply the highest standards of excellence to the purchasing, roasting and fresh delivery of our coffee.
>
> Develop enthusiastically satisfied customers all of the time.
>
> Contribute positively to our communities and our environment.
>
> Recognize that profitability is essential to our future success.

This is a short, concise set of statements that clearly communicates the essence of how senior leaders envision their company. Those same leaders often refer to the guiding principles as keys to the ways they live and work. At the highest levels of the company senior leaders talk about them all the time, and when they start to veer off course they ask "Where is our magnetic north? Let's think about our guiding principles," and those principles help them make decisions that are consistent with their intent.[29]

Conversely, failure to make decisions based on values can sometimes lead to damaging incidents that tarnish a company's reputation. Such was the case recently with Johnson & Johnson, a household name and a leading global provider of healthcare products.

Johnson & Johnson's approach to values-based decision making[30]   The company was founded 125 years ago. Today the firm comprises 250 operating companies worldwide and employs 114,000 people. It generated revenues of $62 billion in 2010.

Dispersed and diverse as this company is, its people are united behind a set of shared values, simply and explicitly set forth in its credo, written in 1943. It prioritizes stakeholders unequivocally. The interests of the company's customers come before all else, followed by employees, communities, and, lastly, shareholders. This order is controversial amid today's pressures to prioritize the interests of shareholders or talent assets. Nevertheless, Johnson & Johnson believes that making customers' interests its top priority is right, both morally and from a business perspective. Only if the company can retain customers' trust can it remain prosperous (twenty-seven years of consecutive earning increases, forty-nine straight years of dividend increases) and live up to its responsibilities to employees, communities, and shareholders.

Here is an example of how the credo drives operating and HR decisions. People at Johnson & Johnson "live and breathe" the company's values. Like those in many companies, they want to make a difference through their work. The company scientist who developed the most effective HIV treatment feels that he was put on earth to wipe out AIDS, hepatitis C, and tuberculosis. Although market factors would allow Johnson & Johnson to price the compound higher than that of competing treatments, the company's commitment to caring about the world's health requires that access to lifesaving drugs factor into the pricing decision, so the drug is priced more affordably. Such allegiance to credo values, even at a significant financial cost, is inspiring to employees, driving uncommonly high engagement.

The strong credo culture also gives Johnson & Johnson a recruiting advantage, particularly among highly principled members of younger generations. Graduates of top universities with plenty of employment options often choose Johnson & Johnson because of its values-oriented culture.

To keep it alive, the credo is embedded in every aspect of human capital management: action plans, onboarding (bringing new employees into the organization), training activities, rewards and incentives, engagement surveys, and performance evaluations. Leaders are held accountable for their actions, and their performance metrics assess not only *what* they accomplished but also *how* they did so, relative to company values. Clearly, Johnson & Johnson's credo is a key force that drives HR strategy.

Consequences of violations of the credo   There were two recent incidents that caused Johnson & Johnson's reputation to take a hit in the rankings of most respected companies. In the wake of these incidents, however, employees' own ratings of the firm's reputation actually fell more than the external benchmarks did, and employee-engagement scores fell even among senior leaders.

One incident was the highly publicized product recalls in the McNeil subsidiary, which undermined the company's reputation for putting customers first. The other related to illegal payments to doctors in Europe, an incident that was found and reported through internal channels. An internal audit process uncovered the corruption, and the company voluntarily reported itself to the government, paid a large fine, and fired the person responsible. Had the credo-based decision process been followed in these situations, Johnson & Johnson would have been spared much cost and reputational damage. Case studies are now being written about the incidents so that the lessons of the painful experiences will not be lost.

Now, in our final section, we look forward with a consideration of some emerging challenges that are helping to shape HR strategy in many firms: virtuality, crowds, and blogs.

Looking forward: virtuality, crowds, and blogs

Close your eyes and imagine this picture on the cover of a popular business magazine: an empty freeway leading to a deserted metropolis. The caption reads: "It's 8:45 a.m. Do you know where your employees are?" Welcome to the new paradigm of work – anytime, anywhere, in real space or in cyberspace. For many employers the virtual workplace, in which employees operate remotely from each other and from managers, is a reality now, and all indications are that it will become even more prevalent in the future.[31] Indeed, for many workers today, their co-workers include people whom they have never met. How is this possible? It happens because they work virtually, in different locations, sometimes on different continents, rather than in the same physical location.[32] David Arkless, president of corporate and government affairs for Manpower Inc., recently stated: "According to our research, roughly 30% of tasks in multinational corporations could be done virtually."[33] This suggests that virtual global mobility and virtual work opportunities for employees abroad may be alternative ways to address shortages of critical skills within a company's workforce or in the external domestic workforce. Can you think of some potential impacts of virtuality on HR strategy?

Crowdsourcing   A second feature of today's world that can potentially affect HR strategy is crowds, or, more specifically, crowdsourcing. Definitions and terms vary, but the basic idea is to tap into the collective intelligence of the public at large to complete business-related tasks that a company would normally either perform itself or outsource to a third-party provider. Free labor is only a narrow part of crowdsourcing's appeal, however. More importantly, it enables managers to expand the size of their talent pools while also gaining deeper insight into what customers really want.

What makes crowdsourcing so powerful is the broad participation that takes place at virtually no cost. Solutions are generated from volunteers or freelance professionals, who get paid only if an organization uses their ideas (e.g., developers of applications for Apple or Google). There is also a wealth of creativity that people are more than willing to share if they only had an opportunity to participate.[34] There are numerous avenues for crowdsourcing, such as enlisting volunteers, hotlines, internet blogs, viewer-participation incentives, idea communities, or free products. Given how powerful this resource is and the very nominal costs involved, it makes good business sense for all of us to think in terms of how we can tap into these global crowds of creativity.[35]

Google uses crowdsourcing in its hiring process.[36] This is what happens. A prospective employee applies for a job. The company uses its applicant-tracking system (ATS) to ask workers to weigh in on applicants who have submitted their résumés online. Information collected about where they went to school or worked previously is parsed and stored in the ATS. The system then matches that information to data about existing Google employees.

Following a match, an e-mail automatically asks employees for internal references. Employees can respond via e-mail, thereby updating the system. This allows recruiters to tap employees who best understand the demands of the jobs and the nature of the culture in assessing the fit of potential hires. It allows current employees to build the community – even if they are not part of the formal interview process. Can you see the similarity with the premise that underlies the creation of Wikipedia, namely that people are willing to contribute to the collective knowledge, especially if they receive information in return? Can you think of some potential applications of crowdsourcing to HR strategy?

Blogs   Much online media research has focused on "having a voice," be it in blogs, wikis, social media, or discussion lists. Social-media monitoring, or brand monitoring, was born as a way to respond to crises and to manage brand reputation. Today there are more than 200 tools and "listening" platforms claiming to be able to help organizations track and assess mentions of their business or brand in social-media channels. They have evolved beyond basic monitoring into an integrated approach that helps inform multiple parts of a business: product development, customer support, public outreach, lead generation, and market research, to name just a few.

In a recent review of the top twenty social-media-monitoring vendors, the top-rated firm was Canada-based Radian 6.[37] Fully automated, it works with companies to help them listen more intelligently to their consumers, competitors, and influencers, with the goal of growing their businesses via detailed, real-time insights. Beyond its monitoring dashboard, which tracks mentions on more than 100 million social-media sites, Radian 6 offers an engagement console that allows organizations to coordinate their internal responses to external activity by immediately updating their blog, Twitter, and Facebook accounts all in one spot.

Successful listening means looking at social data in parallel with business metrics – such as watching spikes in the volume of Tweets around a firm's products and seeing how that impacts website traffic. Once companies understand how social and business metrics relate, they can drive quicker and deeper intelligence through integrated data. By automatically piping in both sets of data to dashboards, scorecards, or custom metrics, organizations are able to learn and act in real time. This kind of intelligence gives teams the ability to capture, manage, analyze, and apply insights from all data points across the organization. Can you see how such insights might drive changes in HR policies or practices?

Conclusion

This chapter discussed seven key contextual factors that are affecting the climate for business: the economy, and the need to retain pivotal talent; globalization; technology; demographics; the nature of work; the nature of leadership; and the growing need for cross-cultural leadership skills. Each of these factors creates internal as well as external human capital risks for organizations, such as the loss of key talent, not investing in the future, a lack of innovation, a lack of emphasis on values, and ignoring social media. To address these risks, firms are driving innovation, using talent (HR) analytics, and emphasizing values. Finally, we considered three emerging challenges that are helping to shape HR strategy in many firms: virtuality, crowds, and blogs.

A final word

Using the broad framework of risk management, this book has focused on formulating, analyzing, communicating, implementing, and assessing HR strategy. We have provided multiple examples of firms that have done so very effectively. Trends under way now are driving dynamic, ongoing challenges in this critical area of human resource management. Your challenge will be to harness these trends for sustained competitive advantage through people. We hope that the tools we have provided will help you in your journey.

Notes

1 *Dayton Business Journal* (2011). Most companies lose top talent. *Dayton Business Journal*, July 26 (available at www.bizjournals.com/dayton/news/2011/07/26/companies-lose-top-talent-n-past-year.html; accessed September 12, 2011).

2 Young, M. B., and Hexter, E. S. (2011). *Managing Human Capital Risk*. New York: Conference Board.

3 Boudreau, J. B., and Ramstad, P. M. (2007). *Beyond HR: The New Science of Human Capital*. Boston: Harvard Business School Press.

4 Boudreau and Ramstad (2007).

5 Kushner, G. B. (2011). Key takeaways from the 2011 Thought Leaders retreat, in SHRM Foundation, *The SHRM Foundation Thought Leaders Retreat: HR's Role in Managing Business Risk: Executive Summaries*, 2–3. Alexandria, VA: SHRM Foundation.

6 Kaye, B., and Jordan-Evans, S. (2008). *Love 'Em or Lose 'Em: Getting Good People to Stay*, 4th edn. San Francisco: Berrett-Koehler.

7 Trevor, C. O., and Nyberg, A. J. (2008). Keeping your headcount when all about you are losing theirs: downsizing, voluntary turnover rates, and the moderating role of HR practices. *Academy of Management Journal*, 51(2): 259–76.

8 Marini, R. (2011). Social media: leveraging the opportunities, in *The SHRM Foundation Thought Leaders Retreat: HR's Role in Managing Business Risk: Executive Summaries*, 12–14. Alexandria, VA: SHRM Foundation.

9 Information in this section comes from Marini (2011).

10 Meister, J. C., and Willyerd, K. (2010). Mentoring millennials. *Harvard Business Review*, 88(5): 68–72.

11 Wilson, P. (2011). Managing global business risk. Presentation at SHRM Foundation "Thought leaders" retreat, Chicago, October 5.

12 SHRM (2011). *2011 Employee benefits: examining employee benefits amidst uncertainty*. Alexandria, VA: SHRM.

13 Meister and Willyerd (2010).

14 Greenleaf, R. K. (2002). *Servant leadership: A journey into the nature of legitimate power and greatness*, 25th anniv. edn. Mahwah, NJ: Paulist Press; Trompenaars, F., and Voerman, E. (2009). *Servant-leadership across cultures: harnessing the strength of the world's most powerful leadership philosophy*. Oxford: Infinite Ideas.

15 Wilson (2011).

16 Kushner (2011).

17 Riegsecker, M., and Swatscheno, S. (2011, Oct.). The Menasha story. Presentation at SHRM Foundation "Thought leaders" retreat, Chicago, October 4.

18 For more information, go to www.menashapackaging.com/index.html.

19 For more information, go to www.prod-dev.com/stage-gate.php.

20 Information in this section comes from DeSai, J. (2011). Making HR the major driver of organizational innovation, in *The SHRM Foundation Thought Leaders Retreat: HR's Role in Managing Business Risk: Executive Summaries*, 7–9. Alexandria, VA: SHRM Foundation.

21 For more information, go to www.coromandel.biz/aboutus.html.

22 Davenport, T. H., Harris, J., and Shapiro, J. (2010). Competing on talent analytics. *Harvard Business Review*, 88(10): 52–8.

23 Roberts, B. (2009). Analyze this. *HRMagazine*, October: 35–41.

24 Cascio, W. F., and Boudreau, J. W. (2011). *Investing in people: financial impact of human resource initiatives*, 2nd edn. Upper Saddle River, NJ: Pearson Education/FT Press.

25 Bryant, A. (2011). Google's quest to build a better boss. *The New York Times,* March 12; available at www.nytimes.com/2011/03/13/business/13hire.html?_r=2&pagewanted=print%20Page (accessed July 29, 2011).

26 Bryant (2011).

27 Davenport, Harris, and Shapiro (2010).

28 See www.myspace.com/youdrinkcoffee/blog/289290652.

29 SHRM Foundation (2007). *Trust Travels: The Starbucks Story*, DVD. Alexandria, VA: SHRM Foundation.

30 Podlogar, S. (2011). Engaging global talent through the Johnson & Johnson credo, in *The SHRM Foundation Thought Leaders Retreat: HR's Role in Managing Business Risk: Executive Summaries*, 21–5, Alexandria, VA: SHRM Foundation.

31 Cascio, W. F. (2000). On managing a virtual workplace. *Academy of Management Executive*, 14(3): 81–90.

32 Johnson, S. A. (2011). We meet again, though we have never met: leading effective teams globally. Paper presented at 7th annual Leading Edge Consortium, "The virtual workforce: designing, leading, and optimizing," Society for Industrial and Organizational Psychology, Louisville, KY, October 14.

33 Arkless, D., quoted in World Economic Forum (2011). *Global talent risk: seven responses*. Geneva: World Economic Forum, 27.

34 Surowiecki, J. (2004). *The wisdom of crowds: why the many are smarter than the few and how collective wisdom shapes business, economies, societies, and nations*. New York: Little, Brown.

35 Evans, M. H. (undated). The power of crowdsourcing, Excellence in Financial Management; available at www.exinfm.com/board/crowdsourcing.htm (accessed November 6, 2011).

36 Wright, A. D. (2008). At Google, it takes a village to hire an employee. *HR Magazine*, 53(12): 56–7 (available at http://findarticles.com/p/articles/mi_m3495/is_12_53/ai_n31152981; accessed November 6, 2011).

37 Lasica, J. D., and Bale, K. (2011). Top 20 social media monitoring vendors for business. Socialmedia.biz, January 12, www.socialmedia.biz/2011/01/12/top-20-social-media-monitoring-vendors-for-business (accessed November 6, 2011).

Index